THE
MONEY
BOOK
for the

young,
fabulous
& broke

ALSO BY SUZE ORMAN

*You've Earned It, Don't Lose It*
*The 9 Steps to Financial Freedom*
*Suze Orman's Financial Guidebook*
*The Courage to Be Rich*
*The Road to Wealth*
*The Laws of Money, The Lessons of Life*

# THE MONEY BOOK

FOR THE  YOUNG,
FABULOUS
& BROKE

SUZE
ORMAN

Riverhead Books   New York   2005

This publication is designed to provide accurate and authoritative information in regard to the subject matter covered. It is sold with the understanding that the publisher is not engaged in rendering legal, accounting, or other professional services. If you require legal advice or other expert assistance, you should seek the services of a competent professional.

While the author has made every effort to provide accurate telephone numbers and Internet addresses at the time of publication, neither the publisher nor the author assumes any responsibility for errors, or for changes that occur after publication.

RIVERHEAD BOOKS
Published by the Penguin Group
Penguin Group (USA) Inc., 375 Hudson Street, New York, New York 10014, USA
Penguin Group (Canada), 10 Alcorn Avenue, Toronto, Ontario, Canada M4V 3B2
(a division of Pearson Penguin Canada Inc.) • Penguin Books Ltd, 80 Strand, London
WC2R 0RL, England • Penguin Ireland, 25 St Stephen's Green, Dublin 2, Ireland (a division
of Penguin Books Ltd) • Penguin Group (Australia), 250 Camberwell Road, Camberwell,
Victoria 3124, Australia (a division of Pearson Australia Group Pty Ltd) • Penguin Books
India Pvt Ltd, 11 Community Centre, Panchsheel Park, New Delhi—110 017, India • Penguin
Group (NZ), cnr Airborne and Rosedale Roads, Albany, Auckland 1310, New Zealand
(a division of Pearson New Zealand Ltd) • Penguin Books (South Africa) (Pty) Ltd,
24 Sturdee Avenue, Rosebank, Johannesburg 2196, South Africa

Penguin Books Ltd, Registered Offices: 80 Strand, London WC2R 0RL, England

Published simultaneously in Canada

Library of Congress Cataloging-in-Publication Data

Orman, Suze.
    The money book for the young, fabulous & broke / Suze Orman.
        p.   cm.
    Includes index.
    ISBN 1-57322-297-6
        1. Finance, Personal.   2. Young adults—Finance, Personal.    I. Title: Money book for
the young, fabulous and broke.    II. Title.
HG179.O7576      2005                    2004062043
332.024—dc22

Printed in the United States of America

10  9  8  7  6  5  4  3  2  1

This book is printed on acid-free paper. ∞

Book design by Platinum Design, Inc., NYC

To Carla and Teddy, a fabulous team

# CONTENTS

INTRODUCTION:

for the
young,
fabulous
& broke

Listen, I know dealing with the responsibility of money, especially a lack of money, may not necessarily be high on your list of priorities. But something motivated you and brought you to this page, so in some way you are telling yourself it's time to start dealing with your financial life. It's time to make some changes.

Most likely, you are young; I hope you feel you are fabulous; and chances are, you are also broke. I've talked to thousands of young people like you over the years, and, for what it's worth, you've got plenty of company.

But you also have a great way out of your current situation. You have time. Because you are young, you have the time to right any missteps, and the time to build a solid financial life. I also know that you have the bandwidth to take the advice in this book and put it into action. You may be intent on feeling beaten up these days, but I'm not going to play along. I admire you for your grit in coping with a lousy job market, skyrocketing real estate values, and hefty student loans. But what I also hear when I talk to you is that you have what it takes to manage the hand you've been dealt.

Now, having said all that, I wouldn't be surprised if you're wondering if this book can really deliver the goods or if it's going to be yet another personal finance book by someone who has no clue about the issues you're dealing with. I guarantee you that this is definitely not your parents' money book. I get *your* situation. The advice in this book is customized to fit your life today. How do I know what you're going through? Because you told me. You were quite blunt about what you want from me, as well as what you don't want.

You want advice that deals with your reality—a set of solutions for the problems you have. You want to be told what to tackle first, and you want clear advice on how to get the job done. And that's what you are going to get here, delivered as concisely as possible. I only dive into details that are absolutely crucial to your success. And you don't need an iota of prior knowledge. I know you've been too busy or uninspired to figure out how a Roth IRA works, what a FICO score is, and why you should even care. No worries. I have written every section of this book so you can quickly and easily comprehend exactly what actions you need to take and why.

What you don't want is yet another personal finance book spewing the same old advice that doesn't work for you. I completely agree. You won't catch me telling you to cut back on the lattes and "simply" save $10 a day. As if saving $3,650 a year when you are broke could ever be simple. Nor will I tell you that credit cards are the devil in plastic (on the contrary, I think they can be good for you) or that you must have eight months of living expenses saved up as your emergency reserve fund before you are allowed past go. *Un-uh*. I know that's not realistic or reasonable for the majority of you at this point in your lives.

Besides, if you didn't have credit card debt and you already had an eight-month emergency cash fund, why would you have picked up this book? You sure wouldn't fit my definition of broke.

**BROKE IS** relying on a cash advance on your credit card to pay the rent or mortgage, and praying that you have enough left on your credit line to do so.

**BROKE IS** having a ton of student loans that make you nauseated when you think about how long it is going to take you to pay them off.

**BROKE IS** not opening your credit card bills because you're terrified to see what you owe and have no way of paying. So instead, you get hit with the late fee and finance charges.

**BROKE IS** wanting to buy a home but having no clue where you can come up with the down payment. So you are stuck renting a small place.

**BROKE IS** counting every coin in your change jar as well as scrounging under the sofa cushions in a desperate attempt to find the dough to cover your bounced check and the $25 fee your bank is going to slap on you.

**BROKE IS** wanting to save for your kids' college educations but not knowing how to swing it because you are already strapped trying to make the mortgage and car payment, and you haven't even started saving for your retirement.

**BROKE IS** not having one penny saved, even though you have a good job. If your car breaks down, so will you. You don't have the money for repairs, but you need the wheels to get to work.

This is by no means an exhaustive list. I'm sure if we all met up, we could have a great time seeing who has the best "Broke is" story. But even though your specific stories may differ, you all want the same thing. You want to fix your situation so you are no longer broke.

That is exactly what this book is about. Our starting point is that you are broke, by your or any definition. Our ending point is that you are not. And we aren't just going to get you past broke, we are going to make sure you never revisit broke. This is such an important point; I see far too many people go from being broke to finally having some money, only to slip back to broke again because they didn't know what to do with their money. I don't want that to happen to you.

Here's the bottom line: You picked up this book because you are broke. Keep reading and you will discover what you need to know—and do—so you will not be broke forever.

OPERATING
MANUAL

Okay, I really meant what I said in the Introduction. The advice I am going to give you is not the same old same old. And I am also not going to deliver it in the same old way.

I have divided this book into ten sections that address the main topics you told me you want help with. At the start of each section, you will find a list of the issues that are most likely gnawing at you, and the pages where you can find the solutions. All you need to do is head over to the section you are interested in, find the topic you want to read up on, and then flip to the right page. But I hope you'll first take the time to read the **Lowdown** that launches each section; it's my spin through the basic information you need to make the smartest moves.

The **Quick Playback** at the end of each section is a recap of the most important do's and don'ts. It's a refresher course on two easy-to-read pages.

Throughout each section, key terms that I suspect you might not know—yet really need to know—are boldfaced in green. When you see a boldfaced word that you don't understand, flip to the **Glossary** in the back of the book for a plain-English explanation that is free of the financial mumbo jumbo that can be so intimidating and alienating.

Speaking of intimidating, I get that for some of you the biggest problem is not knowing which problem to tackle first. If that's your concern, then simply follow the order of the sections; they're arranged in a logical progression. I've also created an interactive **Action Planner** at the **Young, Fabulous & Broke** section of my website to help you get started.

## PERSONALIZED ONLINE ADVICE
## FOR THE YOUNG, FABULOUS & BROKE

As convinced as I am that this book contains all the information you need to start building a solid financial life, I also know it would be even better if I delivered advice tailored to your own unique situations. That's where my website comes in. I have created the **YF&B** section at **suzeorman.com**. It is loaded with tools and resources, including my **Action Planner**.

The book and website are designed to work in tandem. When you see this symbol

in the book, it means there is a tool at the website to give you personalized information that will enable you to take the advice in the book and see what it means for you—not generic advice, but customized advice based on what you plug in: everything from understanding how you can boost your FICO score to how long it will take you to pay off your credit card debt to how much of a home you can really afford.

There is also a message board at the site, so you can swap ideas with fellow YF&Bers.

I encourage you to give the Action Planner a try before you start reading the book. If you spend just five minutes answering a few multiple-choice questions, the planner will tell you what I think your best first move should be in your particular situation. And in the planner, I direct you to the page numbers in the book where you can learn how to do it.

**Password for the Website**

The Action Planner and all the tools at my website are absolutely free to anyone with this book. Here's how to gain access: Go to my website, www.suzeorman.com. Click on the YF&B link and enter this code: **YF&B**. To register, you will need to enter your information, along with this number: 98635472. Then you will create your own password, to use each time you want to sign back on.

I hope that I have thought of everything to make your trip past broke as complete and easy as possible. If you have any questions, comments, or suggestions, you can send me an e-mail from the YF&B section of my website; I will post answers to the topics that seem to be the most popular with YF&Bers.

I know this subject matter is serious stuff. Your future is riding on it. But taking control of your financial life doesn't need to be a solitary and scary process. Fear comes from not knowing what to do or how to do it. And when we are fearful, we do nothing. This book and my website will give you all the information you need to shed your fears and confidently take action. You really do have what it takes to move past broke; you just need to start moving forward.

# know
# the
# score

Nearly every financial decision you make is being watched, with the goal of determining your financial profile.

**THE LOWDOWN**

If you forced me to pick one single bit of advice that would have the biggest impact on turning around your financial situation, I wouldn't hesitate for a second. You have to know the score: your FICO score.

Just about every financial move you will make for the rest of your life will be somehow linked to your FICO score. Not knowing how your score is calculated, how it is used, and how you can improve it will keep you broke long past your young-and-fabulous days.

Yet I also know that you are probably FICO-ignorant; I get a 90 percent failure rate when I ask YF&Bers if they know their FICO score or why it is so important.

That's got to change. Right now.

### FICO FUNDAMENTALS

A Fico score is a three-digit number that determines the interest rate you will pay on your credit cards, car loan, and home mortgage, as well as whether you will be able to get a cell phone or have your application for a rental apartment accepted. FICO stands for Fair Isaac Corporation, the firm that created the formula that seems to lord over your financial life. The way the business world sees it, your FICO score is a great tool to size up how good you will be at handling a new loan or credit card, or whether you're a solid citizen to rent an apartment to. A high FICO score gives you a great reputation with the business world; you'll get the best deals. A lower FICO score translates into paying higher interest rates on cards and loans. Your credit history can even affect your auto insurance premiums or your ability to get that job you applied for. I wasn't kidding when I said it was connected to just about every part of your life.

With so much on the line, I hope it's clear now that you can't afford to stay FICO-ignorant.

Your FICO score is based on your spending and bill-paying habits, and your overall **debt** load. I know this might come off as a bit of disturbing big-brotherism, but nearly every financial decision you make is being watched, tracked, and massaged, with the goal of determining your financial profile. The folks you do business with, from lenders (school loans, auto loans, mortgages) and the phone company to credit card companies, constantly file reports on your financial activity to one of three major **credit bureaus**. These credit bureaus know what you have spent, what you owe, and if you tend to pay bills on time or let them slip. From all that raw personal data, the three credit bureaus calculate your FICO score using a formula developed by Fair Isaac.

Fair Isaac and the credit bureaus make a ton of money sharing your FICO score. Mortgage lenders, auto lenders, employers, cell-phone companies, and insurance companies are happy to pay up to get a glance at your FICO score. They use it just like colleges used your SAT score. It helps them assess whether they want to accept your application, or what terms they will offer you. To the financial world, you are your FICO score—plain and simple.

## THE FICO FORMULA

Fair Isaac sorts the data from the credit bureaus into five broad categories that have varying degrees of importance in calculating your FICO score. Don't worry, this is not going to require dusting off your calculus textbook. It's fairly straightforward.

| Your... | Accounts for this percent of your FICO score |
|---|---|
| Record of paying your bills on time | 35 |
| Total balance on your credit cards and other loans compared to your total credit limit | 30 |
| Length of credit history | 15 |
| New accounts and recent applications for credit | 10 |
| Mix of credit cards and loans | 10 |

On pages 29–32, I explain what moves you can make to boost your score on these five key elements.

## YOUR FINANCIAL LIFE REDUCED TO THREE DIGITS

After massaging all that info, Fair Isaac uses a formula to come up with a score for you that can range from 300 to 850. Anything between 300 and 500 means you are a toxic financial risk and you are going to be hard-pressed to find any business that will want to work with you. Scores between 500 and 850 are sliced and diced to fall into six ranges; the exact cutoffs for those ranges can vary from lender to lender, but typically this is what you may encounter.

### THE FICO RANGES

**720–850** BEST
**700–719**
**675–699**
**620–674**
**560–619**
**500–559** WORST

So your goal is to get your score into the 720–850 range. The good news is that someone with a score of 721 can get just as good an interest rate on an auto loan as someone with an 849. That's true within every score range.

## A MATTER OF INTEREST

The range your score falls into ultimately determines the interest rate that you will pay on loans. Other factors, such as your employment history and salary, will also affect the deal you get, but your FICO score is a major component in determining the interest rate you will end up paying for a home mortgage or car loan.

| | 720–850 | 700–719 | 675–699 | 620–674 | 560–619 | 500–559 |
|---|---|---|---|---|---|---|
| **30-year fixed-rate mortgage** | 6.0% | 6.1% | 6.7% | 7.8% | 8.9% | 9.5% |

| | 720–850 | 690–719 | 660–689 | 625–659 | 590–624 | 500–589 |
|---|---|---|---|---|---|---|
| **Four-year auto loan** | 5.1% | 5.9% | 8.0% | 10.5% | 14.4% | 15.8% |

The rates above were effective in the fall of 2004. But regardless of what current interest rates happen to be as you are reading this, the difference between the highest and lowest of the acceptable FICO ranges is going to remain constant: about 3.5 points on a home loan and more than 10 points on a four-year auto loan.

If percentages don't do the trick for you, let's convert some of this into cold, hard cash. On a four-year, $20,000 car loan, we're talking about paying an extra $103 a month if your FICO score is in the 500–589 range rather than the top range of 720+. That's $1,236 a year, which comes to $4,944 over the four years of the loan.

I think those are 4,944 very good reasons to care about your FICO score.

## FIRST STEP: GET ALL THREE CREDIT REPORTS

Since your FICO score is a calculation based on the history in your credit reports, your first job is to make sure everything in those reports is correct. Don't assume a thing. The rate of mistakes is sickening.

The big three credit bureaus are Equifax, Experian, and TransUnion. You can get the reports online at www.annualcreditreport.com, or by calling 877-322-8228. And you need to check all three. In a clear case of "nothing is simple," each credit bureau receives different info about you from different sources. For instance, your credit card may report to Equifax but not TransUnion or Experian. Or your cell-phone provider may report to TransUnion but not Experian or Equifax. The result is that you have three different reports, all containing different information. You want to make sure all three are sparkling. (By the way, this also means that you have three FICO scores, not just one. But let's not get bogged down with that just yet.)

By the end of 2005, every consumer will be able to get one free report a year from each credit bureau. This is your credit report only; your FICO score is a separate step we will get to in a minute.

If you don't see your state in the freebie phase-in schedule below, it means you can already get your report at no cost. Otherwise, you need to wait till the dates below, or pay about $9 per report from each bureau now.

### FREE CREDIT REPORT SCHEDULE

| | |
|---|---|
| **June 1, 2005** | Alabama, Arkansas, Florida, Georgia, Kentucky, Louisiana, Mississippi, Oklahoma, South Carolina, Tennessee, and Texas |
| **Sept. 1, 2005** | Connecticut, Delaware, District of Columbia, Maine, Maryland, Massachusetts, New Hampshire, New Jersey, New York, North Carolina, Pennsylvania, Rhode Island, Vermont, Virginia, West Virginia, Puerto Rico, and all U.S. territories |

## CORRECTING YOUR CREDIT REPORTS

If you have errors on your credit report, please know that you are in good company. A recent survey by the U.S. Public Interest Research Group found that 25 percent of reports have serious errors, 30 percent listed "old" accounts that should have been deleted, and 79 percent overall had some sort of mistake or error. You can file a dispute with the credit bureau (again, go to their website or call their 800 number to set the record straight), but I am not going to sugarcoat this; it can take a long time to sort through most of the problems and have the erroneous information removed from your record.

Technically, the credit bureau has just thirty days to process your challenge and get back to you with a response. But all that means is that they must contact the company that supplied the data—say, a department store, credit card company, or auto dealer—and ask them to verify the information. In thirty days you may hear back that the credit bureau is keeping the information on your record because the company that charged your account says it was a legit charge. If this happens, you must start dealing directly with that business.

Some good news is that a new federal regulation that went into effect in December 2004 ensures that any business that you are in a dispute with about a charge must share information with you and promptly investigate the problem. As reasonable as that sounds, it clearly has not been the case for many people who have tried to clear up problems. Contact the business's customer service department to request help in investigating your disputed charge.

Another possibility is that you may find that the "mistakes" on your report are actually the handiwork of an identity thief. Don't panic, and don't beat yourself up about it. This is pretty much a national financial epidemic. On pages 36-37, I discuss how to deal with **identity theft** problems.

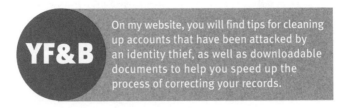

YF&B

On my website, you will find tips for cleaning up accounts that have been attacked by an identity thief, as well as downloadable documents to help you speed up the process of correcting your records.

## GET YOUR FICO SCORE

After you have your credit reports and have taken care of clearing up any mistakes, you are now ready to get your FICO score. Remember, though, that I mentioned that you actually have three FICO scores, based on the different data supplied by each credit bureau. So that can make life expensive, because the charge for *one* FICO score (which automatically includes a credit report) is $14.95.

But don't worry. Unless you are buying a house, there's no reason to get totally FICO'd; you only need to pay for one score, not all three. If you are simply checking your score, take your pick of any of the three. Now, if you are planning to apply for a loan, you need to be a bit more strategic. Typically, a lender you go to for an auto loan or credit card will check just one of your FICO scores. So you want to call them before you apply and find out which FICO score—compiled from the information from Equifax, Experian, or TransUnion—they will use. That's obviously the score you want to check yourself before applying for the credit card or loan.

Here's some trade lingo to help you understand which credit bureau is being used: If the lender says it uses the Beacon score, that means it's Equifax. If they say Empirica, it means they use TransUnion. The Experian name is self-evident— it's Experian/Fair Isaac Risk Model.

A **mortgage** gets a bit trickier. Because this is such a huge financial responsibility, mortgage lenders are going to check all three FICO scores. So in this instance, you need to cough up the money to check all three of your FICO scores. But hey, spending $44.85 to make sure you're in good shape for landing a six-figure mortgage isn't asking much.

I need to stress how important I think it is to make sure you get an actual FICO score. There are other **credit scores** available for just a few dollars, which I know look tempting compared to the cost of a real FICO score and credit report. But saving seven or eight bucks can end up costing you a ton. The problem is that those other credit scores aren't what the majority of lenders and businesses use when checking your history to decide if you are a good credit risk, and those scores can be off by as much as 50 to 100 points from your real FICO score. The FICO score is the industry standard. Consider this scenario: You want to buy a house. So you pay $5 to check your score at one of the "other" services. Everything looks fine, so you go ahead and apply for a mortgage. But when your mortgage lender checks your *real* FICO scores, they aren't as good as you expected, and you end up getting stuck with a higher interest rate on your loan. That could cost you thousands of dollars in extra interest payments. All because you wanted to save a few bucks by not paying for a real FICO score.

## STRATEGY SESSIONS

**PROBLEM:**
There is so much conflicting advice on how to improve my FICO score.

**SOLUTION:**
Focus on what matters to the FICO folks.

Your goal is to do everything possible to please the FICO gods. As the table on page 23 shows, there are **five key areas** that affect your score. So let's just focus on those five areas, in order of importance.

### 1. PAY ON TIME

Your track record in making timely payments accounts for 35 percent of your FICO score. Notice I said nothing there about paying a load of money. All that is required is that you pay the minimum balance due on time. That shows that you are responsible. The longer you manage to be on time, the better your FICO score will be.

Now let's review what qualifies as "on time." Writing the check on the date it is due is not on time. Nor is sending it in three days late but backdating the check. Cute just doesn't cut it.

I want you to write the check and put it in the mail at least five days before your due date. Or if you use online bill pay, make sure you get to it at least two days before the due date. As far as I am concerned, online bill pay is a smart YF&B move. You sit down once a month, and with a few clicks you can have all your bills paid automatically, including your credit card. Just do me a favor: If you have a PDA and use the calendar feature, give yourself a reminder a good three or four business days before the credit card bill is due to sit down at your computer for fifteen minutes and authorize all your online bill payments.

## 2. MANAGE YOUR DEBT-TO-CREDIT-LIMIT RATIO

Your next challenge is to see if you can reduce what is known as your **debt-to-credit-limit ratio**. Your **debt** is the combined balances on all your various credit cards and installment loans—the sum of what you owe. Your **credit limit** is the combined total of the maximum amount each credit card company is willing to let you charge. This calculation plays a big part in determining 30 percent of your score. (Included along with that calculation is whether you carry balances on other accounts, and how much debt you have left on loans such as a mortgage or car loan, compared to the original amount borrowed.)

I bet an example would make this a lot easier to grasp. Let's say you owe $2,000 on one credit card and $4,000 on another. So your combined total debt is $6,000. Next, let's say that the credit limit on your first card is $5,000, and the limit on the second card is $7,000. Add those two together, and you have a total credit limit of $12,000. That means that what you owe ($6,000) is 50 percent of what you are allowed to borrow ($12,000). Voilà; you have a 50 percent debt-to-credit-limit ratio.

Obviously, the lower the ratio, the better. The folks at Fair Isaac say there is no magic cutoff on what counts as a good ratio. Every little increment matters: A 10 percent ratio is better than a 20 percent ratio, which is in turn better than a 30 percent ratio. You get the idea.

One way to get this ratio down is simply to pay down what you owe, but I know that many YF&Bers don't have any extra money sitting around in a bulging bank account. No problem; let's just get a little creative. If you are sure you have the resolve to behave responsibly, I want you to see about asking the card companies to boost your credit limit. Let's say your balance stays at $6,000, but you get your available credit limit bumped up from $12,000 to $16,000. You have now lowered your ratio from 50 percent to 37.5 percent. This helps your FICO score.

The obvious risk with this is that you will be tempted to spend more money because of your higher credit limit. I'll leave it to you to police yourself. It's just a matter of what you want for yourself—a couple new outfits or a higher FICO score so you can spend less on credit card interest and loans.

## 3. PROTECT YOUR CREDIT HISTORY

About 15 percent of your score is based on how long a **credit history** you have. The longer your history, the more "data points" the Fair Isaac folks have in figuring out your money-management habits. That makes them more comfortable in sizing you up.

The big misstep I see so many people make is when they automatically cancel a card. They think they are making a financially responsible move, but it can actually mess up their FICO score because they have just wiped out some important history. Moreover, canceling a card is also going to affect your debt-to-credit-limit ratio, because you have just reduced your "available credit." So here's the deal: Be careful before you cancel a card. If it has a long history, I would opt for keeping it. If you're worried about the temptation of using it, I would simply take a pair of scissors and cut it up. The history stays intact, but you can't use the card. One caveat here, my friends: If you are paying an annual fee for your credit card, I seriously want you to consider replacing it with a no-fee card. Come on, you are broke. You don't have $70 to spend on a fee for "rewards" that you probably can't afford to use.

If you do decide for whatever reason that you want to cancel multiple cards, I would recommend canceling just one at a time; give it at least a month to be picked up by the credit bureaus, and then see how it affects your score. Then proceed with the next card. And always cancel the newest card first; you want to protect your cards with the longest history.

## 4. & 5. CREATE THE RIGHT CREDIT MIX

The final 20 percent of your score is split between your "new credit" activity and your general mix of cards. Nothing too shocking here: Don't apply for a lot of new credit cards or loans all at once. It makes lenders nervous when they see that you are increasing your ability to build up debt. At the same time, lenders always want to see a good mix of credit cards, retail cards, and installment loans, such as car loans or home mortgages, where you make monthly payments for a fixed amount and for a finite period of time. Your ability to juggle those different responsibilities is a measure of your credit-ability. But be careful here. I would not suggest saying yes to every store that offers you its own credit card. That's going to show up as too much new credit. If you have one retail card, great. No need to have three or four—especially if you are going to be applying for a loan anytime soon.

**PROBLEM:**
When I went to check my FICO score, I was told that I did not have one.

**SOLUTION:**
You need to start charging ahead.

This problem is about as common as anyone under the age of thirty not owning a cell phone, but hey, it does in fact still happen. If you find you don't have a FICO score, I bet you also don't have any credit. Remember, your FICO score is merely a calculation based on your personal financial data that is collected by the credit bureaus. If the bureaus don't have any financial dirt on you, then you can't have a score.

While I commend anyone who is able to make their way in the world with no debt, the screwy reality is that you are actually putting yourself in financial danger. The bottom line is that you need a FICO score. You need to be on the financial map, so to speak. Someday, you may indeed want to borrow money—to buy a home or car or to start a new business. Without that FICO score, it's going to be awfully tough to get a loan, or at the very least, you may have to pay a lot more—a higher interest rate—because the lender doesn't have a clue whether you are a good credit risk or not.

Don't worry, this isn't a catch-22; you will be able to get credit cards so you can start building up a history with the bureaus. Credit card companies will be happy to issue you a card based on your income; the only hitch is that the interest rate might be higher because you are an unknown. But hey, you made it this far without a card, so you don't strike me as someone who is going to be running up an unpaid balance. Another option is to open a "retail" card at a department store, which you can use once a month or more. Please be super-careful with a retail card; they tend to charge enormous interest rates, so pay your bills on time. And don't jump at every offer to open a card so you can save 10 percent on your purchases. (How many times have you been hit with that checkout come-on?) Realize that if you open too many cards, you are going to cause some alarms to go off when your FICO score is eventually calculated. Remember, the exercise here is to get one retail card and use it responsibly, so the credit bureaus show a gleaming record of your transaction history. In time, that will give you a good FICO score.

One other option is to take out a secured credit card. With this deal, you get a credit card that looks and smells like the real plastic, but the difference is that your charge limit is whatever amount you have deposited with the card issuer. You have, in essence, secured the card with your own deposit. The same idea applies here: Get the card, use it like a pro, and you will start to build up a sparkling rep at the credit bureaus. Turn to page 95 for information on where to shop for a secured credit card.

Don't worry, I'm not going senile, I know we covered this on page 31, but it is so important that it bears repeating: Do not cancel your cards if you have had them for a long time.

The length of your credit history—how long you have had credit—accounts for 15 percent of your FICO score. If you wipe out your history by canceling cards that you've had for a number of years, you will hurt your FICO score. It is also going to affect your debt-to-credit-limit ratio, which is a big component in figuring out 30 percent of your FICO score. So be very careful before you cancel a card. As I explained earlier, if you want to get rid of the temptation of extra cards, simply give them the scissor treatment. You won't be able to use them, but your history will stay intact. If you absolutely feel the need to cancel—perhaps you have too much total credit available and it is making a lender nervous—be tactical. Cancel your newest cards, not your oldest. Retain the history.

**PROBLEM:**

The interest rate on one of my credit cards shot up from 5 percent to 20 percent, even though I always make the minimum payment on that card on time.

**SOLUTION:**

You need to make sure *all* your card payments are made on time.

There simply is no way to escape a check of your entire credit report.

What happened here is that even though you may have been behaving like a Girl Scout or Boy Scout with this particular credit card—making your payments on time, not running up past your credit limit, etc.—your credit card issuer was doing one of its frequent checks of your credit reports and noticed you missed a payment or went over your credit limit on another card. And that's one big, honkin' warning flag as far as the credit card issuer is concerned. In their world of risk management, the issuer is betting you'll soon fall off the wagon with their card, too. So it is looking for protection if you indeed do become sloppy in handling this card. Jacking up the interest rate is its way of making it worth the while to keep doing business with you. At 20 percent interest, the issuer is getting compensated for dealing with the risk that you may fall behind on payments.

That might be annoying, but it's pretty fair. If you aren't showing them that you are a good credit risk, they have every right to be nervous. But that 20 percent doesn't have to be a permanent situation. Once you work at getting your other accounts in order, and your FICO score starts to climb back up, give your card issuer a call and tell them you deserve to have your interest rate lowered. As I will explain on page 99, when your account is in solid shape, you actually have plenty of bargaining power.

You need to check your credit reports at least once a year to make sure that the only charges and accounts credited to your name are indeed ones you know about. Unfortunately, there is a booming business among financial burglars who steal your financial info—it can take as little as an account number and Social Security number—and then run up charges on your account. Or the thieves use your info to open an account that you don't even know exists (they have the statement mailed to a different address) but is credited to your report and FICO score. This is what is known as identity theft.

It can take months to clear up identity theft issues, but at least you will not be on the hook financially. Your credit card company has the right to hold you responsible for $50 in unauthorized charges, but these days, even that fee is typically waived. The card issuers know they have an epidemic on their hands, and they aren't looking to soak the victims.

If you think someone is illegally piggybacking on your account, contact one of the credit bureaus and put a fraud alert on your account. That credit bureau will send the alert to the two other bureaus. You can contact the fraud divisions at Equifax (800-525-6285), Experian (888-397-3742), and TransUnion (800-680-7289). But it never hurts to follow up to make sure this was done. This alert will require all creditors (card companies, department stores, etc.) to contact you directly before granting any new credit. It will also inform anyone who takes a look at your credit report (such as a mortgage lender) that there may be a fraud problem that could help explain a low score.

The standard fraud alert lasts for as little as ninety days. But thanks to a new federal regulation, you can also opt for an extended alert, which will stay on your record for seven years. Members of the military may request an active-duty alert that is good for at least twelve months; it is designed to protect men and women while they are serving outside the country.

After the fraud alert is in place, you must submit a challenge to the bureau, contesting any charges that you say you didn't make or authorize. And call your local police department to file a criminal complaint. This is an important document in speeding up the process of undoing the damage. You will also need to complete an ID theft affidavit, provided by the Federal Trade Commission. (If it makes you feel any better, ID theft is the number-one consumer complaint made to the FTC.)

The Federal Trade Commission reports that it can take ID theft victims twelve months to clean up their accounts. During that period, you can have a tough time getting approved for any credit. There is no good news in any of this, but I do encourage you to try and keep your head up. It's not your fault. It happens to millions of Americans each year. Don't let it send you into a deep depression. You will get it cleared up.

**YF&B** You can download the FTC's ID theft affidavit form and fraudulent-account statement on my website. It walks you through how to file reports with the credit bureaus and your creditors. I also have a link to great ID theft resource information compiled by the Privacy Rights Clearinghouse, a nonprofit group that follows consumer-privacy issues.

I've been told that too many lenders checking my FICO score can actually hurt my score. I am not clear how I am supposed to comparison shop without causing my score to drop.

**SOLUTION:**
Shop till you drop, just keep it inside a two-week period.

When you shop for a mortgage, the lender is going to want to see your FICO score ASAP. And it makes absolutely perfect sense to worry that if you are doing a lot of shopping around, your credit report is going to have a lot of inquiries. Typically, a lot of inquiry activity is seen as a negative. It is interpreted as a sign that you may be looking to pile on a ton of new debt. But that's not what is going on here. It's not like you are going to take out six mortgages, right? You are going to have only one mortgage, but right now you are shopping among six different lenders. The Fair Isaac brains appreciate that you are just trying to be a smart consumer on what is probably going to be the biggest purchase of your life. So they developed a pretty elegant work-around. If you do all your mortgage shopping in a two-week period, all the inquiries will be combined and will count as just one, so your score will not be hurt.

**PROBLEM:**

My finances are such a mess that I'm thinking bankruptcy might be my only option, but I wonder if that will make my FICO score even lower.

**SOLUTION:**

Don't worry about the FICO score—concentrate on correcting the root of your problem: digging out of your financial mess.

Declaring bankruptcy is going to make a bad situation absolutely awful. A bankruptcy stays on your credit reports for up to ten years. That's ten years of being saddled with a big, ugly demerit. The negative impact lessens with each passing year, but be prepared for a lot of financial hurt, because when you file for bankruptcy, the only way you will be able to get new credit cards or loans is if you pay super-high interest rates.

And when your credit report takes a hit, so does your FICO score. The Fair Isaac crew insists there is no set formula. The higher your score pre-bankruptcy, the farther it can fall; 200 points isn't out of the question. The bottom line is that you are going to feel some real FICO pain if you declare bankruptcy.

With all that on the line, my advice, especially for the YF&B, is to do everything you can to avoid declaring bankruptcy. If you can dig your way out of your financial mess, the sense of accomplishment will be priceless. I discuss bankruptcy in more detail on page 111.

Pay the minimum on time.

That shows that you are responsible.

**PROBLEM:**

I am behind on my student loan repayment and am worried it is going to affect my FICO score.

**SOLUTION:**

You are right to be worried; even your student debt is reported to the credit bureaus, so cut the slacker attitude and make those payments.

I am the first to say that student loans are good debt; after all, they finance your future, not some blowout trip to Cabo. But come on, debt is debt. And if you can't repay your student loans, why should anyone trust you to handle a credit card or mortgage any better? Unpaid student loan debt can also stay on your credit record forever; that's because unless you get a special court order citing undue hardship, your student loans are never "forgiven." Even if you declare bankruptcy, you will still be held liable for your student loans. That means as long as you are on the hook for the loans, your payment (or nonpayment) record is going to stay a part of your credit file. That's gonna be a tough one to explain to anyone wondering why your FICO score is lower than the New Orleans water table. If you need help getting your student loan debt under control, just head on over to page 124, where I walk through how to consolidate your student loan debt and choose the right repayment schedule. Just like a credit card, you need to commit to paying something. On schedule. Every month. That's going to help you boost your FICO score, not drag it down.

**PROBLEM:**

I need to get my FICO score as high as possible before I apply for a mortgage so I can get the lowest possible interest rate.

**SOLUTION:**

Keep your credit card bills super-low in the months before you apply for a mortgage.

As we discussed on page 30, your debt-to-credit-limit ratio plays a big role in determining 30 percent of your FICO score. If you can keep the debt side of the equation to a minimum, it is going to help boost your score. For example, let's say you typically have a $3,000 balance and a $12,000 limit. I want you to do everything you can to pay off or lower that balance. Even taking it down to $2,000 will reduce your debt-to-credit-limit ratio from a good 25 percent to a super-good 16.7 percent. If you don't have any money to pay down that debt, see page 150 for some possibilities for where you might be able to find money that you did not know you had.

Ideally, you want to cut off your credit spending for the two months before you apply for a mortgage. If that's not realistic, just do everything you can to minimize your charges.

And be careful, even if you always pay your balance in full each month. Your credit report can still show your current balance, even though you're in the grace period when your payment isn't yet due. So let's say you have a $3,000 bill this month, which you intend to pay in full, and a credit limit of $6,000. If a lender happens to check your FICO score before you have made the payment, your ratio is going to be calculated at 50 percent. Even though you intend to pay it off by the due date, you have a major ding on your FICO score, because FICO has no way of knowing for a fact that you will indeed pay it off on time. So it deserves repeating: For two months before applying for a major loan, try to keep your credit card spending to an absolute minimum. Ideally, you won't even take them out of your wallet.

**PROBLEM:**

When I tried to buy a new car with the advertised zero-percent-interest-rate car loan, I was told that my FICO score wasn't good enough to get the deal.

**SOLUTION:**

Get your FICO score above 719, and you can drive a great deal for any type of loan.

Please tell me you're really not shocked that what you saw or heard in the ad isn't a slam dunk. Come on, we're talking about auto salespeople here! They are the masters of doing anything to lure you in, get you hooked on your dream ride, and only then hit you with the news that your financial deal isn't going to be as great as the one in the ad because your FICO score isn't in the highest range. Listen hard to the next radio ad you hear, or read the fine print in a newspaper ad; there's always the disclaimer that not everyone is going to qualify for the zero-percent-interest deal. And it all comes down to your FICO score.

Let's try to see this from the lender's perspective. If you were going to lend out the big bucks and not charge any interest on it, would you prefer to do a deal with someone who is a sure bet to pay you back, or are you just as comfortable dealing with a financial flake? Obviously, you want to work with the person who has the highest probability of paying you back. The FICO score is the best tool lenders have in figuring out the probability that someone will repay his or her loan. Walk into the car showroom with a FICO score of 720 or better, and you'll have a shot at a zero-percent-interest deal.

**PROBLEM:**
My life partner/spouse and I want to buy a house together, but our FICO scores are polar opposites. We're not sure how that is going to affect the interest rate we'll be offered on our mortgage.

**SOLUTION:**
Only the person with the good FICO score should apply for the mortgage, so you can get the best interest rate. Once you have the great rate—and great house—you can add the other partner to the title of the house.

If you and your significant other are two or three FICO ranges apart, my advice is for only the person with the highest score to apply for the mortgage. That's your best shot at getting the lowest possible interest rate. Of course, that presumes that you can qualify with just one income. If you need both of you to be on the mortgage application, you are definitely going to get dinged for the lower score.

Lenders typically get all three FICO scores for each person applying for a mortgage. Some lenders might use the lowest of the six scores to determine your interest rate. Others might use the middle score for each of you. A cynic might say they do that to maximize their profit, but you also have to take on some of the responsibility here. If one of you has a lousy FICO score, that means the lender is taking on more risk in offering you a loan. The interest rate is a reflection of how big a risk they feel they are taking. Your best move may be to wait a year and concentrate on improving that lower FICO score.

Now, if you do opt for the one-person application, I want you to know that after you have the mortgage you can add the other person to the title of the house. But I'd actually recommend waiting for your significant other to whip his or her FICO score into shape. Why? Because he or she may in fact be a deadbeat! Also, if you want to refinance or get a home equity line of credit (HELOC), you may have the same problem all over again.

Go to my website and see sample mortgage rates based on your score. You can also use the mortgage calculator to compute the different monthly payments based on whether you can qualify for a lower-rate mortgage or will be stuck with a higher payment because of the "problem" FICO score on your application.

**PROBLEM:**

I want to get my kids started building good FICO scores, but I don't want them to have their own credit cards yet.

**SOLUTION:**

If you have a good FICO score, let your kids piggyback on your credit card so they "earn" your credit score.

Your genes and sparkling personality aren't all that you can pass along to your kids. You can also give your kids your FICO score simply by adding them to your credit card account as authorized users. As long as their names are on the account, they start building a file at the credit bureaus that reflects your credit history. If you have a great FICO score, they will now have one, too.

Technically, you don't even need to tell them that they have a credit card. But I actually think once you have a fifteen-year-old, it is your obligation to teach him or her good money habits. You no doubt remember what happened when you went off to college and signed up for your first credit card and then ran up a whopping bill that you couldn't pay. Wouldn't it make sense to spare your kids that expensive lesson? You can start by giving them a strong FICO score before they even head off to college, and an ongoing lesson in responsible credit card management so they don't fall into the debt trap freshman year.

You can get an authorized card by calling your card's customer service line. One important caveat here: Please don't do this if your FICO score is below 720. The idea here is to help your child, not pass along any bad habits. Check out the story below—it's a telling tale of how parents can financially hurt their kids, which I know is something you would never do intentionally.

**PROBLEM:**

It turns out that my FICO score is a mess because I am listed on my parents' card and they are credit disasters.

**SOLUTION:**

It's easy to get your name off their account and have their bad habits wiped off your credit report.

I know parents are supposed to be the responsible ones in the family, setting a good example for their kids. But when it comes to the baby boomers—your folks—they are not necessarily the most fiscally responsible generation. They have perfected the art of spending, even if they don't have the cash to cover their expensive tastes.

Before you say that that's not your problem, you might want to consider what happened to one YF&Ber who thought he was a FICO star, only to discover that his parents had made his good financial name mud.

Mark was thinking about buying a new car, and decided before heading off to the dealer that he would check his FICO score. The car was a stretch for him financially; his only real shot was if his FICO score was high enough to nab the zero-percent-interest loan deal. He got quite a shock when he saw that his FICO score was 643; he was so sure he would land in the top tier of 720+ because he was so careful about paying his bills on time and not being a charge-a-holic.

After checking his credit reports, he discovered that his problem was all in the family. He was listed as an authorized user on one of his dad's cards, and Dad had not made a payment in three months and was over his credit limit.

At first Mark couldn't believe this was happening. How could Dad be so irresponsible to involve his child in his mess? But then Mark looked closely at his report and realized what happened. Ten years ago, when Mark left for college, Dad added him to his card. Dad wanted to make sure Mark always had the card for emergencies. Mark never ended up using the card, because the first day of freshman year, he signed up for his own card, and has been using it ever since. But according to the credit bureaus, Mark was still an authorized user on Dad's card, and that meant he had inherited his father's credit record, which was now a mess.

The good news is that if you are an authorized user on anyone's card, you have absolutely no financial responsibility for their debts. All you need to do is have your name removed from their account, and their record will be wiped off your credit report. One slight curveball is that the credit card company won't accept the request from the authorized user; they want to deal with the person who is responsible for the account. So in this example, Dad would have to call and make the request that his son be taken off as an authorized user. And you want to get a written confirmation that the change has been made to the account. Trust me, it's going to come in handy for your next chore: dealing with the credit bureaus. And check back with the credit card company in about a month to make sure they are no longer listing you as an authorized user. You just can't be too careful.

Once your name is removed as an authorized user, your credit reports should be updated within thirty days or so. But I wouldn't assume that this will happen automatically. When you check your report after a month or so, if the bad account is still showing up, you need to contact the bureau and press for the change. That written confirmation from the credit card company can come in handy as evidence that you are no longer named on the account. When your credit report is cleaned up, then your FICO score should go up.

# QUICK PLAYBACK

⇨ Check your credit reports at least once a year to make sure there are no mistakes that could make your FICO score lower. By the end of 2005, everyone will be able to get one free report from each credit bureau at www.annualcreditreport.com.

⇨ File a fraud alert with a credit bureau if you think you are a victim of ID theft.

⇨ Complete an ID fraud affidavit if your account has been stolen or "borrowed" by a financial criminal.

⇨ Check your FICO score once a year. If your score is below 720, see the advice on pages 29–32 for ways you can improve your score.

⇨ Always pay your bills on time, even if it is just the minimum, to keep your FICO score strong.

Do not cancel your credit cards as a way to improve your FICO score. It may actually cause your score to drop.

Keep your mortgage shopping to under a two-week period, so your FICO score will not be negatively affected.

Keep a partner with a low FICO score out of the mortgage. If you are buying a home with a life partner or spouse, and one of you has a low FICO score, the partner with the higher score should apply for the mortgage alone. That way, you will get a lower interest rate.

Pass down your FICO score to your kids. One of the best ways to educate your children on smart financial management is to send them off to college with a great FICO score and an appreciation of why that's a very big deal. Add a child to your card and they will inherit your credit profile.

# career moves

chapter **2**

You are way too
young and fabulous
to sign up for a
life of drudgery.

# THE LOWDOWN

Talk about rough starts. Navigating your way in the work world the past five years has been anything but easy. The job market has been so ugly, recent college grads are feeling lucky if they can get any job that pays the bills, regardless of whether it is in a field they are really interested in. And anyone with a few years of real-world experience is itching to move on to something better but not sure there *is* anything better out there right now.

It's not exactly what you were anticipating when you and your parents piled on the debt to finance your college education, is it?

But this is not going to be a pity party. If you are currently stuck in a job that doesn't excite you or a field that you think is a dead-end, your job is to get out. As soon as possible. Please know I say this with the complete awareness that making a switch is not easy. I am not some clueless optimist. I get what is going on in the job market right now for young adults. I know you feel trapped by the economy and you think you should just settle for any job that you can land, and hold on to it. That is absolutely understandable.

But I am writing this book to help you build a strong future. And from my vantage point, you are setting yourself up to be one unhappy puppy five, ten, or twenty years down the line if you settle into a career today that doesn't really interest you. Each year you stay, it will become harder and harder to make a change; the reasons to stay put will keep piling up: You don't want to start over if it means making less money; after a few years working, you can't imagine the financial hit of going back to school; you take on some big-ticket responsibilities (a house, kids, etc.) that make it tougher to move. So you stay put. And you wake up a few years later and can't believe you are the middle-aged, slump-shouldered person you vowed you would never become.

Look, I told you this book was going to come flying at you from a fresh angle, and that is going to start right here. Conventional wisdom says that you should be grateful you are employed in today's economy, period. I think that's dangerously shortsighted. Try hard to picture yourself in your current career ten or twenty years down the line. If it's not a pretty picture, you should be thinking about planning a career switch now. It may take you a few years to figure out what you want to do and to get yourself started down that path. But the point is that you are working today to put yourself in a position to enjoy what you will be doing years down the line. That's not pie-in-the-sky career advice. That's Life Management 101. You are going to be working for thirty or forty more years! Why would you want to set yourself up to spend your life miserable five days a week?

I know what I am talking about. After I left school, I spent seven years working behind the counter and waiting on people at a restaurant. At my peak, I was earning $400 a month—twenty-nine years old with an annual salary less than $5,000, and the sinking feeling that I was going to be a waitress forever.

How's that for a rough start?

But I didn't settle. I just made up my mind that there was a big difference between a job that simply paid the bills and a career that I could enjoy and grow in. I wanted a career. I want you to make that same choice for yourself. Yes, I know it is hard. Yes, I know it takes courage. But at the same time, you are in a perfect position to make that change. When you are YF&B, you have far more flexibility than you will ten or twenty years down the line. Use that to your advantage today to build that better future.

## INVEST IN YOURSELF

After the waitressing stint, a fluke set of circumstances landed me in a training program to be a stockbroker. Forget all the crap about P/E ratios, growth rates, and market share. Here's the big lesson I learned from my clients and colleagues: The best way to make money is to look for an undervalued asset, borrow money to invest in it, and then hold on until it appreciates enough that you can sell it, pay off your loan, and pocket a nice profit.

What does this have to do with your career? Don't worry, I am not suggesting that you become a stockbroker. But when I look around these days, I don't see too many surefire great, undervalued assets. As I write this book, real estate in many areas looks a bit pricey and risky. Stocks aren't screaming "buy." But *you* strike me as an incredibly undervalued asset. You have a great education, great skills, and great energy. You have what it takes to succeed in a career that truly interests and excites you. If that sounds too rah-rah for you, that's your first problem. If you don't think you are fabulous, if you don't have incredible confidence in yourself, you will never have the strength to go after what can make you happy. Don't tell me you are willing to sell yourself so short.

Please just focus for a moment on the Y part of YF&B. I want you to use it to your advantage. All you need is time to make your mark in the field of your dreams. The time to pay your dues is now.

And I know how you can buy yourself the time to do just that.

## TAKE CREDIT

Before you hit me with, "But Suze, I can't afford to follow my dreams because I won't make enough money starting out [or starting over]," I want you to listen up. I know passion alone doesn't pay the bills. If the career that gets your motor running doesn't bring in enough money during the dues-paying years, I want you to use your credit cards to fill in the gaps.

Yep, you read that right. It is so important to spend your YF&B years focusing on getting started in a field that makes you happy to wake up Monday morning, I am giving you the green light to use your credit cards. If your salary doesn't cover your bills and living costs during your dues-paying years, then charge it. Notice I said "bills and living costs." Those are *needs,* not desires. And the trick is to know how to play the current credit card environment to your advantage. The average interest rate is about 15 percent, but if you know what you're doing, you can get an initial rate as low as zero percent that eventually adjusts to less than 10 percent. If you think about it, that's an incredibly great way to give yourself a career loan; you can take the low-paying job and finance your extra living costs on a low-interest-rate credit card.

In Chapter 3, Give Yourself Credit, I will talk a lot about my credit theory for the YF&B crowd and give you the rules of the road for accumulating debt. But for now, let's focus on making sure you are building a great career for yourself rather than settling for a job that does nothing for you but pay the bills.

# STRATEGY SESSIONS

**PROBLEM:**
I'm being given more responsibility but not more money.

**SOLUTION:**
That's actually a very good thing, if you know how to play it right.

Early in your career, you are looking for every opportunity to climb a rung. Money should not be your focus. Gaining responsibility and exceeding expectations are your goals at this stage. If you consistently impress your manager and colleagues, you are going to continue to step up the ladder. Eventually, that will bring plenty of opportunity for more money. But that's for later. Right now, you just want to get yourself off the ground.

Lauren, a YF&Ber who went to the Rhode Island School of Design to become a shoe designer, is exhibit A for my do-more-for-less theory for the YF&B.

After graduation, Lauren turned down a $65,000-a-year job as a toy designer to take an entry-level job at less than half that salary at a company that had a shoe-design division. She was fine with the dues-paying work but didn't see how she could make it in New York City on such a low salary. I told her to go for it. When you are in your twenties and thirties, you have the time—and flexibility—to pursue your dreams.

Every few months, Lauren would check in with me; she was taking on more and more responsibility—which thrilled her—but she was still stuck at what she felt was a low salary. She wanted to know how to ask for a raise. I told her that was a big mistake. Her goal was for her boss to notice her work and dedication, not to make more money. This stage of her career should focus on her opportunity to become more, not to ask for more.

She moved to an apartment closer to where she worked so she could save on transportation costs and spend more time at the office. She threw herself into the work, always looking to do more than was expected of her. Within a year she finally got the recognition she deserved. All those long hours and extra unpaid chores did not go unnoticed by the people who make the decisions; she was promoted to shoe designer. Though Lauren was told she would be getting a raise, she didn't know how much, and she asked me if she should step in and tell her boss what level raise she was expecting. I told her no. At this stage in her young career, her goal was simply to concentrate on doing the work to put her career on a great path, and be patient about the money. She didn't have to be too patient; within a few more weeks she got a great raise without having to do any lobbying. And the added bonus is that she loves what she is doing and is on course to create a lifetime career for herself. That's smart job management when you are YF&B.

## DELIVER THE GOODS

What Lauren did so successfully was switch the balance of power in her office. When you first start work, it's perfectly natural to think your boss has all the power. You are the eager beaver who feels you need the job more than your boss needs you. That's a logical starting point. But I want you to do a 180 here. Your goal is to work so hard and be so productive that your boss and your colleagues become totally dependent on you. Don't just do what is expected of you. Anticipate what needs to be done and just go for it without having to be asked. Now, I am not talking about being presumptuous and stepping on toes. A little common sense here, folks. When you perform an expected task, suggest to your supervisor the additional work you might do to follow through on the project. I'm talking about showing initiative, showing you are engaged and enthusiastic.

As you excel at what you do, your value—and power—will grow. You will have your manager appreciating—and worrying a bit—that she couldn't get the job done without you. Once you have made yourself a valued asset at the office, you will have the leverage to negotiate a better salary. Or, as Lauren saw, the money will follow the work.

But notice the order there. Don't expect or demand the money before you have done the work. That will actually hurt you, because you will feel pressure to live up to the raise, or your manager may push you harder and faster because she gave you the raise.

At the point that you are a most valued player in the office, you'll have plenty of options. Not only will it be easy to make your case for a raise to your boss, you also will have the ability to leave. In the process of making yourself indispensable at your job, you have learned a lot and achieved a lot. Your résumé is stronger than ever. So if your boss won't cough up the dough, you'll have the experience to jump back into the job market with new successes to add to your résumé.

**PROBLEM:**
## How do I negotiate a raise without resorting to begging?

**SOLUTION:**
## Let your work make your case for you.

Even though Lauren's bosses eventually got on the stick and gave her a raise, I realize there are plenty of bosses out there who need a serious nudge. And asking for a raise is one of the biggest job stress points I hear about. I think that's sort of silly. It's a sign that you don't think you have earned it. Let me ask you something: If you don't value your work, then how can you expect someone else to value it?

## RAISE THE ISSUE

As we just discussed, first you need to make yourself indispensable to your manager and your team. When you do that, there is absolutely no reason to be stressed out about asking your manager to discuss your compensation. Remember, it's all about the power you have created on the job. Once you have made your colleagues appreciative of your effort and dependent on your work, you will have yourself a nice negotiating position. Come at it with a sense of strength. This is to be a no-begging zone.

What trips up so many of you is that you don't keep your raise rationale confined to your job performance. You include all sorts of external issues that have no place in making your case. Whether you suddenly owe $3,000 in car repairs or you are helping out your retired parents—whatever the strains on your income that arise from your life—these issues, even unspoken, tend to cloud the discussion of why you merit a raise. Your raise negotiation needs to focus solely on your achievements on the job—not what is happening in your personal life. You need to stay clear and single-minded on this point to make the most compelling case.

## STATE YOUR CASE

Before you sit down with your manager for a chat, I want you to submit a written record of your responsibilities and achievements over the past year. You don't want to write a book; remember, you need your manager to read it, not get all glazed-eyed. I suggest keeping it to one or two pages. Try a very direct format. State a responsibility, task, or project you were assigned, and then give your evaluation of how well you performed. Did you meet the deadline? Was your work accepted, or did it require many revisions? If you have responsibility for any budget or revenue items, did you exceed expectations? Ask your manager to solicit feedback from at least three of your coworkers, people you work with in different capacities.

Make sure your manager has your self-evaluation at least a week before your meeting. There are to be no excuses that she didn't have time to read it. In fact, if you end up in the meeting and it is clear that she hasn't read it, do not get frustrated. Be professional but firm and suggest: "Why don't we reschedule this so you have a chance to read through my memo? I think it will help us have a more productive conversation."

## BE CENTS-IBLE

I hope during the review conversation your boss will let you know that you are getting a raise. But if she doesn't, you are to take the lead. I wouldn't phrase it as a question. Rustle up that confidence and try this approach: "Given how much I have achieved and the fact that I fulfilled my responsibilities and took on additional work, I believe I deserve an increase."

If your boss refuses a raise or does not give you the raise that you want, ask for an explanation. If it is because the company is struggling, ask when you can expect your situation to be revisited. In three months? Or in a year? Get that commitment in writing, if you can. If not, make a note in your file of the date the meeting took place and what was discussed for your follow-up effort. Then it's up to you to decide what to do. If you feel you aren't being truly valued or your manager isn't being straight up about the company's financial position, then it is probably time to job hunt. But if you really like your job and the company, talk to your boss about some creative alternatives to a pay raise. Would an extra week of paid vacation make a difference for you? How about taking a class that can help you professionally, and having your company pay the tuition? Or maybe you ask for Friday afternoons off in the summer. If you are a truly valued employee, your manager should be willing to consider any of these options.

## BOW OUT GRACEFULLY

If you are turned down for the raise, and you don't buy the reasoning, then it is time to look elsewhere. Take the high road here. Don't sulk on the job. Don't fume. Just start moving forward. Continue to be the model employee, but also start your hunt for the next job. It may take you a month to find a new job. It may take you a year. Be patient. You don't need a new job; you simply *want* a new job. I also wouldn't be surprised if when you finally do give notice at your job, your manager will kick into high gear and scramble to keep you. At that point, it's up to you to decide which job you want. You have all the power.

I have a boss who does hardly any of the work but takes all of the credit.

**SOLUTION:**
Focus on the big picture. If your boss does well, so will you.

I know it can be difficult to swallow your pride and let others take the acclaim. But often, that's part of the dues-paying that is a necessary phase in every career. As far as I am concerned, every YF&Ber has the same job description. Whether you are an engineer or a chef, your task is to make your boss look good—even a lousy boss who takes credit, doesn't share it, and uses the "me, me, me" management technique.

When you are still establishing your career, you shouldn't be concerned about having the spotlight trained on you at center stage. You are the supporting player in the background who makes your boss—the star in this drama—shine.

But that doesn't mean I am suggesting you resign yourself to a life of professional servitude. First, don't be too myopic here. Your boss may be a jerk, but there are plenty of other folks who you interact with, right? They will see your work; they will appreciate your effort. And hey, don't you think they know all about your boss anyway? My point is that even though your boss isn't giving you credit, your colleagues are going to be well aware of what you bring to the game. You are building a reputation throughout an entire organization, not just with your boss.

At the same time, making your boss look good is good for your career. Stop for a moment and think about your manager. She probably reports to someone, and that boss probably has a boss, too. That's the nature of the business world, right? Everyone is "managing up," trying to impress their boss so they can get promoted. Well, let's say you make your boss look so fabulous that she gets promoted. That means her spot is now open; don't you think you might be in the running for that position?

In the meantime, one way to deal with your frustration is to turn it into resolve. Make a promise to yourself that when you become a manager, you will treat your staff with all the respect you wish you'd gotten when you were an underling.

**PROBLEM:**
My résumé is posted on all the best online job sites, and I spend hours each day sending e-mails to prospective employers, but I am getting nowhere.

**SOLUTION:**
You need face time, not computer time. When you're in a tough job market, it's the personal touch that gets you the job.

Look, I love the Internet and e-mail. I couldn't survive without them. But if you are completely relying on your computer to nail a job, you are nuts—especially in an economy where there aren't enough jobs to go around.

I am all for using websites to see what jobs are out there, and I have nothing against filling out an online application and attaching your résumé with it. But that is only your start. You must also press the flesh. You have got to get your face in front of someone in the HR department or, even better, the person who is doing the hiring. If it's a small company, shoot for a meet-and-greet with the boss.

Making personal contact is an essential job-hunting technique. Just think about it for a moment. There literally may be thousands of résumés submitted online or via e-mail for any one job. And we all know the horror stories that some recruiters and hiring managers use search tools that scan résumés for key words. If your résumé doesn't have the secret word, you are out of luck—even if you are a perfect fit for the job. That's what is so crazy about everyone relying on computers to find jobs and screen candidates. It completely overlooks the human component.

That's why you need to get a chance to sell yourself face-to-face.

Blair, a YF&Ber with two degrees from the University of Wisconsin, diligently sent off her résumé to every school system near her home, in hopes of landing a teaching job. Nothing happened for weeks. Weeks turned into months. Finally, Blair simply decided to call ten schools to tell them she would like to drop off her résumé and hand it directly to the person in charge of hiring. Five of the ten schools told her to come on by. By the end of the day, she had delivered five résumés and met three principals. Each of those principals sat her down for a chat. She got job offers from all three.

Now, as much as I want you all to have such success right out of the box, I realize it can take a lot of persistence to get what Blair landed on her first up-close-and-personal jaunt. But what I hope you'll appreciate is that it won't *ever* happen for you unless you are willing to get out there.

You also need to be packing a big dose of confidence. Whether you are looking for your first job or shopping for your next job, the confidence you bring to the hunt is just as important as your résumé. Timid and cowering aren't going to get anyone's interest. You need to reek poise and self-assurance. And that needs to come through in every interaction with a prospective employer: your e-mails, your calls to their admin staff to ask for an interview, the voicemails you leave. Getting a job these days requires selling yourself. Confidence is one of your most important selling points.

## MAKE CONTACT

When pulling a Blair and making a cold call isn't plausible, you need to find a contact inside the company for help. If you don't know anyone, spread the word that you're looking for an in. Hit up family, friends, and even friends of friends for any connection. Call the cousin of your mother's bridge partner, even if you've never met Mom's bridge partner, let alone her cousin.

Don't be shy or feel desperate because you are asking for help. Come on, in a tough job market, it shows determination and initiative. And remember, every person you come in contact with during a job hunt was, at one time or another (and probably multiple times), looking for work, too. That's a feeling no one ever forgets. You'll also find that there are people who love to help out because it feeds their sense of power and importance. Whatever. All you care about is getting the help, no matter what the motivation behind it is.

When you contact someone for help, make it clear that you are not asking that person to find you a job. You are asking them to help you identify the right people you can meet for informational interviews. That removes any pressure. Be respectful and realistic. If your uncle knows the CEO of a multibillion-dollar company you want to work for, I wouldn't recommend asking for an informational interview with the CEO. What you want to ask is for his suggestion of whom you might contact for an informational interview. Then you get to contact that person and slip in, "Joe CEO suggested I contact you...."

## SHOW YOUR FLEXIBILITY

If you're unemployed or underemployed, you can play that to your advantage by volunteering for part-time work. If there is someplace you really want to work and they give you the "We have no full-time positions" brush-off, push back by asking if they have any contract work. The goal is to get your foot in the door any way you can. Show your enthusiasm and determination by making it clear that you will consider any work.

And I do mean *any*. You are looking for the perfect opportunity, and that's not the same as the perfect job. If your dream is to be the product manager for the coolest widget company in the country, be excited if what you are offered is a job as assistant to the assistant to the product manager. The point is that you will be on the team. Don't worry about where you start in the lineup.

# You can't afford to stay put if you are unhappy.

**PROBLEM:**

How will I know when it's the right time to leave my job?

**SOLUTION:**

Listen to your stomach.

Here's my foolproof method for understanding when you need to leave a job: Give yourself a gut check at 6 P.M. Sunday. If your stomach is tightening and you feel nauseated, I suggest you take that as a pretty clear indication that you need a new job. When the specter of another week of work has you sick to your stomach, you don't need a PhD in clinical psychology to figure out that something is very wrong.

I have a Friday test, too. If all you can think about on your way to work every day is how close it is getting to Friday, you clearly aren't loving the job.

And there's no reason you should stay unhappy. I know I said it earlier, but let's just review one more time: You are at the perfect stage of your life to make a change. If you have yet to start a family or take on a big, honkin' mortgage, you have the ability to make a move. Even if it is to a lower-paying job that excites you. Work is not like school; it doesn't end in four years. It is your life for a very long time. If you don't like your work now, are you telling me that you are just going to stay where you're at, even if it means thirty or forty more years of just making do? You are way too young and fabulous to sign up for a life of drudgery.

**PROBLEM:**

I hate my job and want to go back to school.

**SOLUTION:**

Don't use school as an escape hatch.

I can't tell you how many times YF&Bers tell me that going back to school will solve their problems. But what I sense is that for a lot of you, the back-to-school strategy is an excuse—an easy out, not a solid career move.

There are two basic scenarios at play here. The first camp of back-to-schoolers are YF&Bers who were laid off during the lousy economy of the past few years and haven't been able to get another good job. They may have part-time jobs, but they are what our government bean counters annoyingly refer to as "under-employed." Then there's the other group: those who just hate their jobs and want to escape.

In both cases, you need to have an honest chat with yourself. If the first time you thought about going back to school was after you got laid off, I am highly dubious about your motives. If you want to quit your job and go back to school for a degree that isn't necessary or even related to any specific career, you are in for a bunch of trouble. You won't really solve anything. You are just trying to avoid a situation you don't like right now.

As I will explain in a moment, making a career change must be carefully thought out. You want your motivation to be all about the excitement you have for a new career, not merely the relief of getting out of one you currently hate. If you can honestly say that you are going back to school for all the right reasons, then I say go for it.

**PROBLEM:**

I really want to change careers, but I am afraid I won't be able to pay my bills, especially if I go back to school.

**SOLUTION:**

This is the perfect time to go for it, even if it means a short-term money squeeze. Use your credit cards to make ends meet while you build a better future.

It is understandable that money concerns make you feel stuck. You pretty much live paycheck to paycheck, so you don't even allow yourself to dream about doing something different if it means taking a pay cut or, even worse (money-wise, that is), going back to school.

I get where your head is, but I want you to fight the temptation to let money concerns keep you stuck. You can't afford to stay put if you are unhappy. You have got to make the change. I don't care if I sound like a broken record: The best part of being young and fabulous is that you have the flexibility and time to start over, even if you just got started a few years ago. Sure, it takes a bit of money discipline to finance the shift to a new career, but that's a short-term situation that will put you in position to enjoy a long career.

One of the reasons I was so excited to write this book is because you have the opportunity to change anything—*yes, anything*—in your life that you don't like—including rebooting your career. Do you realize how young twenty, twenty-five, thirty, or even thirty-five is? There's a pretty good chance that you are going to be living well into your nineties. That shouldn't be depressing; that should make you excited. Even if you start over right now, you have plenty of time for a successful (new) career *and* a long retirement.

If you are a YF&Ber who has yet to start a family or pile on a hefty mortgage, you can't tell me you are shackled by too many financial burdens to be able to take a short-term hit to your income. There's no reason you can't think outside of your unhappy career box. Sure, it is going to require some trade-offs. Maybe you find a roommate for a few years so you can afford to go back to school or take a lower-paying job. Or you find the resolve to reduce your living costs a bit. If making a change is a priority, you will find the means to get the job done.

## RESEARCH, DON'T RUSH

We are so programmed for immediate gratification—and the pressure to succeed ASAP—that we move way too fast in just about every aspect of our lives. When it comes to pondering your career, slowing down is so crucial. The goal here isn't to make a rash decision in one week. It's about spending a few months, maybe even a year, exploring, researching, and plotting a change that will work for the rest of your life.

Think of yourself as a growth company, and you'll want to map out a business plan to grow your business over the next few years. You don't want to simply make a move away from something you don't like into something else that won't hold your professional attention. It can take time to figure out what it is you really want to do.

If you know you hate your job but don't know what you want to do, then give yourself a project each week to research different careers that might interest you. Talk to friends, go back to your school's alumni association, and see if there are other alumni in that new field who you can talk to. Sign up for a night class at a local university to see if a new subject area really interests you. If you are considering studying in an area that is at all related to your work, talk to your boss and HR rep about having the company pay some or all of your tuition.

## CREATE A CUSHION

If your new career involves going back to school, even part-time, or taking a new job at lower pay, I want you to take the time to build up a bit of a cash cushion to help you through this transition. I know this is a touchy subject; you get to the end of the month and you can't pay the bills, let alone save any money. So you're probably sitting there shaking your head at me right about now.

All I am asking is that you take a serious look at your life and see if there is any opportunity to squeeze some money out of what you make today to set aside in savings. Maybe there isn't; if you're eating ramen noodles for dinner every night, then you most likely have made every cut you can. But give it a hard look. If you live alone, what about taking on a roommate to save on rent and split utilities? Steer clear of $10 martinis when you are out with friends. Spend a vacation at home or visiting nearby friends, rather than booking a cheap flight and staying at a modest hotel. All that still adds up. You get where I am going here; I know it's not fun to scale back, but it's just temporary. Remember, we're aiming to get you onto a career path you love. Down the line, that is going to make you happier and more productive. And with that will come the money to live your life without penny-pinching. For more details on how to unearth money from your life without making more money, see page 150.

Remember, we're aiming to get you onto a career path you love. And with that will come the money to live your life without penny-pinching.

# QUICK PLAYBACK

➡ Focus on the right career, not a job that simply pays the bills. There is no reason to settle for less when you are so young.

➡ Aim for the best opportunity, not the best salary. The right job at the right company in the right field is your goal early on. Follow your passion. There will be plenty of time to make money down the line.

➡ If following your dreams means having a measly salary for a few years, use your credit cards to fill in the income gap. You are not to use money as an excuse for sticking with something you hate.

Work hard; make yourself indispensable. When others are dependent on you, you have the power.

Your job is to make your boss look good. Period. And remember that your coworkers will be well aware of who's doing the heavy lifting.

There's no need to beg for a raise if you know you've earned it.

Going back to school makes sense only if it is a necessary step in a well-conceived career change. Otherwise, it's just a bad excuse to get out of a situation that isn't working for you.

give yourself credit

Used correctly, your credit cards may be your ticket to living out your career dreams.

# THE LOWDOWN

Check your expectations at the door before you read any further. You're probably expecting me to jump all over you about how evil credit card debt is, and what a financial hole you are digging for yourself if you run a high credit card balance. Don't sell me short.

It is true that I have spent the past ten years telling the OF&B generation (Older, Fabulous & Broke) that running up credit card debt to finance an indulgent lifestyle is flat-out stupid. But that is not advice for the YF&B, who are just trying to make ends meet and live off their credit cards.

I'm changing my hawkish debt stance for you because I understand that you are Generation Broke. By that, I don't mean that you were born broke, but that what many of you have had to face in the early years of adult life has made you broke. You have had the bum luck of stepping out into the work world during an incredibly tough period when it seemed impossible to get ahead financially. Good jobs with good pay are hard to come by for recent grads. As if that's not stressful enough, you break out into hives every time you think about how long it is going to take you to pay off your student loans. The average debt load for a bachelor's degree is close to $19,000, and a grad degree adds another $31,000 or so to your debt.

Those of you who have been out of school for a while haven't had an easy ride, either. Since 2000, your jobs may have disappeared, or your paychecks may have shrunk along with your company's balance sheet. Career advancement has taken a backseat to career survival.

At the same time that you are struggling to get by, your cost of living keeps climbing. Real estate prices are out of sight in many pockets of the country; the down payment for a starter home in some areas is probably more than what your parents paid for their first home.

Put that all together, and it's clear that many of you are legitimately living in the red; you don't make enough to get by. So I am not going to feed you some head-in-the-sand position that credit cards are the devil in plastic. This book is all about advice that makes sense for your reality—advice that you can act on. So here's my forward-looking advice: Credit card debt can be a financial lifeline in your YF&B years, a temporary tool to fix your broke situation.

Not what you expected me to say, eh?

## JOB 1: A POSITIVE SPIN ON LIVING IN THE NEGATIVE

In case you happened to skim past Chapter 2, Career Moves, I want to quickly review a few key points that tie in to the topic of credit cards. The single most important move you can make right now is to choose a career over a job. A career is work that you are truly interested in, that you will want to do for decades. A job is what you settle for today because the job market is lousy and you've got bills to pay.

I want you to focus on the long view and build a career. If that means taking an entry-level position right now and paying some dues, I say go for it. Yes, it may take a few years to gain traction, but it makes a lot of sense to take the time now to establish yourself in a career that will bring you satisfaction for years. However, many YF&Bers feel so much financial pressure that they lose sight of the long term. Some of you feel forced to give up on your dream careers, while some leave jobs that you truly love—and that offer great long-term opportunities—because you can't afford to live off the starting salary.

That's where credit cards can come to the rescue. I want you to stay focused on your career. Put in the time and effort to prove yourself at work, and don't worry if the pay is pathetic. The early years are all about becoming indispensable in your job so everyone becomes dependent on you. The opportunity to gain experience and traction in your career comes before your income.

Don't worry, I haven't lost it. I know you need money to live on, so you are going to use your credit cards to make up the shortfall between what you earn and what you need to pay your basic monthly living costs. Used correctly, your credit cards may be your ticket to living out your career dreams. If you follow my advice for *responsible* credit card usage, your cards can close the financial gap if your current salary in a career you are excited about doesn't cover your basic living expenses.

## FINANCIAL FOOLS NEED NOT APPLY

Let's make sure we are on the same page here. This isn't some free pass to blindly pile on debt. Don't you dare try to twist this around in your head and interpret my advice as a ticket to live a party-hardy lifestyle courtesy of your credit cards. That is *not* what I'm suggesting. If you think you are entitled to use your credit cards for blowout vacations, a closetful of expensive clothes, and going out four times a week, you are financially deranged.

Are you thinking that you'll be able to pay off the debt as you begin to make more money? Come on, you and I both know that isn't how it works. Look at what has already happened to your finances. A few years ago, you were fresh out of college with no job and $3,000 in credit card debt. When you landed your first job with the starting salary of $25,000, you didn't pay down your card balance; instead, you amped up your spending. Nice vacations, $150 jeans, and an endless stream of meals out with pals ballooned your card balance to $8,000. And if you don't wake up fast, it will double in no time. The simple truth is that the more you make, the more you spend. It's a financially lethal habit. If you don't kick it now, you are going to be staring at some ugly realities in a few years; bankruptcy could be your only way out, or you may feel pressured to take a crappy job that you hate just for the better pay, so you can deal with your credit card debt.

My credit card strategy is solely for expenses that you need to live on — not expenses that finance your living the high life. The only YF&Bers who should try this are those of you who are conscientiously doing everything you can to get your living costs as low as possible but are still coming up a few hundred dollars short each month. In Chapter 5, Save Up, I will provide a slew of cost-cutting ideas. If you give those a shot and are still in the hole at the end of the month, then you can turn to your card for some relief.

Because I want this strategy to be nothing but a lifesaver, we need to lay down some basic parameters. While you are starting out in your career, I think it is perfectly reasonable to lean on your card for monthly living expenses, but you are to keep those charges to less than 1 percent of your annual gross income. For example, if you make $30,000, I don't want you to use your card for more than $300 in monthly living expenses. After two years, that would mean you have charged $7,200 on your credit cards. That's the upper limit of what I think is "safe" for you to take on, given your current earnings. My thinking is that within a few years, your career should be picking up some steam, and you can stop adding to your card debt. Ideally, at that point you would be able to start paying down the balance. And I don't want you to get cowed into thinking that the balance is so big that you will never wrestle it to the ground. Committing to a plan where you add $50 to $100 a month to your required monthly payment will shave down your balance a lot faster than you would imagine.

Ultimately, though, you need to police your own card. It is up to you to gauge whether giving yourself another six months or year to lean on your card will make a big difference in getting your career over the initial dues-paying hump. Just be careful that you don't dig yourself such a large debt hole that you will spend the rest of your life trying to climb out.

Now, if you are going to rely on your credit cards to stay afloat during the formative stage of your career, I want you to understand how to charge smart. That means knowing the difference between necessities and indulgences, keeping your borrowing costs low, and doing everything to keep your FICO score high.

## SAFE AND UNSECURED

Before we start our card strategizing, you need to understand a very important fact about credit card debt. The technical term for credit card debt is **unsecured debt**. What this means is that there is no underlying asset that the credit card companies can come and take away if you do not pay your bills. But that doesn't mean you can skip out on your obligation, nor do I advocate being irresponsible. But I do want you to understand that credit card debt doesn't have the same penalties as secured debt.

With **secured debt**, you offer up an underlying asset that the lender can grab if you fail to make your payments on the loan. This type of loan is more "secure" for the lender, because they have a backup plan if you become a financial flake. For example, if you use a loan to buy a car, the car is the secured asset that the lender will use as collateral. If you can't make the payments, the loan company will come and take your car away (yep, the repo-man scenario). A home loan is another form of secured debt—this time, the house is the collateral. If you can't keep up with the payments, the mortgage lender can force you to sell the home in what is known as a **foreclosure**, so they get their money back.

With your credit card, there is no "secured" asset that the card company can come after. That's one of the reasons interest rates on credit cards can be so high; lenders are looking to make as much money off high interest payments as possible to offset the losses they incur from deadbeat cardholders.

## TAKE CHARGE: GOOD AND BAD USES OF CREDIT

Giving you the green light to use your credit cards to make up legitimate shortfalls when you are YF&B is dependent on you being ultra-conscientious. I know I am repeating myself, but I want to make sure you really got it the first time I said it: Using your credit cards to live off only works if you limit your card spending to truly necessary expenses. Let's face it, there are good uses and bad uses, and you cannot afford to mix up the two.

Buying groceries so you don't go hungry is a good use. Flipping the card on the table to pay a $40 bill for a quick bite out with the gang after work is a bad use. A good use of your credit card is filling the gas tank so you can get to work. A bad use is renting a car for the weekend so you and your pals can head to the beach and run up a tab at a hotel that you really can't afford.

That's just a sampling, but you get the idea. We're talking necessity vs. indulgence. There is no room for negotiation here, no "I deserve a splurge" rationalizations. You can't afford it. Plain and simple. Here is your challenge anytime you take out your credit card: Stop for three seconds. Ask yourself: Good use or bad use? If it's a good use, hand the card to the cashier. If it's a bad use, the card goes back in your wallet.

Now, if you are on the fence about whether a purchase makes the "good" cut, I have an easy tie breaker for you to use: Just ask yourself if the purchase is worth double or triple its cost. I am not being unreasonable—just incredibly practical. What you need to understand is that when your purchases end up on a credit card that you pay 18 percent interest on, and you only send in the minimum amount due each month, the net cost of that purchase once you factor in paying interest is going to be double or triple the initial price tag. So that $150 pair of jeans you've been eyeing carries a real price tag of $300 to $450. That kind of clarity helps, doesn't it?

## FOOD FOR THOUGHT

I get that being so cost-conscious is tough, especially when it comes to certain charges, such as eating out. Sitting down for a restaurant meal with friends is an important part of life; it is how we socialize and relax. That's not to be minimized. But I am constantly amazed when I hear YF&Bers tell me that they can't make ends meet, but then tell me that they eat out four times a week with pals, and it probably ends up costing them about $100 each week. Save the pricey restaurants and clubs for special occasions. Once again, I am not a killjoy, telling you to go monastic. Do you know that a recent report found that on average, people eat 83 meals out a year, and that figure climbs to about 220 when you add in takeout? If we conservatively assume that the average restaurant bill is $20, then the cost of all these meals out and takeout comes to about $4,400 a year. Put that on a high-rate card where you just pay the monthly minimum, and you're probably looking at a net cost of about $10,000 once you factor in all the interest charges over the years. No wonder you're broke!

And you have got to stop being such a wuss when it comes to splitting the bill. You know what I am talking about: You're out for a simple bite to eat with the gang; your pals all order appetizers and entrées, but you stick with a bowl of soup because you're not hungry. Yet when the bill comes and one of your pals suggests just splitting it evenly, you don't make a peep. That's just got to stop. You are to pay only your fair share. Your friends have to respect that. And don't tell me I am being unrealistic, and that you are too embarrassed to let on that you are watching your money. Come on, these are your friends, they understand. And besides, my guess is that they are just as B as you.

You may need to let your friends know ahead of time that you can cover only the cost of what you order. You're in no position to share in the cost of expensive wine or the fact that two of your pals love to have a few rounds of expensive mixed drinks. Do not be ashamed. You are never to apologize for being responsible. If you charge up your credit cards to pay for food that you didn't eat, drinks you didn't have, or a fancy tip that one of your friends decided to leave, don't come crying to me when you don't have money to pay your bills.

## HOLD THE RIGHT CARDS

Now that we're square on good and bad credit card use, your next task is to make sure that the cards you are using give you the best deal. My guess is that you probably are still using the card that you got at freshman orientation years ago. Remember those nice folks who gave you a T-shirt or calculator for simply signing up to get a card? Then a few weeks later your new card showed up in the mail and you became a full-fledged member of Charge-It Nation. No questions asked.

It is time to start asking a lot of questions. If you are going to use your credit cards to live on, you can't afford to spend a penny more than necessary in interest rates and fees. And if you aren't paying attention to the rates and fees, I can guarantee that you are paying too much. Credit card companies make billions of dollars a year off unsuspecting customers who don't realize that they are getting soaked with high fees and interest rates. You need to give your cards a thorough exam to make sure you are doing everything to minimize your costs.

## TAKE INTEREST IN YOUR RATE

If you are going to run up a credit card balance, you want to pay the lowest interest rate possible on that sum. If you don't know your interest rate, check your statement or call the customer service number on the back of your card. If your FICO score is in the high range of 720 or above, and if you have a steady income without a ton of debt, you should not be paying a rate above 10 percent. If you are, it's time to get strategic.

I want you to look around and see if your rate is as good as it gets. See what other offers are out there. You are looking for a card company that will give you a lower interest rate than you currently pay, if you do a **balance transfer**. A transfer involves moving the money you owe on your current card to a new card. (We'll walk through the details of balance transfers in a minute.)

You should be able to get a card that has an introductory rate for six months or a year that is below 5 percent; in many cases, you could get a zero-percent rate for the intro period, after which the rate adjusts to a "regular" rate. Shopping around for a bet-

**YF&B**

On my website, you can find a list of the best credit card deals out there.

ter deal is not an automatic win. If your FICO score is below 720, you may not qualify for the low-rate offers. In that case, you'll have to dedicate some time to improving your FICO score.

## CONSIDER A TRANSFER

When you find a card that offers you a better interest rate—as well as other key features discussed below—do not automatically apply for the card. Before you apply, you are to call your existing creditor and tell them that you want them to lower your interest rate to whatever the balance-transfer rate is on the card that you are considering. Don't ask—tell them. Because of your strong "credit profile," you are in the driver's seat. Let them know that there's another card out there that would love to have your business. I bet they will give you the better deal. If they turn down your request, go ahead and apply for the new card.

When—and if—your application is accepted, you are to see how much of a credit limit they have given you and decide if you will be able to transfer your entire balance from your higher-interest-rate cards. Ideally, you will be able to transfer all of your balance to the new card. But if you can't, then transfer as much as possible. At the same time, call back your "old" card company and bring it to their attention that you have indeed started to transfer your money to a new card. Tell them that to keep the rest of your business, they will need to lower your interest rate. If they don't offer you the lower rate, please be patient for six months, then apply for another new credit card that offers you a better deal and do another transfer. I want you to wait the six months so you don't get dinged on your FICO score; too many new accounts in a short period can hurt your score.

It is important to understand that the super-low rate on a new card is good only on the balance that you transfer. If you make additional charges on the new card, then a higher interest rate will likely kick in. For example, you might get a zero-interest rate on the balance that you transfer to the new card, but you will be hit with 15 percent interest on all new charges that aren't immediately paid off. So use your smarts here: Shop around for a balance-transfer deal where the rate on new purchases isn't too high, or use the new card for the balance transfer only, and use an existing (or new) card that charges a low rate for your regular purchases.

A final note on transfers: You also want to look out for any charges to make the transfer. The card you are leaving could levy a fee for saying adios, and your new card may hit you up, too. These fees are typically a percentage of the balance-transfer amount—say, 3 percent or 4 percent—and some issuers cap it at a max of $50. But that could still mean a stiff $100 fee to move your money from one credit card to another. You obviously want a card that does not do this, or one that charges a low fee.

Now, if your FICO score is too low for you to qualify for a good balance transfer, head on back to pages 29–32 to brush up on ways you can boost your score. If you feel you are in a deep debt hole that you can't see your way out of, don't miss the advice on page 112 about working with a credit counseling service.

## WATCH YOUR GRACE PERIOD

Credit card companies lend you money in the hopes that you will not pay off your balance at the end of every month. They make their big bucks when you have to pay interest on unpaid balances. That's fair business. But the question you have to ask is: When does that interest clock start to tick? You are entirely captive to the good graces of your company. I am talking about the grace period that your card company imposes. This is the time between the statement end date (the closing date of your monthly statement) and the date when your payment is due. If you pay off the bill in full during the grace period, you will owe no interest on any of the purchases you make the next month. But the moment that you carry a balance and do not pay off your bill in full on the due date, you will start to pay interest on every additional purchase from the second you use the card during that month. You will no longer have any grace period, even if you make the minimum payment on time; the grace period works only if you pay off your entire bill on time. Obviously, the goal is to shop for the card with the longest grace period. Twenty-five days used to be pretty standard for grace periods, but many issuers have cut that down to twenty days, and some have no grace period at all. That is unacceptable.

I also want you to actually read each statement you receive; don't assume that just because your due date has always been around the twenty-seventh of the month, it is going to stay that way. Your card company may switch the grace period, and the new due date could move to the eighteenth of the month. Oh, sure, they will tell you about this in those annoying fine-print inserts that no one ever looks at. My advice is simply to check the due date each and every month, to see if they have shortened your grace period.

## KNOW YOUR BILLING CYCLE

This one is buried in the fine print, too, and it can cost you a ton. Credit card companies use one of two basic methods when computing your bill: average daily balance or two-cycle average daily balance. You can find out which one governs your bill by calling your customer service line or looking at the back of your statement. If you carry a balance, the two-cycle method is going to hurt you. If your card uses this method, I want you to stop using it and transfer your balance to a card that uses the average daily balance system.

The problem with the two-cycle method is that you get stuck with higher interest-rate charges. Let me explain. Let's say last month you charged $1,000, and you paid $900 of it. Then this month, you did not ring up anything. So you figure your bill is going to be the $100 and the interest owed on that $100 balance. But instead you have a bill that is charging you interest on the entire $1,000. That's because you have a two-cycle method that looks at the balance for both months, not just the current month. It is a rotten deal that you are to avoid at all costs.

If your card used the average daily balance system instead, you would have been hit up for interest on only the $100 that you didn't pay off. That's a big difference. Check how your cards compute your interest; make sure you do not have any cards that charge on a two-month billing cycle.

## MINIMIZE YOUR MINIMUM AMOUNT DUE

Pop quiz: Do you have any idea how your card company computes the minimum amount due that shows up on your bill each month? It's a simple calculation based on a percentage of your outstanding balance. It typically ranges from 1.5 percent to 2.5 percent; with some cards, the percentage can be even higher. If you are cash-strapped, it can make sense to go with a card that has the lowest minimum. For example, if you have a $3,000 card balance and must pay a 2.5 percent minimum, that is going to run you $75 a month. But at 1.5 percent, your monthly minimum due falls to $45. That's a nice $30 savings.

But I do need to explain that there is a tradeoff here: Because you pay less each month, your balance will get larger than it would if you paid a higher minimum.

That means that it is going to take you longer—and more in interest payments—to eventually pay off your entire balance. I think that's okay; as I said, this is *only* for your YF&B years, when you aren't yet making enough to live on.

## LOOK OUT FOR MISTAKES

Before you pay your bill, scour the statement. Accidents happen. I am not talking about identity theft, but the fact that you can sometimes be double-charged for something due to a processing snafu. Or that credit that you got when you returned a purchase doesn't show up. If you don't make sure everything on your bill is legit and up-to-date, who do you think will?

## PUNCTUALITY COUNTS

There is no bigger way to sabotage the low interest rate that you pay on your credit cards than to not pay your bill on time. There is really no excuse here; you simply need to pay the minimum amount due on your card, not the entire balance. Come on, that's not asking a lot.

You need to get inside the head of the bean counters at the credit card company to win at the rate game. You're not naïve, right? You understand that the card companies hate offering you a low-rate card. They only do it to get you to sign up, and then they start working overtime to see if they can trick you into screwing up on something so they will have an excuse to bump up your rate. Just envision a typical staff meeting at your credit card company. The boss walks in and tells the troops that corporate wants the card division to come up with another $500 million in income from fees next year. So everyone puts on their brainstorming hats to think up new rules that can be buried in the fine print of those super-annoying mailing inserts that no one reads—rules that will allow the credit card company to boost the interest rate on those great teaser deals that they offer you.

Trust me, that's exactly what is going on.

And one of their favorite fine-print games is to change your interest rate the first time you are late with a payment. That can mean kissing an introductory rate of 4 percent good-bye and getting stuck with 21 percent—just because you didn't pay the minimum amount on time.

And if you have multiple cards, you'd better make sure everyone gets paid on time. Card issuers love to check your payment record on any other cards you might have and use it as ammunition to boost your interest rate. Let's say you have a great new card with a 4 percent interest rate. You treat it like a piece of plastic royalty, always being sure to get the payment in on time so you don't lose that great rate. But you aren't as conscientious with your other credit card, and a few times a year you are late with payments. If the card issuer for your low-rate deal checks your payment record and sees you have blown it a few times on your other card, that's enough to boost your great 4 percent rate; it could more than triple as a result.

If you are one of the legions of YF&Bers who tend to leave the credit card bill unopened for weeks rather than face the depressing numbers, you need to change your attitude right now. Do not be bummed or ashamed. If you are using it wisely—for good uses—you can open it when it arrives and pay it on time, even if it is just the minimum. Hey, take pride in knowing that you screwed the bean counters this time.

And let's just review a tidbit from Chapter 1, Know the Score: It is so silly to try to outsmart the card companies by sending in the payment the day it is due. Their computers don't have a heart or a sense of humor. If it doesn't arrive by the due date, your interest rate will be in jeopardy, you are going to get hit with a late fee of $15 to $35 or more, and your credit report is going to show that you were late, which means your FICO score will take a hit.

## CUT THE ANNUAL FEES

If you are paying $50 or $75 in annual fees, there'd better be a really good reason. Most cards are not worth that much—not when you are so broke.

When you are shopping around for a new card, don't let the "bonus" points blind you. Yeah, miles are great, but only if they come with a card that has a great low interest rate, uses the average daily balance billing method, and doesn't charge a big annual fee. Once you make sure those key items are a good deal, then by all means go ahead and sign up for a bonus card. But I also want you to take an honest look at what type of program you will be signing up for. With the super-competitive airfares these days, you can fly to most places in the country for less than a few hundred bucks if you plan in advance, so saving up miles for a few years for one ticket that would cost you less than $300 doesn't necessarily make the most sense. Aim for a more practical bonus card. For example, a card that offers you a discount and rebate for gas can be a great way to earn a little money back on something that you really need today to get by.

## DON'T PAY RETAIL

Credit cards offered through stores, which are known as retail cards, tend to have super-high interest rates. No matter how great your FICO score is, you are going to pay 20 percent interest or more on any unpaid balance. The smartest move is just to say no every time a cashier offers you a 10 percent discount on a purchase if you apply for their card. If you have a regular credit card, you certainly don't need a retail card. The only exception is if you need a retail card to help build your credit reputation; a full explanation is provided just ahead.

**STRATEGY SESSIONS**

**PROBLEM:**
I can't get a credit card.

**SOLUTION:**
Start with a secured credit card and a retail card.

If you are one of the rare birds who doesn't have a FICO score, or if your score is so low that you can't get a credit card, I want you to get a secured credit card. A secured credit card looks and smells like regular plastic, except that your credit limit typically can't exceed the amount of money that you have deposited ahead of time with the card company. That's the "secured" part of it; the card issuer doesn't have to worry too much about you being a credit risk, because they have a security deposit that they can use if you bail on your payments. As long as you are able to make that security deposit, you should be able to get a card. Your goal then is to use the card responsibly—pay on time, don't run over your credit limit, etc.—so that within a year, you will have established a track record at the credit bureaus and will be able to apply for a regular credit card. Think of a secured card as a necessary baby step.

If you have sworn off credit cards and stuck with a debit card that automatically deducts your payments from your bank account, I want you to rethink your strategy and consider moving to a secured card so you can eventually get a regular credit card. One of the biggest problems with a debit card is that you aren't building up a payment history at a credit card bureau. And as I explained in Chapter 1, Know the Score, if you ever plan on buying a home or taking out a car loan, you need that history so you can get a FICO score. Besides, plenty of banks just love to hit you with "small" charges every time you use your debit card; maybe it's 50 cents or $1 each time you use the card. Add up the cost over a year, and I bet you would be talking about a serious chunk of change. It's just another reason not to be so wedded to your debit card.

I don't think prepaid cards are a viable option, either, since they also aren't going to help you build a reputation at the credit bureaus. If you can't get a regular credit card, you are to get yourself a secured card and use it as a stepping stone to a credit card.

A secured card works just like a regular card; you get a monthly statement, and if you pay the bill in full, there is no interest charge. But if you carry a balance, you are going to get smacked silly. That's because secured cards tend to have very high interest rates, above 20 percent. So you need to be super-careful here and avoid running a balance. You also need to shop around for the best secured card deal that charges you the lowest annual fee—it can be $50 or more—and make sure you understand all the various fees that the secured cards love to hit you with. Read the fine print of any offer; with that bit of elbow grease, you can make the secured-card strategy work to your advantage. It's just a short-term solution to get you to your real goal: a regular credit card with a low interest rate.

You can shop for secured cards at www.bankrate.com and www.cardweb.com. Quite often, you can get the best deals through a credit union, which operates a lot like a bank for its members. Membership is typically based on some organization or group, such as teachers or members of the military, though you can often join if you simply know someone who is a member of that particular group.

Go to my website for a link to a credit union finder for your area.

Before you sign up for a secured credit card, call its customer-service line and ask which credit bureaus your record will be shared with. Not all secured cards share their data with the bureaus, and signing up with those cards will defeat your whole strategy. Remember, you are using the card so you can start building a reputation at the credit bureaus. Ideally, you want your information to be shared with Equifax, Experian, and TransUnion, but if your card reports to only two of the three bureaus, that's fine, too.

In addition to a secured card, I also want you to apply for one retail credit card, such as a department store card. Each month, you are to buy one item that you need and pay the bill immediately. Just like the secured card, your retail card activity will be reported to the credit bureaus. But only go for the retail card if you have 100 percent confidence that you will never run a balance; 20 percent interest rates are common on these cards. That's insane. So go for a card only if you have the discipline to make a purchase and pay it promptly in order to build a great credit report.

**PROBLEM:**

The only debt I have is my hefty balances on five credit cards. I want to begin to pay them off, but I don't know where to start. I worry that it will take forever to get the balances down to zero.

**SOLUTION:**

Pay the minimum on all five, and pay extra on the card with the highest interest rate. You will be amazed at how quickly you can dig yourself out of debt.

Getting out of credit card debt is not as hard as you think. You just need to outsmart the credit card company. Let's say you have a $5,000 balance that you pay 18 percent interest on, and your minimum amount due each month is 2.5 percent of your balance. If you pay just the minimum amount due, that will work out to a payment of $125. Then the next month, assuming you have made no new purchases on this card, your minimum amount due will shrink, because it is constantly recomputed to be 2.5 percent of your remaining balance. That recomputing is the credit card company's friendly way to keep you indebted (at 18 percent!) as long as possible. In this example, if you constantly stuck to the minimum payment, it would take you twenty-six years to get the balance down to zero. Oh, and you'll have forked over more than $7,000 in interest payments. It's a nice business those credit card companies have going, right?

But here's what the credit card companies don't want you to know. Let's say that you just keep paying that $125 a month (hey, you found the money to pay it the first month, so you can do it again), even though your required minimum payment is going to be lower. Your balance would be paid off in just five years or so, and your total interest charges would be $2,693.

The following table shows how long it takes to pay off a $5,000 credit card balance.

|  | Initial Minimum Due | Time to Pay Off Balance if You Pay a Recomputed (Lower) Minimum Each Month | Time to Pay Off Balance if You Keep Paying the Initial Minimum Due Each Month |
|---|---|---|---|
| 21 percent | $125 | 33 years, 9 months | 5 years, 10 months |
| 15 percent | $125 | 21 years, 5 months | 4 years, 8 months |
| 9 percent | $125 | 15 years, 11 months | 4 years |

**YF&B** Use the get-me-out-of-debt calculator on my website to see how making extra payments above your monthly minimum will shorten the time it takes you to get out of debt.

When you have multiple cards that carry balances, you need to come up with a unified strategy for all the cards. Here's what I want you to do: Call every card company and see if they will reduce your interest rate; it's worth a try. If you have a good FICO score, you will have more bargaining power. Or look for new cards that will give you a lower interest rate, and transfer your balance.

Once you've done all the rate negotiating or balance transfers that are possible, it's time to start paying off the debt. Your game plan is to concentrate on the card with the highest interest rate, not the card with the highest balance.

- List your cards in order from highest interest rate to lowest—not highest balance but highest interest rate.

- Next to each card's interest rate, write down the minimum that the card company is asking you to send in.

- On the credit card with the highest interest rate, you are to pay as much over the minimum as you can afford. I want it to be at least $50 extra. So if the minimum payment on that card is $50, try to pay at least $100 total on that card.

- On all other cards, pay only the monthly minimum due. And pay it on time.

- Keep paying the extra amount on the highest-rate card until the balance is gone.

- When the first card is paid off, take all the money that you were paying on that first card (which is now paid off) and apply it to the card with the next highest interest rate. So, for instance, if you were paying $100 a month on the highest card and $45 a month as the minimum payment on the next-highest-interest-rate card, you would then take $145 and apply it to the second card.

- Keep paying that $145 per month on the second card until the balance is down to zero. Then take the money that you were paying on the second card ($145) and pay it—plus the minimum amount due—on the card with the third highest interest rate.

- Continue for as many cards as you have.

**PROBLEM:**

The 21 percent interest rate on cash advances is crazy, but when I need the cash, what other option do I have?

**SOLUTION:**

Charge more on your credit card so you don't need to take a cash advance.

Cash advances are the biggest wet kiss you can ever lay on a credit card company, but they leave an awful taste in your mouth. Here's the deal: You take out the cash advance, and your card company starts charging you a super-high interest rate—20 percent or more is common—and there is absolutely no grace period. Even if your regular card transactions have a twenty-five-day grace period, you'll start paying interest on cash advances immediately. But wait, it gets even worse. You won't be allowed to pay off the cash advance until you pay off any balance on your credit card. That's because the credit card company wants you to keep paying the 20 percent or more in interest for as long as they can make you do it. Oh, and did I mention that when you take out an advance, you also could get hit with a fee of 2 to 4 percent of the withdrawal amount?

The best advice I have for you is to avoid taking a cash advance unless it is absolutely necessary. If you tend to take out an advance a day or two before payday because your wallet is empty, think about ways you can use your credit card more during the month—but only for the good uses—so you have more cash around.

If you are already stuck with a credit card where you have a large cash advance that you are paying off at sky-high interest rates, consider a balance transfer to another credit card with a lower rate. And do your best not to use cash advances in the future.

**PROBLEM:**
I have $5,000 in credit card debt that I am paying 18 percent on. I'm thinking of using the $3,000 that I have in savings and a loan from my 401(k) to pay it off.

**SOLUTION:**
Raid the savings account, but don't touch the 401(k).

If you are paying 18 percent interest on a credit card and earning just 1 or 2 percent on interest, which is going to be taxed, in a savings account, then you may be Y&B, but you're shaky on the Fabulous front. It makes no sense to pay 18 percent when you have money sitting around earning just 2 percent or so. You can't stop being broke by volunteering to lose 16 percent a year.

Of course, I understand the urge to have a savings account. I am a huge fan of the emergency fund; it is the ultimate in financial security. But if you have credit card debt, you don't really have financial security, no matter how big your savings account is. So my advice from both a financial and emotional point of view is to use your savings to pay off as much of your credit card debt as possible. Don't panic about not having any emergency money. In a true emergency, you can always use your credit card to pay bills. And as I discuss in Chapter 5, Save Up, there are other creative places to find emergency cash while you are rebuilding your savings account.

But you are never to touch your 401(k) account to pay off a credit card. I know everyone at the office says it's a great deal, but they don't know what they're talking about. Here's the problem: The money that you originally invest in a 401(k) is pretax, meaning it came out of your salary before taxes were deducted. But when you repay the 401(k) loan, you do so with after-tax money. Later in life, when you start to withdraw money out of your 401(k), you will pay taxes on it again. Oh great, you just volunteered to pay Uncle Sam twice on the same amount of money. That's smart?

Cash advances are the biggest wet kiss you can ever lay on a credit card company, but they leave an awful taste in your mouth.

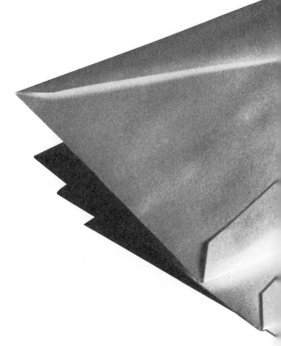

The other reason I don't want you to do this is that if you decide to switch to a new job—or are laid off—most companies will require that you pay the loan balance back within a few weeks or months after leaving. If you don't have the cash handy, you will be in a big jam. The amount that you still owe will be treated just like a withdrawal, and that means you will pay tax at your ordinary income-tax rate, plus a 10 percent penalty because you are not at least 59½. And if you don't have the money to pay it, the IRS will take it right from your 401(k) plan. And just so you know, keeping your money in your 401(k) offers you some nice protection if, God forbid, you ever end up claiming personal bankruptcy; assets in these plans cannot be used to settle your debts in a bankruptcy.

**PROBLEM:**
I cosigned for a friend's credit card, and now that she is deep in debt and not making any payments, the card company is coming after me to pay the bill.

**SOLUTION:**
It's completely legit; push your friend to get the debt paid, or help her out, before your FICO score turns to mud.

This is one of those instances when being a good buddy has bad consequences. When you cosign for a credit card or any type of loan, you are agreeing to take on the financial responsibility. Cosigning is not the same as being a character reference. Cosigning is not merely being a good friend. By cosigning an application, you are saying, "Hey, if my bud doesn't make good on the bills, just come knock on my door. I've got her back."

When your friend first approached you to do this, a few warning bells should have been ringing. If someone needs a cosigner, it means that the credit card company, car financer, or even mortgage lender sees something funky—maybe a lousy FICO score or a very low salary—which makes them nervous. So they tell your pal they will only give her the card or loan if she arranges for a Plan B if she can't pay the bill. Your signature makes you Plan B—B as in "I will happily go broke covering the payments if my friend flakes." Come on, there's no rule of friendship that says you have to be a coconspirator in financial irresponsibility. Even worse is that by cosigning, this credit card becomes part of your FICO score.

Now let's talk about what you can do if you're already in too deep. Ideally, you could sit your friend down and guilt her into getting you out of this mess. You can try, but we both know the chances are pretty slim that this will work. Let's face it, there was a reason she's been avoiding you at parties and not returning your phone calls. She knows what is going on and can't deal with it. So I am not too hopeful that she will snap into shape here. But hey, give it a shot.

The bottom line is that you are going to have to bite the bullet on this one and pay off the debt. It's your very big problem. Friends and finances can be a lethal mix. In Chapter 10, Love & Money, I talk about how to ask friends and family for money and, more important, how to respond if you are the one being hit up for money.

## PROBLEM:
My mother recently passed away, and I am her only heir. She left behind $15,000 in credit card debt—do I have to pay it off?

## SOLUTION:
Unless you cosigned for the credit cards, you have no obligation to pay off the debt, though your parent's estate is responsible.

The only ways you can ever be held directly responsible for someone else's debt is if you were married to them at the time they took out the credit card—even if they took it out in their own name—or if you cosigned their loan or credit card application. So unless you cosigned for your mom's credit card, you have no obligation to pay her bill.

Now, even though you aren't personally liable for your mother's debt, her estate must pay off all her debts before distributing any of the assets to you and any other beneficiaries that she named in her will or trust. Assuming Mom's estate had assets worth at least $15,000, they would need to be sold to pay the debt. Assets can be anything from a bank account to the equity in a house. If she died without any assets, you will not be held responsible for the debt.

**PROBLEM:**
We own our home and don't know if it is okay to use a home equity line of credit (HELOC) to pay off our credit card debt.

**SOLUTION:**
Using a HELOC can be a dangerous way to get rid of high-interest credit card debt. Getting a lower card rate is a smarter move.

It's time for a quick review. Your mortgage is secured debt. That means that if you mess up and miss enough payments, your lender—the folks who loaned you the money for the mortgage—can force you to sell your home in a foreclosure so they can get their money back. Now, if in addition to your mortgage you add a Home equity line of credit (HELOC), you will be increasing your risk. (For more on HELOCs, head to Chapter 9, Big-Ticket Purchase: Home.) You now have two big secured debts. Fall behind on either one, and you could be out of your home.

Credit card debt is unsecured debt. If you cannot pay off your card debt, there is no way the card company can force you to sell your home to pay the bill. So I wouldn't recommend using a HELOC to pay off your credit card debt. What happens if you get injured or laid off? If you can't make the payments, you will be in a fix.

And don't get all worked up about the great tax savings on HELOCs. Yes, I know the interest payments on a HELOC are tax-deductible (up to $100,000), but tax rates right now are at a historical low. I'm not so sure it makes sense to risk your home for a relatively small tax break. Think this through: If you are in the 25 percent tax bracket, all we're talking about is getting 25 cents back for every dollar that you spend in interest payments.

My other concern is that I see so many people go for the HELOC, pay off the credit card debt, and then turn around and charge up their cards again. So now they have to repay their HELOC *and* they have a mountain of credit card debt. That's when foreclosures happen. So you need to be really careful and honest here. If you think you could fall into that trap, don't open the HELOC.

The better move is to do everything you can to get your credit card rate lower. Head back to page 88 for advice on how to snag a low-rate card that you can transfer your balance to. Your debt will still be unsecured, but now you will be able to pay it off at a low rate.

## PROBLEM:
I want to start my own business, but I can't get a bank loan, so I'm thinking of using my credit cards to finance my dream.

### SOLUTION:
Take this step only if you have low-rate cards, and keep your spending below $15,000.

Hey, I love reading stories of daring entrepreneurs who started their now-thriving business by tapping out every credit card they could get their paws on. But I guarantee you that for every feel-good financial story that relied on credit cards, there are at least 100 folks who did the same and failed.

If you are going to start your own business, I want you to be realistic. Yep, you read that right. I want you to dig a financial hole that you can climb out of, not one that you are going to be flailing about in for the rest of your life.

First, if you want to go into business for yourself, please spend lots of time researching your idea before you spend a penny. Whims and hunches are not good business ideas. And I am doubly skeptical of any business idea that suddenly pops into your head after you are laid off from work. If it was such a great idea, why weren't you planning and saving up for it while you had a job?

If you are determined to launch your own baby, I want you to first make sure that your credit cards have the lowest possible interest rate. If you can't get your rate below 10 percent, I have to question whether you are ready to run a business. If you can't qualify for a good interest rate, you obviously have some financial blemishes in your life.

Once you have a low rate lined up, I want you to subject business expenditures to the same bad-vs.-good test that we discussed earlier in this section. No fancy high-end furniture or expensive leased cars. Stick to the bare necessities to get your business launched.

And you must set a limit on how much money you will plow into the business the first year. I recommend sticking to a $15,000 cap. I don't care if your combined credit card limit is $25,000. If you tap all that credit and the business doesn't fly, you are going to be in a huge hole. Give yourself $15,000 for the first year. If the business is growing after that first year but you still need a little help, then you can tap some more. But if at eighteen months the business can't stand on its own, you are to call it quits. I don't want you to put another penny into it. You will still be young enough to pay your way out of the debt, but only if you stop piling on more.

**PROBLEM:**

I have a $4,000 credit card bill that I haven't paid for four years, but now the card company is coming after me, and I don't know what to do.

**SOLUTION:**

Taking full responsibility is always the best move, but you may be able to hide behind your state's statute of limitations on collecting bad debt.

Okay, I want to be really clear here: If you have punked out on paying your credit cards, that's really bad behavior. And you should do everything possible to pay them off. Earlier in this section, I discussed how paying even a small amount each month is going to help you pare down that balance in a matter of a few years. Or you can work with a reputable credit counseling service for advice on how to devise a workable repayment plan.

All that said, I want you to understand that each state has a limit on how long a credit card company or collection agency can legally come after you to try to make you pay off the balance. That's what is known as a statute of limitations. The last time you paid your bill is the start date for figuring out whether you are under or over the statute of limitations. If your state has a four-year statute of limitations on credit card debt and you last made a payment on your card four

On my website is a state-by-state list of the statutes of limitations for debt collection.

years and one day ago or longer, you are under no legal obligation to repay the debt. But be careful: In some states, if you merely tell a debt collection agency that you intend to repay the debt or that you will send in a check,

and you do, the day you orally make that commitment or send in a check, you'll start the statute of limitations all over again.

If you have collection agencies contacting you, please understand that they are not allowed to harass you. Here are some of the protections you have:

- A debt collector cannot contact you at unusual or inconvenient times or places—that is, before 8 A.M. or after 9 P.M.

- A debt collector may not contact you at work if they know that your employer prohibits you from receiving collection calls at work.

- If you have an attorney, a debt collector may not contact you directly. They must work with the attorney.

- A debt collector may not threaten to use violence against you, another person, or your or another person's reputation or property.

- A debt collector may not publish your name on a "deadbeat" list, as a person who doesn't pay bills.

- A debt collector may not list your debt for sale to the public.

**YF&B** For a complete list of consumer protections against debt collectors, go to my website; I also have information about what to do if you feel a collection agency is treating you unfairly.

**PROBLEM:**
I am drowning in so much credit card debt that I feel like bankruptcy is my only option.

**SOLUTION:**
If you got yourself into this situation, you owe it to yourself to try to fix the problem rather than run away into bankruptcy.

Personal bankruptcies keep reaching record levels, which doesn't really surprise me, given that consumer debt levels are also reaching record highs. You don't need a Nobel Prize in economics to see how one plays into the other.

When you are so young, I want you to think very long and very hard about whether you really need to declare bankruptcy. Oh, sure, it sounds like such a nice escape route. No more debt! But what does it say about you? Will you ever be able to recover from the sense of defeat? Besides, when you declare bankruptcy in your YF&B years, you do serious damage to your FICO score. And that is going to have a huge impact on the cost of getting loans after your bankruptcy. That's what everyone seems to overlook; they focus on getting their current debts "forgiven," but they fail to think through the impact on the rest of their lives. If you want to buy a home or a car anytime within the next seven to ten years, I am here to tell you that bankruptcy is going to cost you big-time.

For example, on a $150,000 mortgage, someone with a good FICO score could expect to get an interest rate of about 6 percent (based on rates as I am writing this, in the fall of 2004). Someone with a bankrupt FICO score is going to get stuck with a 9 percent or so interest rate. That works out to an extra $370 a month. Over seven years, that's an extra $31,000 that you would be paying as a result of having declared bankruptcy. And that's just for a home. Let's also remember that you will have high rates on any car loan you take out and credit cards you use. I bet the extra costs you would face after bankruptcy exceed the amount of money you owe today. So why not spend the time and elbow grease to see if you can dig yourself out of your debt hole without filing for bankruptcy?

Before you opt for bankruptcy, try to get some help sorting through your options. There is an entire industry built on providing help to consumers who are overwhelmed with their debt. Some of the debt-help businesses are not exactly legit; they force you to cough up a lot of money, and sometimes they can do more harm than good. You are to work only with debt counselors that are recommended by the National Foundation for Credit Counseling (www.nfcc.org; 1-800-388-2227).

When you meet with an NFCC-recommended agency, you will lay out your financial situation; if they think they can help you dig out of your debt within five years, they will sign you up for a repayment plan. All your debts will be gathered together, and you will make one single payment to the counseling agency, which will then work with your creditors to get your debt repaid. Quite often, the credit counselors negotiate deals on your behalf where either part of your debt is forgiven or your interest rate is reduced. You will probably be required to pay a monthly fee for this repayment-plan service, but it should not be more than $25 a month. In addition, the credit counselor should also discuss programs and classes that you can enroll in to learn some tricks for better budget and credit card management.

Now, if your debt load is so large that the credit counselor doesn't think you can dig out within five years, you probably aren't going to be offered a repayment plan. In that case, I want you to contact each credit card company or lender to whom you owe money. Tell them you want to pay back the money, but you are having a tough time. Ask them if they have any special programs to help people in your situation. If your debt is unsecured—which all credit card debt is—it is in the lender's interest to work with you to get some payment. If you declare bankruptcy, they may never get a penny.

Finally, please, please, please do not run into bankruptcy protection. Do everything you can to solve the problem without taking that drastic step. I would even recommend swallowing your pride and asking any family members with a strong balance sheet to loan you the money so you can get rid of your credit card debt and start fresh.

Please, please, please do not run into bankruptcy protection. Do everything you can to solve the problem without taking that drastic step.

Credit cards are a great lifeline when you don't yet make enough money to live on, but only if you are truly committed to using the card solely for necessary expenses, not indulgences.

The true cost of a purchase can be double or triple its price tag if the charge goes onto a card where you pay only the minimum amount due and have a high interest rate.

Cash advances are a big-time rip-off. The interest rate is typically above 20 percent, and you'll start paying interest the minute the money is spit out of the ATM.

Credit card companies can use a late payment on another loan or credit card as an excuse to boost the rate they charge on their card. Always pay at least the minimum amount due on time for all your cards.

The due date for your credit card payment can change; check each statement to make sure you know when the bill needs to arrive at the card company.

The higher your FICO score, the more bargaining power you have to push for a lower interest rate on your credit card.

Transferring your balance to a card with a low interest rate is a smart way to reduce your debt costs. Before you transfer your balance to a new account, ask what the "real" rate will be after the introductory tease rate expires. Also find out if your old card will charge you a fee for the transfer.

Cosigning a credit card application for a friend is a disaster waiting to happen. You will be on the hook if your friend can't (or won't) pay his or her bill.

Don't use a home equity line of credit or a loan from your 401(k) to pay off credit card debt.

Do everything you can to dig out of a big debt hole; declaring bankruptcy is a lousy solution that can end up costing you more than your current debt would.

# making
# the grade
# on

# student
# debt

Remember, this debt was for a truly necessary and worthwhile cause: your education.

# THE LOWDOWN

Right now it may not feel like it, but that pile of student debt that's got you bummed out is a terrific investment. A few years ago, Census Bureau wonks calculated that a college education gives you nearly double the earning potential of a high-school degree. Over the course of your working life, a bachelor's degree is estimated to translate into $2.1 million in lifetime earnings, compared to $1.2 million for those with only a high-school degree. Collect a master's degree, and you'll be up to $2.5 million. A professional degree (M.D., law degree, etc.) bumps your potential lifetime earnings to $4.4 million. Of course, what you ultimately earn is going to be based on your specific career path and how long you stay in the full-time workforce. But there's no denying that the benefit of your education is going to greatly surpass its cost.

Let's say you have $30,000 in loans. If you lock in an interest rate of 4.25 percent (more on this in a sec) and take twenty years to pay it off, you're looking at a total bill of close to $45,000. I absolutely respect that that is one scary number, and that it is tough to come up with the money to start paying the loan back now while you are YF&B. But in return for that $45,000, you have a good shot at an extra $900,000 in excess earnings over what you'd have made if you'd never gone to college. That's a 1,900 percent return on your investment; over a forty-year career, that works out to an average annual "earnings" bonus of nearly 8 percent.

So chin up. You made an amazing investment.

## STUDY UP ON YOUR REPAYMENT OPTIONS

Having said all that, I realize that the future economic value of your college degree doesn't help you make your present-day debt payments. And on a limited YF&B income, your student debt can feel more like a ball and chain than your ticket to riches.

But you're not nearly as shackled as you think. Yes, you must repay the loans. But I have to tell you that the financial planets are completely aligned in your favor right now. As I write this in the fall of 2004, interest rates on student loans are at incredibly low levels, and the lenders you owe are standing by with a slew of different payment options to give you as much flexibility as you need. All you need to do is study up on what works best for you.

## WHAT HAPPENS AFTER SCHOOL

Let's do a quick review of what's at play here. Throughout your college education, you took out a bunch of loans. The most popular type of loan is the Federal Stafford loan. You may also have Perkins loans, and your parents may also have taken out PLUS loans on your behalf. In this book, we're going to concentrate on your personal debt, and for most of you that means Stafford loans.

You probably didn't pay anything on those loans while you were in school, but interest was building on the amount you borrowed. If you qualified for **subsidized loan**s, the federal government covered those interest payments for you while you were in school. If you didn't meet the financial need requirements, your loan was *unsubsidized*—meaning that you're on the hook for the interest that accrued while you were in school. But instead of paying the interest while you were in school, you probably took the option to have those interest payments tacked on to what you would owe once you got out of school and started your repayment.

Before you graduated, someone from the financial aid office, or your lender, should have contacted you and told you what needed to happen once you left school. But that was spring semester of senior year, when you weren't exactly very focused. All you heard was that you had a six-month **grace period** after you left school, during which you wouldn't have to start paying back the money.

That six months is long gone for many of you; still, I bet some of you are not on the ball about starting the repayment. I know it's tough to face, especially if, given all your moving around, your lender hasn't yet tracked you down. It's tempting to just let it slide—tempting but stupid. As I will explain in a few minutes, defaulting on your student loans is a seriously bad move.

It's time to get committed to a loan repayment program. If you don't have a clue where your paperwork is, just head over to the National Student Clearinghouse loan locator at www.studentclearinghouse.org. Click on the Students & Alumni tab to get to the loan locator. After you plug in some basic personal data, you will have info on all your loans and who your lender is; don't worry if the name is different than the institution you originally borrowed from. It is common for your loans to be resold to other lenders. You can also track down your loans through the National Student Loan Data System, maintained by the U.S. Department of Education (http://www.nslds.ed.gov/).

# DELAY TACTICS

Alright, so now that you know what's on your loan plate, you are beginning to get the financial sweats. Calm down. It's not as bad as you think. We'll run through your repayment options in a moment, but first I want you to understand that you may be able to delay your payments and maybe even get them canceled.

The odds of getting your Stafford loans canceled outright are pretty slim; total and permanent disability is usually required. You may be able to get $5,000 of your Stafford loans forgiven if you agree to teach in a low-income public school. There are more

**YF&B** For a complete list of occupations that will get your loans canceled, go to my website.

cancellation options with a Perkins loan. In addition to the teacher forgiveness program, volunteer work in the Peace Corps, certain military service, or a career in law enforcement can qualify you for full or partial forgiveness.

If cancellation isn't in the cards, your next best alternative is to get a deferment. As the word implies, with a deferment you get to delay payment until a later date. If you have a federal Stafford loan that was subsidized, your loan will not accrue any interest while it is in deferment. With an unsubsidized loan, you won't have to pay interest while you are in the deferment phase, but the interest meter will continue to run, and that interest will be added to the loan amount that you will eventually need to repay. In other words, deferment on an unsubsidized loan is going to cost you more in the long run, so only go this route if absolutely necessary.

A deferment is an entitlement, meaning that if you meet the qualifications, you must be granted a deferment. There's no judgment involved. There are a variety of circumstances under which you can qualify for a deferment of your Stafford loans. Some of the most common reasons are: you, your spouse, or anyone who is dependent on you becomes disabled; or you are unemployed, join the Peace Corps, go back to school, or work with underprivileged children. You may also be eligible for deferment if you work in law enforcement. In cases of unemployment, you may be able to get a three-year deferment, but you will need to reapply every twelve months.

If you don't qualify for a deferment, your next option is to ask for forbearance. It's up to your lender to grant your request. In this setup, you can get your pay-

The eligibility rules for deferments vary according to the type of loan you have and when it was issued to you. For detailed information about deferment, go to my website.

ments delayed, but during the period in which you are not making any payments, the interest on your loan will continue to accrue, whether your loan is subsidized or unsubsidized. Forbearance is easier to get than a deferment; again, you need to contact the lender and discuss their qualifying standard.

## A MOMENT OF INTEREST

When you repay a loan, you owe both the principal (the amount you borrowed) and the interest to the lender who was nice enough to front you the money for school. That interest rate changes every July 1, based on the going rate for a Treasury bill index. The maximum interest rate for a Stafford loan is 8.25 percent; Perkins loans top out at 5 percent. That means that come every July 1, you hold your breath and see if your payments are going to rise or fall.

Here are the current Stafford loan rates until July 1, 2005:

| The Date the Loan Was Issued to You | Current Interest Rate Until July 1, 2005 |
| --- | --- |
| After June 30, 1998 | 3.37% |
| Between July 1, 1994, and June 30, 1998 | 4.17% |
| Before July 1, 1994 | 4.17%–4.32% |

Those are some incredibly great rates. The technical term is *cheap*. But come July 1, there's no guarantee that they will stay low. That's the big problem with student loans; because the rates are variable, you'll have a hard time predicting what your payments are going to be, year to year.

YF&B — Student loan interest rates are adjusted every July 1. You can find updated rates on my website.

## THE CONSOLIDATION SOLUTION

You can get around the variable-rate stress by **consolidating** your student loans. When you consolidate, you pile all your loans together into one giant loan. And you get to lock in an interest rate that you will pay for the rest of your repayment. No more sleepless nights on June 30 for you. As I write this in the fall of 2004, you have a very good chance to lock in a repayment deal where your interest rate could be about 4.25 percent or less for the rest of the loan life. You don't need a PhD in economics to know that that is a ridiculously great deal. By consolidating and locking in a rate, you are protecting yourself from future rate shock. And if you consolidate during the six-month grace period (the time between graduation and the date you must start your repayments), you can get an even lower rate.

I need to pause here and offer some important caveats. Once you consolidate, you are no longer eligible for deferment or forbearance; you are now on the repayment train and won't be able to get off until you have paid the balance of your loan. And be extra-careful consolidating Perkins loans; you may jeopardize your ability to apply for complete forgiveness if you take up one of the aforementioned careers that qualify for loan cancellation. The obvious advice here is that if you are interested in consolidation, take the time to have your lender slowly explain all the pros and cons.

Most school loans are eligible for consolidation. If your loan falls into one of the following categories, you can indeed consolidate:

- Federal Stafford loans: subsidized and unsubsidized loans in the Federal Family Education Loan Program and Direct Loan Program

- Federal PLUS (parent) Loans

- Federal Family Education Loan Program and Direct Loan Program

- Federal Perkins or National Direct Student Loans (NDSL)

- Federal Insured Student Loans (FISL)

- Federal Supplemental Loans for Students (SLS)

- Federal Nursing Student Loans (NSL)—subsidy lost upon consolidation

- Loans for Disadvantaged Students (LDS)

- Health Professions Student Loans (HPSL)

- Health Education Assistance Loans (HEAL)

If all your loans are from the same lender, you must consolidate with that lender. If you have loans from a variety of lenders, you can shop around at banks, credit unions, and other loan sources, such as Sallie Mae, to consolidate. Contact Sallie Mae at 800-448-3533 or www.salliemae.com. To contact the Department of Education's loan consolidation program, call 800-557-7392, or learn more at their website: http://loanconsolidation.ed.gov.

If your loans are from a private lender that does not offer consolidation, ask about the different repayment options that you can choose from. For each option, ask the lender to tell you your monthly cost, how long you will be making the payments, the total interest charges, and whether the interest rate will be adjusted (and how often). If you own a home, go to Chapter 9, Big-Ticket Purchase: Home, and check out my advice about how a home equity loan or line of credit can be a viable option for repaying your student loan ahead of schedule.

## PICK YOUR PAYMENT SCHEDULE

When you consolidate, you have the opportunity to choose a payment plan that fits your financial comfort zone. With the standard repayment plan, you pay a fixed amount each month—$50 is the minimum—and can take up to ten years to repay the loan. With the extended payment plan, you'll still have minimum monthly payments of at least $50, but you can take from twelve to thirty years to repay, depending on the size of your loans. One caveat: Only folks who took out Federal Family Education Loan Program (FFELP) loans after October 7, 1998, and have debt exceeding $30,000 are eligible for the extended payment option. With the graduated repayment plan, your payments increase every two years but will never exceed 1.5 times what you would pay under the standard plan. The income-sensitive and income-contingent plans are designed to help those who are working on a limited salary find a reasonable payment plan. Under this arrangement, you can take from fifteen to thirty-five years to repay.

Ideally, your goal is to get your debt paid off as quickly as possible; the longer you take, the more interest you will end up paying. So if you can comfortably handle paying down your loan in ten years, go for it. If paying your loan down in twenty or even thirty years is what you can afford, then go for the extended payment schedule; just remember that you always have the option down the line to pay it off ahead of schedule, and there is no prepayment fee.

Here's how the payment period affects your total interest costs:

| A $35,000 loan with a 4.25 percent interest rate, paid back over... | Monthly Payment | Total Interest Paid over Life of the Loan |
|---|---|---|
| 10 years | $358.53 | $8,024 |
| 20 years | $216.73 | $17,016 |
| 30 years | $172.18 | $26,984 |

**YF&B** On my website, the student loan repayment calculator will show you your monthly payments and the total interest costs of these various payment options.

## EXTRA CREDIT: HOW TO GET YOUR RATE EVEN LOWER

Lenders love it when they can rely on you to pay on time. In fact, if you promise to be punctual with your consolidated Stafford student loans, some lenders will cut you breaks that can save you big bucks. Agree to have your loan payment automatically deducted from your bank account every month, and some lenders will reduce your interest rate by 0.25 percent. Manage to be on time for thirty-six straight months, and starting in month thirty-seven, your interest rate will decline a full percentage point. So the combined bonus for merely being on time is a huge 1.25-percentage-point reduction in your interest rate. And let's not forget that paying on time is also going to do wonders for your FICO score.

The way these breaks typically work is that your monthly payments don't drop, but you run up a smaller interest bill. The net effect is that you will pay off the loan faster. Remember our $35,000 loan that we're repaying over ten years at 4.25 percent? Simply dropping the rate to 4 percent will save $1,681 in interest costs and get your loan paid off four months early. If you opt for a twenty-year repayment period, your interest savings would be $5,522, and you would finish paying the loan twenty-five months ahead of schedule.

# TAKE A TAX BREAK

Regardless of whether you consolidate, there's a very good chance that in your YF&B years, you can get a tax deduction of up to $2,500 a year in interest payments that you make on your student loans. Remember, your loan payments are made up of principal (what you originally borrowed) and the interest that the lender is charging you on that principal. The interest portion of your payments is what's eligible for the deduction.

Here's how it works: All deductions are based on the federal **income tax** rate that you pay. For example, let's say you are in the 25 percent tax bracket and you paid $1,000 in interest on your student loans this year. All you need to do is multiply your interest payment by your tax rate to find out how much Uncle Sam is going to let you take off your tax bill. So in this example, $1,000 x 0.25 = $250. In other words, the true cost of your interest payments just fell from $1,000 to $750. If you are in the 15 percent tax bracket, your deduction on $1,000 in interest payments would work out to a $150 break. Not bad, right?

But not everyone gets this nice tax break from Uncle Sam. If you are single and make less than $50,000, or if you file a joint return and your combined income is below $100,000, you will qualify for the federal tax break. The deduction is phased out—meaning you won't get the full deduction—if you are single and your income falls between $50,000 and $65,000, or if you are married, file a joint return, and your combined income is between $100,000 and $135,000.

While I know you would love to be able to click your heels and be transported to a new land where your student debt would be automatically forgiven, you have to admit that you've got some nice repayment options these days. You can lock in at a low rate that could eventually fall to just 3 percent, and you might be able to snag a nice tax deduction. And remember, this debt was for a truly necessary and worthwhile cause: your education.

# STRATEGY SESSIONS

**PROBLEM:**
I finally have a little money left after paying my monthly bills, but I don't know if I should use that cash to pay off my student loans or to invest in my 401(k) or a Roth IRA.

**SOLUTION:**
Investing in a 401(k) that gives you a company match should always be your top priority.

Here's a quick trailer of what we're going to cover in detail in Chapter 6, Retirement Rules: If your employer offers a company match on your contributions to a 401(k), you are to jump at it. Snubbing your nose at this deal is tantamount to turning down a bonus. So if you have been feeling too pinched to join your company's 401(k) plan, you should definitely use your improved cash flow to start contributing to the 401(k) rather than use the money to speed up your student loan repayments.

After you contribute enough to get the maximum company match, you can opt to stop your contributions for the rest of the year and concentrate on other financial goals. Your initial focus should be on your debt payments. Let's say you have a credit card balance with a 15 percent interest rate, and your student loan rate is 8 percent, because you consolidated when rates were much higher than they are today. Concentrate on the credit card debt; always pay down the most expensive debt (that is, the debt with the highest interest rate) first. When you've got that polished off, you can attack the student loan debt that is running you 8 percent.

Now, if your student loan's interest rate is lower than 8 percent, there is no reason to rush to pay it off, especially if you qualify for the tax deduction on your interest payments. The better move is to just keep up with the required payments and use your extra cash to invest in a Roth IRA. As I explain in Chapter 6, Retirement Rules, Roths are as close to the perfect investment as there is.

**PROBLEM:**

I just got married, and both my spouse and I have student loans. Should we pay them separately or consolidate all of our debt?

**SOLUTION:**

I am a big believer in combining finances when you marry—but not your student loans.

Any debt that you took on before you got married is not the responsibility of your spouse after you get married. You're only on the hook for debts that you both run up during the marriage. But if you consolidate your student loans together after you marry, then you are both on the hook for the other spouse's debt. I think that's a dangerous move. Let me explain why I believe student loan debt is one of those financial obligations that you shouldn't ever merge. I wish you and your honey a life of shared happiness, but with the divorce rate at about 50 percent, I am going to be a bit pragmatic here. If you and your spouse consolidate your loans and decide to separate, that big loan is now going to be a big bone of contention. Let's say your student loans accounted for 35 percent of the total, and your spouse's loans made up the other 65 percent. When you separate, your debts are going to be part of the divorce settlement. You could be on the hook for a lot more of the debt than you brought into the marriage.

Now let's take the gloves off and be brutally realistic. If you consolidate and one of you dies or is permanently disabled, you may be able to get only a partial discharge (forgiveness) of your consolidated loans. But if you had kept the loans separate, the surviving spouse would be able to apply to have the deceased's loan canceled. I hope none of this ever comes into play for you, but I need to share one of my secrets of attaining financial security: Hope for the best, but plan for the worst. Another problem with merging your student loan debt is that if one of you decides to go back to school, you won't be able to take the regular in-school deferment.

While I don't want you to mix your student debt, I do think there are many important ways that couples must merge their finances if they are to have a truly successful relationship. Read Chapter 10, Love & Money, to help you and your significant other learn what it takes—financially speaking—to thrive.

**PROBLEM:**

With credit card debt, car loan debt, and student loan debt, I am ten feet under and want to declare bankruptcy.

**SOLUTION:**

If it takes you the rest of your life, you need to pay off your student loans.

Bankruptcy is simply not an option for dealing with your student debt. You can have all sorts of other debt, such as credit card debt and auto loans, "dismissed" through bankruptcy, but your student loans stick with you. Unless you get a court to let you off as a hardship case—which typically requires permanent disability— your student loan debt will stay with you until you die. If you step back for a minute and take a look at all your repayment options, you will realize that the student loan industry bends over backward to help you find a solution that you can truly manage. Sticking your head in the sand and hoping the problem will go away is guaranteed to make it worse. You also have to remember that the credit bureaus will track your payment record. If you screw up with your student loans, it will lower your FICO score. That, in turn, means that the interest you pay on your credit cards, car loan, or mortgage is not going to be rock-bottom. See why I don't want you to mess up with the student loans? So call your lender, tell them your situation, and work with them to come up with a plan that won't break your bank account. Committing to a payment schedule is the best move you can make for your entire financial well-being.

And don't delay. If you neglect to send in student loan payments for nine months, you are technically in default on your student loan, and you are in for some serious hurt. Among the ways your lender can come after the money is to get the IRS to send any tax refund check you are due to receive to them, not you. Your state income tax refund could also be hijacked. You may also find that 10 to 15 percent of your paycheck is being siphoned off to pay back the loan. That's what is known as wage garnishment. If none of that works, the lender can take you to court. A defaulted student loan sticks with you like a tattoo. The only laser removal treatment is to pay it off. Period.

And you will seriously mess up your future if you don't pay. Just consider some of these consequences of not paying your student loans:

- You won't receive any more federal financial aid (and possibly state aid) unless you make arrangements to repay what you already owe.

- You may be ineligible for assistance under most federal benefit programs.

- You'll be ineligible for deferments or forbearances (more on these in a minute).

- You'll be liable for the costs associated with collecting the payments for your loan, including court costs and attorney fees.

- You may not be able to renew a professional license that you hold.

- Your loan may be given to a collection agency; that's not something you want to experience.

That's the bad news. But the student loan industry isn't trying to make this an impossible task. If you commit to any one of the repayment plans mentioned earlier, and if you pay on time for at least twelve months, your "default" demerit will be removed from your credit report. That's a sweet deal. Normally, bad behavior sticks on your credit report for many years, but the student loan folks will report that you are "rehabilitated" if you stay on the straight and narrow for twelve months.

So it's time to suck it up, call your lender, and figure out a plan that works for both of you.

**PROBLEM:**
I consolidated years ago when rates were a lot higher. Can I get a lower rate now?

**SOLUTION:**
Unfortunately, you can't refinance consolidated loans, but if you own your home, you may have another option.

Consolidation is a onetime deal. Unlike a home loan, where you can always refinance again and again to take advantage of a mortgage with a lower rate, the rate at which you consolidate your student loan will be yours for the life of the loan.

The only possible way to lower your rate is to go back to school and take out new loans. You can then do a new consolidation loan that piles together your old consolidated loan with your new back-to-school loans. But as with all consolidated loans, your interest rate is the weighted average of the old loan and the new loan. So let's say your old 7 percent loan has a $20,000 balance, and you take out a new loan at 4 percent for $10,000. If you were to consolidate these loans, your new rate would be about 6 percent.

But for those of you who are stuck and cannot get a better interest rate on your student loans, if you are willing to get creative, there are a few things you may be able to do.

If you own a home that has equity in it, you could use either a home equity loan (HEL) or a home equity line of credit (HELOC) to pay down or pay off your student loan. But I want you to be very careful before using either one. Your home becomes the collateral for the loan; if you can't keep up with the payments, you run the risk of losing your home.

A HEL is where you borrow against the equity that you have in your home (more on this on page 312). You can use that money for absolutely anything. The interest rate on a HEL is fixed. With a HELOC, the interest rate is adjustable; it will rise and fall along with the general direction of interest rates in the economy. So that creates some risk for you; you would be giving up the known fixed interest rate of your consolidated loan for the unknown adjustable rate of a HELOC. In both cases, however, if the loan is less than $100,000, the interest payments are tax-deductible, no matter what your income is.

So here is the bottom line: If the difference between your student loan and the HELOC is just 1 percentage point or so, I don't think it's worth the risk of using the HELOC, since the interest rate could rise in the future. I would go for the HEL rather than the HELOC. You want that fixed interest rate so you don't have to be worried that your payment will skyrocket if interest rates head north over the next few years. The only time to use a HELOC is if you think rates will remain stable or decline during your payback period.

But if you consolidated years ago at an interest rate of 8 percent, and you can get a HEL (or HELOC) for 6 percent or lower, then you might want to use one of these options to pay off all or some of your student debt. It makes even more sense if your income is now too high to qualify you for the student loan interest deduction (the full deduction is available only if you are single and your adjusted gross income is below $50,000, or $100,000 for married couples filing a joint return). Just think about it: Your HEL or HELOC interest rate would be lower than what you are paying on your student loan debt, but you would also get the interest tax deduction on your HEL or HELOC payments.

And I want to be really clear that I am recommending this HEL/HELOC strategy only to repay student loan debt that carries an interest rate above 6 percent. If you can pay it off with better terms by using a HEL or HELOC, that makes sense. But you are never to use these home loans to pay off credit card debt.

Now, for those of you who do not own a home, or don't have any sizable equity in your home, I have another option for you. If the interest rate on your consolidated loans is 8 percent or more, you might want to look into trying to get a low-interest-rate credit card (anything below 8 percent) that issues transfer checks. All you have to do is take one of the checks that comes with the card and pay off as much of your student loan as possible. The idea here is that the interest on the new card will be lower than the 8 percent that you are paying on your student loan. Of course, you'll need a high FICO score to qualify for this kind of card deal, but if you can get it, it could be a great way for you to reduce the interest rate on all or some of your consolidated student loans, especially if the fixed interest rate on the card after the intro period is below 8 percent.

But you need to be super-sharp about how you handle all your debt payments. Remember, your credit card company is going to be on the lookout for any excuse to boost your interest rate. If you are late on any debt payment, you could see the interest rate on your new card get raised all the way to 20 percent or more. You obviously don't want to find yourself suddenly paying 20 percent interest on money that you used to pay off at 8 percent. So please only consider this repayment option if you are absolutely sure that you will be diligent about paying all your bills on time. The only way this plan makes sense is if you keep the rate on your card super-low.

Normally, bad behavior sticks on your credit report for many years, but the student loan folks will report that you are "rehabilitated" if you stay on the straight and narrow for twelve months.

**PROBLEM:**

I just received an inheritance, and I can't decide if I should use it to pay off my student debt or for a down payment on a house.

**SOLUTION:**

If you consolidated into a low-rate loan, then go for the down payment.

If you have been fortunate enough to consolidate your student loans into a low-rate deal—say, less than 5 percent or so—then you should be in no rush to pay it off. That's cheap money.

But there's one important caveat that you need to consider. When you apply for a mortgage, your lender is going to go through all sorts of calculations to determine your financial strength. Remember, the whole game with lenders is making them comfortable that you are a good risk—that you are going to repay your loan on time and in full. So one of the calculations that the lender will run through is your income-to-debt ratio. Your student loans are considered part of your debt, and thus are going to have an effect on how comfy you make the lender feel. To learn more about the specific ratios that lenders look for, and for a worksheet to figure out where your ratio falls, turn to page TK; I cover all of this in detail in Chapter 9, Big-Ticket Purchase: Home.

If you find that your income-to-debt ratio is too high, then you may want to use some of the inheritance to reduce your total debt so you can then qualify for a mortgage with the lowest possible interest rate. But that doesn't mean automatically paying down your student loan. If you have other installment debt, such as an auto loan, and it has a higher interest rate, get that paid down first. Always pay off the highest-interest-rate loan first.

**PROBLEM:**
I lost my job, and now I can't afford my student loan payments.

**SOLUTION:**
Work with your lender to see if you can qualify for a deferment.

I think the student loan industry does a pretty admirable job of trying to work with the realities of the YF&B. Whereas a mortgage lender isn't going to let you off the hook if you lose your job, you can catch a break with your student loans. If you are unemployed but looking for work, you may be eligible for a deferment for as long as three years. (Remember, though, if you have consolidated you are no longer eligible for a deferment.)

If your loans were subsidized, you won't have any interest build up while your loan is in deferment. If your loans weren't subsidized, the interest clock keeps running during deferment. You won't have to pay it while you are in deferment, but the interest is added to the balance of your loan, so when you do start repayment, you will have the added cost of whatever interest was charged during the deferment period. Contact your lender and request an application for the unemployment deferment.

The interest rates charged on federal student loans are reset each year on July 1.

Even if you claim personal bankruptcy, you will still need to pay back your student loans.

Your student loans are reported to the credit bureaus. If you fall into default, you will damage your credit report and hurt your FICO score.

Work with your lender to find a repayment plan that fits your current financial situation. Remember, though, if you extend your repayment period, you will increase your total interest costs over the life of the loan.

A deferment with a subsidized loan will not accrue any interest. With an unsubsidized loan, or if you are in forbearance, interest will continue to be added to your loan amount.

Once you consolidate, you are no longer eligible for deferment or forbearance.

If all your loans are from the same lender, you must consolidate with that lender. If you have loans from a variety of lenders, you can shop around at banks, credit unions, and other loan sources, such as Sallie Mae, to consolidate.

If you have a low-rate loan, don't rush to pay it off; it can make more sense to use any extra money for other goals, such as paying off your credit card debt or saving for a down payment on a home.

Have your consolidated loan payment automatically deducted from your checking account and you may be able to get your interest rate reduced by 0.25 percent.

On your federal taxes, you can deduct up to $2,500 per year in student loan interest if your income is less than $50,000 (or $100,000 if you are married and file a joint tax return).

Don't consolidate your student loans with your spouse's student loans.

If you consolidated at a high interest rate, consider paying off your loan with a low-rate credit card or a home equity line of credit (HELOC).

save up

Saving is for a short-term goal that you hope to reach within five years or so. Investing is for the long term.

# THE LOWDOWN

Congrats on making it to this section. Until now, we've been talking about how to make the best of the debt you have—how to minimize the costs of credit card and student loan debt. Now it's time to shift gears in your journey out of broke and concentrate on how to save up for your big-ticket goals: buying a car, buying a home, and security in the form of an emergency cash fund.

Reaching this stage is a great step forward. But I have a gut feeling that you're not feeling totally triumphant, right? Your salary is on the rise, yet your bank account isn't. You're doing better, but it's still tough to make ends meet. Your salary has finally started making a noticeable climb, but it seems that the more you make, the more you spend. And you're not really sure where it's all going.

I know the feeling. When I became a stockbroker after seven years of waitressing, I was finally making real money. At the age of thirty, my annual income shot up from $5,000 to more than $50,000 within one year. I was on Easy Street, right? If only. The crazy thing was that I had more debt when I was making $50,000 than I did when I was pulling in $5,000 as a waitress. The next year, I was making $100,000, and I still wasn't getting ahead. Oh, sure, I looked like I was doing great: my wardrobe got a serious upgrade; I had better furnishings; my lunches had moved from Taco Bell to pricey restaurants with tablecloths; I went from a fourteen-year-old, beat-up car that I owned outright to a brand-new one (which I financed); and my weekends were a lot of fun, courtesy of my friends Mr. Visa and Mr. MasterCard. My income was a lot bigger, but my bank account had more holes than a sieve. Whatever came in went out even more quickly. I got trapped into thinking that because I was earning more, I could afford to have more debt; at one point, my credit card balance broke the six-figure mark and I was paying 21 percent interest. I was more broke than ever.

Think that's odd for a financial adviser? Give me a break. I was just like most people who finally had money. Rather than act responsibly with my newfound cash flow, I felt I was entitled to make up for lost time by eating out every night, hitting the clubs, taking nice vacations, and filling my life with whatever gadgets I wanted. I thought picking up the tab was a great way to impress people; so what that I couldn't really afford to do it? In the end, I had to learn the hard way that success is not solely about making more money. It is about knowing where the money you make is going.

## SCREW BUDGETS

Is it a good idea to take a look at where your money is going in order to figure out how to keep more of it around? Sure. But I'm not going to be pushing Budgeting 101 on you. I heard from so many YF&Bers who said they wanted help with budgeting. No, you don't! Budgets are about as successful as fad diets where you lose a ton of weight at first and then gain even more back. Big surprise. Operating on denial, constant worrying, and incessant monitoring is not sustainable. The same is true with money. If you force yourself onto a strict budget, chances are you'll never be able to stick with it, and you'll end up with more debt than you started with. So we're going to come up with a more rational approach. Instead of financial crash-dieting, we are going to look for some reasonable changes you can make in order to "find" money to put toward your savings goals.

Normally, this is where a personal-finance book comes to a screeching halt and hits you with an ugly spreadsheet to figure out where you are spending your money each month. Not here. This is a spreadsheet-free zone. I know you don't have the time or inclination to pore over the nitty-gritty. Besides, there are far faster ways to determine if you've got cash flow issues, including the following examples.

- You are finally making more money, but your bank balance is the same as it always has been.

- You hold your breath every time you use your credit card, waiting to see if the charge will be accepted or denied.

- Your credit card balance keeps growing.

- You consider it a good month if you bounce only one or two checks.

- Your closets are a designer showcase, yet you are never sure you'll be able to pay all your bills each month.

If any of this rings true, you've got some work to do. Perhaps you're bringing this on yourself by buying stuff that you can't afford. It's time to get responsible. There is no magic bullet here. You have to make the decision that saving is more of a priority than spending on indulgences. That's your call.

But I also bet that for many YF&Bers, the problem is not that you are living large; it's that you simply don't make enough to cover your basic living needs. Let's see if we can free up some more money for you by reducing some basic costs without taking a bite out of your lifestyle.

**YF&B**

As I said earlier, I'm not going to insist that you spreadsheet your spending to see where your cash is going. But I also figure that some of you are closet spreadsheet geeks who might actually want to take a detailed look at your finances. On my website, you will find spreadsheets and worksheets that you can download or fill out online to assess where your cash is really flowing.

You want to play it safe with your savings.

# DIGGING FOR DOLLARS

I want to be straight up about this: If you aren't yet making enough money to live on and are using your credit cards to fill in the shortfall, I'm not going to sit here and tell you there are plenty of ways you can find money. That's just insulting. The truth is that it's really tough to make a lot out of a little. My guess is that you might be able to tell me a few things about creative penny-pinching. But I do want to throw out some additional ideas that just may have passed you by.

## STOP GETTING A TAX REFUND

Obviously, each and every one of us has to pay income tax on the money that we earn. But a lot of you have too much withheld from each paycheck. You may think that's just fine because when you get around to filing out your tax returns, you get all excited about your nice, fat refund. That's a big, big mistake, my friends. You are simply being repaid your own money that you never should have paid in the first place. Making it worse is that you didn't get to earn interest on the money you overpaid. Your Uncle Sam did. As nice as it is to give our cash-strapped government a free loan, you can't afford it!

I want you to change your withholding so less money is subtracted from your paycheck. Contact your HR rep and ask for the paperwork to adjust the exemptions that you claim on your W-4 form. The more exemptions you claim, the less money will be withheld from each paycheck. The less money that is withheld, the more you will have to pay your bills on time each month. But be careful; the idea is not to get so much money back that you end up owing the IRS more money when you file your tax return. You're going for the perfect solution: not too much and not too little.

YF&B

On my website is a link to a withholding calculator to help you determine how to fill out your W-4 form.

## STEER CLEAR OF LIFE INSURANCE

If you are young, single, and broke, and have no one who is financially dependent on you, you most likely do not need to have life insurance (see page 330). If your employer offers you coverage for free, that's fine. But if you are paying for a policy through your employer, contact your HR department and cancel your coverage.

## RAISE YOUR INSURANCE DEDUCTIBLE

As I explain on page 265, the higher your **deductible**, the lower your annual **premium**. Now, I know you think a low deductible—what you pay before the insurer covers the cost of a loss—is a must, because you don't have the money to cough up if something happens. But this is a deceptive game. If you go for the low deductible and end up making claims, your insurer is going to either raise your premium or cancel your policy outright. So your low deductible will end up costing you more in the long run. I want you to boost any $250 or $500 deductibles to $1,000. If your insurance currently runs you about $800 a year, that could reduce your premium by $100 or more. If you do need to make a claim, and you don't have the cash to cover the deductible, then you will use your low-rate credit card, because by now you've moved your FICO score into the top range and will qualify for a card with a low interest rate, right? (See Chapter 3, Give Yourself Credit.)

## CELL IT

Do you really need your phone line at home, or can you get by with just your cell phone? Maybe boost your minutes on the cell phone but get rid of the home line. You'll still save $30 to $50 a month. That's a nice chunk of change.

## LOOK AT YOUR BANK STATEMENTS

I bet many of you don't even bother to open your bank statement each month, and even if you do, the only number you focus on is the end balance. Spend an extra forty-five seconds with the statement, and you could save yourself some big money. Did your deposits get credited? Are the withdrawals all kosher, or is there a debit you didn't authorize? Give your next statement a good scan and add up your ATM and bounced-check fees. Then multiply by twelve. That's real money you're throwing away each year. If you are constantly using ATMs that are not part of your bank's system, switch banks to one that has plenty of ATMs along your route.

I know the bounced-check issue is a sensitive one; it's not as if you *want* to be screwing up here. Look, it's all about finding the resolve to stay on top of your cash flow. Don't cross your fingers and hope there is enough money to cover your checks. Make sure. One common bounced-check trap is that you deposit money in the bank and then pay a bill immediately, thinking that the money you just deposited will cover it. Then, on the next statement, you see that you were hit with a $25 charge because the check bounced. That's because banks can take anywhere from two to five business days to clear your deposit—or eleven days if the check is for more than $5,000. That's between the time you made the deposit and the time the bank credited your account. But when you write a check, it gets processed the day it is received. So if you write a check against the deposit before it has cleared, you have now bounced a check. And this is what the bank is hoping you will do.

There's plenty you can do to avoid this problem. First, if your employer offers direct deposit of your paycheck into your bank account, you are nuts not to enroll. Direct deposits clear immediately. Next, if you do deposit checks on your own, don't write checks on the deposit until you are sure it has cleared. You can always call customer service or check online to confirm that it has cleared.

And I also want you to be on the lookout for an especially sneaky fee. You are to call your bank and ask if your account has free bounced-check protection or courtesy overdraft protection. If they say yes, you are to tell them that you want to opt out of this coverage, and have them send you a written confirmation. Why am I telling you to turn down something that's free? Because you don't really think it's free, do you?

The way these schemes work is that the bank automatically covers every check you bounce. They call it "free" because you are not required to enroll in a typical overdraft plan, where you pay an annual fee of $10 to $50 to have the bank take money out of your savings account (or off your credit card) when you are about to bounce a check. With the free bounced-check protection, the bank coughs up their own money to cover your checks. And for that bit of financial chivalry, you get hit with a fee that is typically $25 per check. Not only that, there also can be additional charges of about $3 a day until you pay back the bank for the amount they covered, and if it stays unpaid, you can have a collection service knocking on your door within a few weeks.

If, after checking your statement and getting up to speed on your bank's fees and policies, you want to look for a better deal, shop around with banks as well as credit unions. A credit union is a financial coop that offers banking and loans to its members. Each credit union is composed of members linked by some common bond—their employer, a club, a union, a church, etc. Quite often, you can join a credit union simply by knowing someone who is a member. The neat thing about credit unions is that since they are nonprofits, they tend to offer low interest rates and fees on their financial products; to find credit unions in your area, go to http://www.creditunion.coop/, and poll friends and family to see if they are members of credit unions. You can shop for banks in your area at www.bankrate.com.

## BALANCE YOUR CHECKBOOK

Okay, I'm going to get parental on you here. Looking out for wayward fees is not enough. You also need to balance your checkbook to make sure all your deposits have cleared. It's also a great way to stay on top of your cash flow; you'll know when you are getting within dangerous check-bouncing territory.

The balancing act is not rocket science. Sign up for online banking; it's free at many banks. Then all you need to do is fire up your computer once a month and check that every deposit you made has been credited to your account, and that the only withdrawals are for checks you wrote or cash you withdrew. It should take less than a half hour to complete your balancing act. And do I need to state the obvious—that you should shop around for free checking, and make sure you can comfortably meet any required minimum balance?

For those of you who are overwhelmed by the prospect of balancing your check-book after years of "guesstimating," don't worry. Here's what I want you to do:

Right after you have paid all your bills for the month, I want you to take your next paycheck and open up a brand-new checking account. It can even be at the same bank. From that point on, you are not to write any checks on your old account. Now, because you have opened up a new account and you know exactly what's in there, you have made a fresh start. You have absolutely no excuse not to balance your account each month. From now on, you are to keep every ATM slip and record every check you write. With those documents, it will be easy to balance your account at the end of the month. You simply add the deposits and subtract the payments. Obviously, you don't want to run up extra fees on your new account, so look for a bank that offers free checking.

We've got one last step with this balancing exercise. Remember your old account? Once you're sure all the checks you wrote on it have cleared, you can close it and take whatever money is in that account and transfer it to your new account.

## CHECK YOUR CREDIT CARD STATEMENTS

I know, I know, enough with the "checking statement" advice. Well, just give me one more shot here. I am mentioning this again—for credit card statements this time—because there are plenty of opportunities for mistakes on your statements. Double billing for a purchase, or a return that was never credited, or some phantom new fee that shows up for a service you didn't ask for. Think it doesn't happen? You are so wrong. I will bet you that if you did this every month, you might find $100 or more a year that you have been shelling out just because you haven't bothered to scan your monthly statement.

## SWEAT THE SMALL STUFF

I need you to indulge me for a sec on this one. You've probably already heard a lot of the "small" savings tips I am about to run through, but my guess is that you haven't really given them a fair shake. So please just take a look and size up if scaling back on just one or two of these items could save you $25 or more a month.

- **Wait an extra week or two to get your hair cut.** Switch from a six-week cycle to an eight-week cycle, and you cut out two appointments a year. Same goes for hair coloring and manicures—skip the polish and they last longer.

- **Wash more, dry-clean less.** I'm not talking about the office wear that you must dry-clean, but what about all the other clothes that end up at the cleaner just because it is more convenient?

- **Drink economically.** Okay, you're out with your buds and you order a $10 martini. Two, in fact. That's $20 before tip. How about some wine or beer instead? You can cut the bar tab in half. Or, better still, head across the street to the old-school bar with the rock-bottom prices. It's the company that makes the evening, not the décor.

- **Brown-bag it.** Try it one or two days a week. Rather than spending $10 to $15 at lunch places near your office, bring your lunch to work.

- **Go public.** This is for those of you in big cities. Yes, taxis are most convenient. They are also a huge cash drain. Taking a cab should be treated as a special occasion or reserved for when it's really the only safe alternative to public transportation.

- **Be a good sport.** Let's face it, sports like golf and skiing are big-ticket outlays. So think strategically. Buy your equipment off-season or used, and you will save some major bucks. And scale back on the swank. Work on your golf game on a public course, rather than paying up for a private club course. With the skiing, do the math on whether shelling out for the season pass up front will end up costing you less than paying à la carte each time you head to the slopes.

# WARNING: SUGGESTED LIFESTYLE CHANGES AHEAD

I have just outlined some ways to save money without drastically changing your way of life. Below are just a few more that do ask you to make more changes. It's up to you to decide if you want to make the trade-off; it's all about weighing what you are willing to do now, so you will have more later.

## STAY HOME FOR THE MOVIES

If going out to the movies every weekend ends up costing you $30 once you figure in the beer and pizza afterward with your friends, how about going to the movies just two times a month? Save yourself $60 a month, $720 a year. I know you've heard this before, but the problem is that you just have not been motivated enough to do it. I figure if you're reading this section, you're ready now.

## GET A ROOMMATE

Okay, wait, wait, wait. Come back here. Let's face it, your rent is your biggest fixed cost; bring that way down for a few years, and it will give you an opportunity to save up some serious funds. If you don't already have a roommate, it may be time to ponder the possibility. I know it is a major lifestyle change, but think about the struggles and sacrifices you're already making, and consider how many of them could be alleviated if you found some relief from your housing costs. I know that many of you feel that living roommate-free is a privilege of adulthood and a price you're willing to pay. I'm only asking you to envision the upside of a short-term roommate arrangement before you dismiss the notion out of hand.

## GET *AHEAD* OF THE HOUSING TREND

If you live in a city with a high cost of living, you have to recognize that it is by choice. No one is making you. It is your decision, and that's great. Go for it. But if you are so YF&B that you can't make ends meet, at least fight the urge to live in the hippest, trendiest neighborhood or block. Set your sights on finding the next hot neighborhood.

That worked for David, who, back in his YF&B years in the late 90s, wanted to live in the trendy East Village neighborhood of New York City. He loved the restaurants, bars, and proximity to other great downtown neighborhoods. But the rents were sky-high. So he expanded his sites and started exploring surrounding areas. Way across town, on the outskirts of Chelsea, he noticed art galleries, cafés, and shops sprouting up. And the rents were seriously cheaper than in the East Village. David found a great studio, and he was just a couple subway stops away from the East Village haunts he loved. Fast-forward a few years, and David's quiet Chelsea neighborhood had indeed morphed into one of the city's hippest areas. David's rent was raised now that his neighborhood was hot, but it was nowhere near what it would be if he moved into that same apartment right now.

Don't get stuck with tunnel vision about where you "have to" live. Expand your housing horizons. Spend some weekends driving or walking around town, looking for any signs of a neighborhood that looks like it is making a turn: a new café or restaurant that looks like your kind of place, etc. And check in with real estate agents and rental agencies in your area; tell them you are thinking of moving and want their spin on what neighborhoods are up-and-coming.

## DRIVE YOUR CAR LONGER

Rather than trading in your car every three or four years and taking out another loan for a new car, how about holding on to it for six, seven, or eight years? That way, there will be three or four years when you own it outright—no monthly loan payment. You get where I am going here? If you aren't spending $300 a month on the car loan, that's $300 a month you have for your savings fund.

**YF&B** I would love for anyone with a useful cost-saving move in the YF&B years to post their strategy on the message board on my website. As I said, I bet I could learn a few tricks from you.

**PROBLEM:**

I want to start my own savings account, but everyone tells me I should pay off my credit card debt first.

**SOLUTION:**

Let the interest rates on your credit cards be your guide.

A lot of people get confused about what to do first when it comes to saving money: pay off debt, save for their retirement, or just put money away for an emergency fund. Listen, if you are paying 18 percent interest on your credit card debt, it makes absolutely no sense to start a savings account where you will be lucky to earn 2 percent interest. And that 2 percent is taxable, which reduces your real return even more.

Now, I know you think that having some money in the bank will make you feel more secure. But the reality is that it will make it impossible to get out of your broke situation. If you are paying 18 percent and just earning 2 percent, that means you're losing 16 percent.

Here's what I want you to do: Look at the interest you are paying on your credit cards. If that interest is higher than the interest you can earn in a savings account, then pay off your credit card debt first. If the interest on your credit card debt is lower or essentially the same as the interest on your savings account, then you can put more money into savings if it will make you feel more secure. It really is that simple.

**PROBLEM:**
Whenever I manage to save some money, my car breaks down or something else happens that forces me to use all my savings and go further into debt.

**SOLUTION:**
Keep an "emergency" credit card around.

Cash should be your first line of defense when you are hit with unexpected expenses. But I know that in the YF&B years, you might not have had the time or money to build up a large enough cash reserve to cover life's inevitable surprises. That's where your credit card can come to the rescue; when you use your card for emergency repairs, that's a good use of debt.

But we need to review how you are to use the card *smartly.* It is far better to make a regular charge than to take out a cash advance. The cash advance typically has a much higher interest rate—it can be more than 20 percent—than the rate for your regular charges. So charge your repairs; do not take a cash advance to pay for them.

If your credit card isn't an option, you might consider tapping your Roth IRA if you have one. As I explain on page 187, you can always withdraw your contributions (though not your investment gains) without any penalty or tax. And if you have a traditional IRA (see page 188), you are allowed to withdraw your money for sixty days without tax or penalty. But if you don't repay that money into the account by day sixty, you will have to pay income tax on the withdrawn amount, as well as a 10 percent penalty. And I always want you to think long and hard about raiding your retirement funds; you are cutting back on a long-term goal to solve a short-term problem. I realize that sometimes this may be necessary. Just please make every effort to replenish your retirement kitty as quickly as possible. The one retirement fund you are not to touch is your 401(k). As I explain on page 186, taking a loan from your 401(k) is a dangerous and expensive move.

Of course, the best solution would be to have an emergency cash fund. Now, for some reason, every time I suggest to YF&Bers that you should have an emergency cash fund, you jump all over me, insisting that there is absolutely no way you can afford to set aside money for emergencies. Sure, that probably isn't in the cards when you are just starting out and don't make enough to live on. In both Chapter 2, Career Moves, and Chapter 3, Give Yourself Credit, I have been quite clear on how to cope when you are super-young and super-broke. But there will be a time when your salary does get to a more comfortable level and you have your credit card debt and student loans under control. When that happens, it's time to concentrate on building an emergency cash fund.

Ideally, you would build up a cash fund that is equal to at least six to eight months' living costs. That's my super-safe strategy to make sure you won't be up a creek if your car breaks down, or if you lose your job and it takes a while to get another one. But don't slam this book down in disgust just yet. I know that's a lot of money. Relax. I am not suggesting that you have the emergency fund taken care of tomorrow. You can build up a stash over time.

I am a big believer in the power of incentives. The table on the next page gives you a sense of how putting away a little money each month can help you reach your goals over a few years.

**YF&B**

On my website, you can use the periodic investment calculator to see how putting aside a set amount each month can grow into a sizable sum over time.

| If your monthly saving is... | ...And you earn 2 percent a year, your account will be worth... | | | |
|---|---|---|---|---|
| | 3 years | 5 years | 7 years | 10 years |
| $100 | $3,714 | $6,315 | $9,023 | $13,294 |
| $150 | $5,570 | $9,473 | $13,535 | $19,941 |
| $200 | $7,426 | $12,630 | $18,047 | $26,588 |
| $250 | $9,283 | $15,788 | $22,559 | $33,235 |
| $300 | $11,140 | $18,946 | $27,070 | $39,882 |

**PROBLEM:**

I am finally making a decent sum of money, but I still have nothing left at the end of the month after paying all my bills.

**SOLUTION:**

You have plenty of options if you are ready to make some trade-offs today in order to reach tomorrow's goals.

Warning: This riff is not for the YF&B who are cash-strapped, because they simply don't make enough money to cover their living costs. This advice is for the YF&-not-so-B who are finally bringing in some money but still can't finish a month with something left in the bank. If that's your MO, you are what I call "broke by choice." You are making enough to live on, but you are making choices—conscious or not—to spend all, or more than, you make.

You are spending money that you don't even have to impress people you do not even know or like. It is such a colossal mistake. When you waste money simply because it's easier to do so, or because you feel you're entitled to it, that is just plain stupid. And don't feed me the crap that you only live once and you deserve to have fun while you're young. Hey, there is a ton of fun to be had later, too—when you can afford it! If you don't make the right choices now, you are going to be so broke when you are older that you will be absolutely miserable. Look, I'm not going to tell you what you can live without. You're looking to pare back, not cut out.

If you are having trouble deciding what is good spending and what is bad spending, I ask you to head over to your bedroom closet. Open it up. Any item you have not worn or used in one year, or that still has its price tag on or is sitting in its original packaging, is to be placed in the center of your living room. While you're at it, check under the bed, in the garage, and in your bathroom. Take out all your unused or hardly used cosmetics, video games, and any sports gear you haven't touched in eons. Get it all in one big pile.

I bet if you sat down and added up the cost of everything in that pile, it would account for a high percentage of the credit card balance you currently have. When you say you don't know where the money went, a lot of it is sitting unused in your closets.

So here's what you are going to do with all that junk. (Yes, it is junk. It can be the most gorgeous outfit or coolest toy, but if you aren't using it—if you don't need it—it is junk.) You can sell it on a website such as eBay (www.ebay.com) or Craigslist (www.craigslist.org), but I also recommend looking into donating it to a charity and taking a tax deduction on the value of your contribution. You may just find that the value of the deduction beats what you can get for it online. My friend tried to sell a $1,000 purse she got as a gift on eBay, and the only bid she got for it was $10. She was far better off donating it and getting a tax write-off.

The ItsDeductible software program ($19.95; available online at www.shop.intuit.com) will help you place a value on your donated goods.

After going through this closet-cleansing ritual, I hope you will have found an incentive to curb your spending appetite. Just remember that three-second trick from the Give Yourself Credit chapter: When you are ready to whip out your credit card, ask yourself if it is for a good use or bad use. If it's a bad use, the card goes right back into your wallet. That unspent money is going to mean that your bank account should be bigger at the end of the month—big enough, let's hope, for you to start saving.

**PROBLEM:**

I don't have enough money to invest in my company 401(k) *and* start my own savings account; I don't know which one to do first.

**SOLUTION:**

Go for the 401(k) if you can get a company match; after that, start your own savings plan.

We will talk about 401(k)s and retirement savings in detail later, in Chapter 6, Retirement Rules, but right now I just want you to understand one important 401(k) fact: Many plans offer a company match. This means that if you contribute to your plan, your employer will kick in some money, too. The amount of the match varies; some employers do a dollar-for-dollar match up to a certain level, say $1,500; others may offer a 50 percent match on the first $2,000, $3,000, or $4,000 you invest in the plan.

This is free money that you are not to pass up. Let's say your employer offers a 50 percent match up to $1,500 a year. That means for every dollar you put into your plan, your employer will give you 50 cents, up to a maximum of $1,500. So if you invest $3,000 in your 401(k), your employer will kick in another $1,500 (that's 50 percent of your $3,000) to your account. You just made a 50 percent return on your investment. It gets no better than that.

So if your employer does indeed offer a company match, I want you to sign up for your 401(k) and contribute enough each year to get the maximum company match. You are to do this no matter how much credit card debt you have. You are to do this before you save one penny outside of a retirement account. This is your number-one priority when it comes to savings. But again, do this only if your company matches your contribution.

If you aren't sure how much you need to invest to get the max out of your employer match, just call up your HR department and ask. After you get the maximum company match, you have the option of suspending your contributions for the rest of the year. That will free up some money for you to start your own savings account or to pay off your credit card debt. (See page 193 for details on how to stop your contributions.)

**PROBLEM:**
I have no clue where to save. And I don't know if I should invest in stocks or just keep my money safe and sound in a boring savings account.

**SOLUTION:**
Keep it simple and safe. A bank, credit union, or discount brokerage can set you up with a money-market account or money-market fund.

Saving is not the same thing as investing. Saving is for a short-term goal that you hope to reach within five years or so. Investing is for the long term. You save for the down payment on a house that you hope to buy in a few years. You invest for your retirement in a few decades.

The big difference is the risk you are willing to take with your money. If you need your money in less than five years, your money does not belong in stocks. I will discuss this more in Chapter 7, Investing Made Easy, but here's a quick preview: As we all learned from the 2000–2002 market collapse, stocks can crater. And there is no guarantee how quickly they will rebound. So if you intend to use your money in the next few years, you don't want to run the risk that your account will have taken a downturn just when you need it.

You want to play it safe with your savings. You won't have the big upside that stocks offer, but you also won't have any of the downside. Your money will grow, earning interest at a modest rate. In the fall of 2004, safe savings rates ranged from 1.5 percent to 3 percent. But you have the peace of mind that when you need the cash, it will all be there, with no losses.

The types of safe investments appropriate for your savings are called certificates of deposit (CDs), money-market deposit accounts (MMDAs), and money-market mutual funds. CDs and MMDAs are offered by banks and credit unions. A CD requires you to leave your money untouched for a predetermined period of time. This can be just a few months, or a few years. The longer the period, the more interest you will earn. In the fall of 2004, you could earn 1.3 percent a year on a three-month CD, and 2.9 percent if you agreed to invest for two years. The only thing you need to be careful about is that you will have to forfeit a portion of the interest you have earned—the penalty can be 50 percent or so—if you try to take your money before the CD matures—meaning before the term is up. With a CD, you need to invest a set amount, typically at least $500 or so.

If you want more flexibility, banks also offer MMDAs; you earn less interest than with a CD, but the money is never tied up, and you can even write checks on your account, though there is typically a minimum of $250 or so per check. One nice benefit of CDs and MMDAs is that if your bank is a member of the Federal Deposit Insurance Corporation (FDIC), your investment is insured up to a $100,000 max. Now, the incidence of banks going belly-up is pretty rare, but for worrywarts, it's nice to know the government will take care of you if something happens. The interest rate you earn on your account varies according to the size of the minimum balance. As with a CD, the minimum is typically $500 or $1,000.

You can shop for the best CDs and MMDAs at www.bankrate.com. You do not need to use a bank that is in your state. You should also check with the bank where you have your checking account; sometimes, if your combined balances are above a certain level, you can qualify for a higher interest rate.

Another option is a money-market mutual fund, which is a mutual fund that invests in the same sort of low-risk short-term securities as a CD or MMDA. The one drawback with investing in a fund is that you do not have FDIC insurance. That said, if you stick with a reputable mutual-fund firm, the odds of running into any trouble are extremely low. Money-market funds can also be a terrific option if you don't have the $1,000 or so that many banks require to open a CD or MMDA. A handful of mutual-fund companies will let you open a money-market fund account with an investment of as little as $50. You must sign up for their Automatic Investing Plan (AIP), where you agree to have a certain amount directly invested in the account each month; again, it can be just $50 or so. The TIAA-CREF (800-223-1200) mutual-fund company and T. Rowe Price (800-638-5660) both offer money-market accounts that you can start with as little as $50.

**PROBLEM:**
I just found a $100 Series EE savings bond that my grandparents gave me years ago, and I have no idea what it's worth or how to cash it in.

**SOLUTION:**
It might not be worth as much as you think.

There are a variety of savings bonds issued by the U.S. Treasury. I am going to cover the popular Series EE here, but you can learn about all the varieties at the Treasury Direct website, www.treasurydirect.gov.

When you purchase a Series EE bond, you pay just half the face value of the bond. So in this example, your grandparents paid $50 for a $100 bond. How's that? Well, you have to hold on to the bond for a bunch of years to be able to redeem it for $100. During that period, all the interest the bond earns is plowed back into the bond until it has earned enough interest to make up the difference between what your grandparents paid for the bond ($50) and its face value ($100).

The interest rate is set by a formula that follows the movement in the five-year Treasury note. You are guaranteed that your bond will reach its face value within twenty years, but if you don't redeem it then, it can continue to earn interest for up to thirty years from its issue date. That said, you don't have to wait for the bond to reach its full maturity to redeem it; you can redeem it once it is at least twelve months old, though you will be hit with a three-month interest penalty on any bond that you have held for less than five years.

When you eventually redeem your bond, you will owe federal income tax on the interest the bond earned. The only tax escape is if you happen to have been older than age twenty-four when the bond was given to you, and if the bond was issued after December 1989. If you meet those criteria, and you intend to use the bond to pay for college costs, your federal tax will be waived.

YF&B On my website are links to learn more about Series EE bonds, Series I bonds, and Series HH bonds.

I know this is another round of confusing Washington rules and regs, so let's concentrate on the key info:

- You can redeem any EE/E bond that is at least one year old; but if the bond is not five years old, you will forfeit three months' interest as a penalty for your early redemption.

- You are guaranteed that your bond will reach its full face value within twenty years. Redeem before then, and you may not get the full face value.

- Bonds that have reached their full face value can continue to earn interest for an extended period: up to thirty years past the original issue date of the bond. The guaranteed minimum interest rate during this extended period varies.

| Bonds issued between... | ...Earn a guaranteed minimum of... |
| --- | --- |
| 11/82 and 10/86 | 7.5 percent |
| 11/86 and 2/93 | 6 percent |
| 3/93 and 4/95 | 4 percent |
| 5/95 and the present | No guaranteed rate |

My advice is to head over to the Treasury Department's website; they know this is crazy stuff, so they have a calculator where you can plug in your savings bond info and see what it is worth today and what it is currently earning in interest. The savings bond calculator is located at: http://www.publicdebt.treas.gov/sav/savcalc.htm.

If you do decide to redeem your savings bond, take it to a bank or brokerage where you have an account; bring some photo ID along with the bond, and they will be happy to cash the bond for you.

Success is not solely about making more money. It is about knowing where the money you make is going.

# QUICK PLAYBACK

➡️ You don't need to make more to save more; you can "find" extra cash by raising your insurance deductible (and lowering your premium), stretching the time between haircuts by a few weeks, and using just a cell phone, rather than paying for a line at home.

➡️ Your bank statement can be a treasure trove of "savings"; add up all your ATM and bounced-check fees. If it's more than zero, you are wasting money. Switch to a bank where the ATMs are more convenient, and curb your bouncing habit.

➡️ Before you start a savings account, your first priority is to invest in your company 401(k) to get the maximum company match.

➡️ A savings account that pays 2 percent interest makes no sense if you also have a credit card balance that costs you 18 percent interest. Use your savings to pay off the credit card debt.

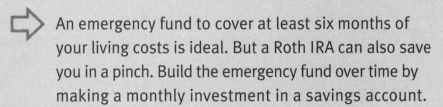 An emergency fund to cover at least six months of your living costs is ideal. But a Roth IRA can also save you in a pinch. Build the emergency fund over time by making a monthly investment in a savings account.

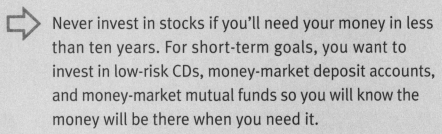 Never invest in stocks if you'll need your money in less than ten years. For short-term goals, you want to invest in low-risk CDs, money-market deposit accounts, and money-market mutual funds so you will know the money will be there when you need it.

# retirement

## rules

chapter **6**

Unlike your grand-parents and maybe even your parents, you are going to be pretty much on your own for funding your retirement.

# THE LOWDOWN

I wouldn't be surprised if you took a look at the title of this section and rolled your eyes, thinking, *Oh, sure, Suze, let's talk about all the money I need to save for retirement, when right now I consider it a triumph to be able to pay my bills every month. Give me a break.*

I want you to approach this section with an open mind. I am not interested in guilting you into saving for your retirement. I'm going to lay down what is at stake here in clear terms, so you can make the right decisions for yourself. And what I have to tell you is going to be quite a different spin than what you may have heard elsewhere. I am a big believer in retirement accounts such as 401(k)s, but I think there is also a compelling argument to be made today—thanks to our current tax rates—to postpone your 401(k) investment and invest in a Roth IRA instead, or to invest in your 401(k) up to the point where you have qualified for the maximum company match, and then invest any additional money elsewhere.

So please stick with me. I have a lot of strategies designed just for YF&Bers with limited budgets. And I am totally sensitive to the irony of talking about retirement goals when some of you are still scrambling to establish yourself in your first job. But the reality is that you have been dealt a tough hand, and that requires getting an early jump on your retirement savings, because your best friend right now is time.

Let's do some brief scene-setting, so you get what I am talking about. Unlike your grandparents and maybe even your parents, you are going to be pretty much on your own for funding your retirement. You have to invest your own money in retirement plans known as 401(k)s and IRAs. Your grandparents never had to invest in their pensions; they got it along with a gold watch when they retired after working for the same company for years. They also could rely on Social Security to provide a chunk of their retirement income. But I'm not sure Social Security is going to be around when you need it.

While you are paying into the Social Security system with every paycheck (it's the deduction listed under FICA), it's pretty clear that you are not going to get any-where near the benefits that older folks who are already receiving Social Security are currently entitled to. The entire system is based on the simple premise that the benefits paid to today's retirees are financed by the contributions being made by today's workers. That worked fine when Social Security was first created and most people were only expected to live into their sixties. Now that your gener-ation is expected to live well into your eighties, the system can't possibly keep up with the demand for benefits from people who will spend twenty or thirty years in retirement, not just five or ten, to say nothing of the fact that the benefits due to your parents' huge boomer generation are going to seriously strain the system. That means, in the simplest terms, that you can't rely on the federal government to support you during your retirement.

That's not intended to depress you. I just want you to understand who you need to rely on: you and only you—not your employer, and not the federal government. And don't expect any inheritance to bail you out, either; the great news is that your parents are living longer, too, so they will probably be using their money until you are in your sixties.

## IT PAYS TO BE YOUNG

After saying all that, I figure I owe you some good news. Here you go: You are actually in a sweet spot for dealing with investing for your future. I know that many of you think the path to getting rich is to pick the can't-miss stock du jour.

Nice theory, but I am here to tell you that wealth is not built by chasing hot stocks; success is rooted in how long you are invested. Of course, it does matter what you invest in, and I will explain what you need to know in the next chapter, Investing Made Easy, but what I want you to get right now is that the number of years that your money is invested is the most important ingredient in your YF&B financial recipe. And if there's one thing the YF&B have lots of right now, it is time. But notice the words *right now*. While money will always come and go, when time goes, it is gone forever, so you can't afford to waste it.

The time factor I am talking about is what is known in financial circles as the power of compounding. It's a pretty simple concept. Let's say you have an initial investment of $100, and it earns 10 percent in a year. That's $10. So you now have $110. If you earn 10 percent the next year, it will be 10 percent of $110, not $100, so you will actually make $11 in year two, not $10. That gives you $121. The next year, let's say you earn 10 percent again. That's $12.10 (10 percent of $121). Get it? Your money keeps feeding off itself.

Let's walk through an example where you take $300 from your paycheck every month and invest it in a retirement account; that's $3,600 a year. And let's assume that your money earns an average annual return of 8 percent. Why 8 percent? Well, as I will explain in the next section, stocks, on average, have gained about 10 percent a year for the past six or seven decades. But I want to be conservative here, so we're going to dial back and work up our numbers based on an average annual rate of return of 8 percent.

Now, a word about **average annual return**. It's one of the most misunderstood numbers. When I say the average annual return for stocks has been 10 percent, I am not suggesting that each year you will get a 10 percent return. Far from it. Behind that average are years when stocks gained 20 percent or more, as well as other years when they lost 20 percent or more. When I use the term "average annual return," I am in no way saying that there is a straight-line trajectory where your investment gains 10 percent each and every year. It is a long-term average of market returns.

You have been dealt a tough hand, and that requires getting an early jump on your retirement savings, because your best friend right now is time.

Back to our example. You invest $300 every month and earn an 8 percent average annual return on your money. If you do this from the age of twenty-five to the age of forty—just fifteen years in total—you will have invested $54,000, and your account will be worth $104,504. Next, let's assume that you never invest another penny. You keep that $104,504 invested, and it continues to earn an average annual return of 8 percent, but you stop adding any money to the account.

When you turn seventy years old, your investment will be worth:

A. $450,089

B. $622,489

C. $1.05 million

More good news. The answer is C. By letting that $104,504 compound at our assumed average annual rate of return of 8 percent for the next thirty years, you will become a millionaire. So think about this: You actually invested only $54,000, and now you have more than $1 million.

Now let's see what difference a few years will make on your bottom line. Instead of starting your investing at twenty-five, you wait until you are forty when midlife panic strikes and you realize you need to get serious about this retirement stuff. As with our earlier example, you invest $300 a month, but in this case you do it for the entire thirty years, all the way until you turn seventy. Once again, you'll earn an average annual return of 8 percent. So how much do you think you will have if you invest the same amount each year, but you keep up the investments for twice as long?

A. $450,089

B. $622,489

C. $1.05 million

The answer is A. Yup, you read that right. Even though you actually put in double the amount of money ($108,000 vs. $54,000), you will have less than half as much in your account. That's because your money has just thirty years to com-

180

pound, whereas if you had started at twenty-five, it would have forty-five years to compound until you reached seventy. The amount of time was twice as important as the amount of money that you invested.

Just FYI: If you start at forty and want to end up with the same amount of money as someone who started at twenty-five, your monthly investments would need to be about $700 instead of the more manageable $300. And you would have to make that investment for the full thirty years, not just the fifteen years of investing that you would need if you started at twenty-five years of age. In your twenties and thirties, you've got the one key ingredient that people in their forties and fifties would kill for.

Do I have your attention now?

Go to my website, where you can play with the compound interest calculator to see how investing now and letting that money work for you over decades can make reaching your retirement goals a lot easier than you thought when you first settled into reading this section.

## INVESTING WITH A TAX BREAK

Where should you invest to start your money on its compounding journey?

Welcome to the wacky world of retirement plans. I say "wacky" because you have to understand a slew of odd rules and regulations, and make some choices. I am here to serve as your retirement simplifier. We are going to focus on the two smartest retirement investing options:

- **A 401(k) that offers a company matching contribution**
- **A Roth IRA**

Ideally, you will be able to invest in both the 401(k) with the company match and the Roth IRA. You are indeed allowed to do both, and they are an unbeatable one-two punch in investing for your retirement. Now, if you have a 401(k) at work but the boss doesn't offer a company match, I want your first priority to be funding your Roth. I will explain more about this in a bit, but I know that so many of you are twisted in knots about what to do first, and what to do if you have the money for only one investment, not both. So now you know: 401(k) with a company match is job one. Then comes the Roth. If you have the money to pull off both, go for it.

## THE MATCH GAME

The most common type of retirement account that is offered by your employer is known as a **401(k)**. Some nonprofits offer a similar type of plan called a **403(b)**. The military offers what is known as a Thrift Savings Plan or TSP. Tax-sheltered annuities (TSA) are a type of 403(b)s, and are sometimes called tax-deferred annuities. Employees of public schools, tax-exempt charities, self-employed ministers, and members of Indian tribal governments are eligible to invest in TSAs. Because all these plans are so similar, please know that when I say "401(k)," I am also referring to 403(b)s, TSAs, and TSPs, too.

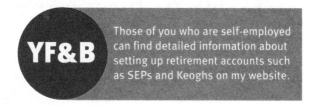

**YF&B** Those of you who are self-employed can find detailed information about setting up retirement accounts such as SEPs and Keoghs on my website.

I want to take you slowly through how 401(k)s work. I know that many of you have been turned off by the HR presentations and either haven't started to contribute or are contributing but have no clue what is going on.

The odd name 401(k) comes from the part of our federal tax code that deals with these plans. There are a few moving parts to a 401(k). Let's knock them off one at a time. First, there are your contributions—the money that is taken out of every paycheck and invested in your 401(k) account. There are limits to what your annual contribution can be.

| Year | Annual Limit |
| --- | --- |
| 2005 | $14,000 |
| 2006 | $15,000 |

After 2006, the maximum pretax contribution limit is indexed in $500 increments for inflation.

The great thing about your contributions is that they are taken out of your paycheck pretax. That means that you get to put the money that would normally go to Uncle Sam to work for you instead. Let's say you are in the 15 percent federal income tax bracket. That means that 15 cents out of every dollar you earn goes to pay your federal tax. That leaves you with 85 cents in after-tax income to invest or spend. When you contribute to a 401(k), 100 cents of every dollar goes straight into your account. There is no money siphoned off for taxes. One way to look at this is that you just got a 15 percent bonus for agreeing to invest in your 401(k). The higher your tax bracket, the higher your bonus, so to speak.

But wait, it gets better. As I began to explain in Chapter 5, Save Up, many companies (though not all) pitch in and add money to your 401(k) account—what is called the employer match or company match. Every company has a different system. Typically, your boss will kick in a percentage of your contribution up to a specific dollar limit. For example, your company match might be 50 percent up to $2,000 per year. So what this means is that for every dollar that you contribute to your 401(k) plan, your boss will throw in 50 cents, up to the company's maximum of $2,000 per year. You would have to invest $4,000 to get the maximum match from your boss (50 percent of your $4,000 is $2,000). You can still invest more on your own, but your boss will not match it.

I cannot stress this one point enough: Any retirement plan where your boss kicks in a matching contribution belongs at the top of your retirement investing to-do list. I do not care if you have a mountain of credit card debt, or if you want to save up for a home or car. If your company gives you a matching contribution on your 401(k), you must enroll in the plan and invest enough to get the maximum company match. This is free money! In the example above, it would be like getting a 50 percent return on your money without any risk. You are nuts if you pass that up.

I knew a guy by the name of Mike, who was working his tail off to impress the bosses at the architecture firm where he worked. He was doing really well, but he couldn't get his boss to cough up a raise. Mike loved the firm, and he knew it was the right place for him to build his career, but he was getting frustrated on his $30,000 salary. When we talked, we agreed that in the current job market, he would be lucky to get a 5 percent raise. That would be $1,500. And he would then have to pay tax on that $1,500. At the 15 percent federal income tax rate, he would pay $300 in tax, reducing his "raise" net to just $1,200. He came to me looking for advice on how to snag the raise. Instead, I asked him if he was enrolled in his company's 401(k) plan. He told me he wasn't; he said he didn't have the money to spare, and he looked annoyed with me for changing the subject. I told him to give me a call the next day once he found out if his boss offered a company match on the 401(k). It turns out that his employer offered a 50 percent match, up to $1,500 a year. Here he was, knocking his head against the wall to get maybe a 5 percent raise that would be taxable, when he could have a $1,500 gift from his boss without any taxes. In the three years that he had failed to participate in the company plan, he had essentially lost out on $4,500 in "bonus" money from his boss.

# VESTED INTEREST

Now, there is usually a string attached with the employer match. The money that the company contributes goes into your 401(k) account, but in most instances, you don't really own that money until a few years have passed; this is what is known as **vesting**. Think of it as your employer making an investment in you. Your company doesn't want to give you the money and then have you leave your job in a year. This is a long-term incentive for you to stick around. So they use what is known as a vesting schedule. All this means is that each year, a little more of your company match becomes yours to keep forever. Each company has a different vesting schedule, but typically you have 20 or 25 percent of the company match vest each year. So if you start a new job in 2005, and vest over four years, then the employer match for the amount you invested that year will be 100 percent yours in 2009. Leave after 2009, and you'll get to take all of the match with you. Leave before 2009, and you can take only the portion of the match that is already completely vested. And I want to be really, really clear on this: I am only talking about your employer match. The money that *you* contribute to your 401(k) is always 100 percent yours. It does not have to vest.

One bit of strategic advice: If you anticipate that you will be job-hopping in the next year or so, you might want to skip the 401(k), since you won't be around long enough to "collect" the vested company match. Instead, focus on funding a Roth IRA.

# TAX POLICY

While your money is invested in a 401(k), you pay no tax on your earnings. The technical term for that is **tax-deferred**. The taxes are deferred, or postponed, until you take the money out. But during all the years that the money stays invested, no taxes are due. This adds to the compounding, or growth, factor of your money in a 401(k) plan. But when it comes time to start taking money out of your 401(k)—you can start as early as 59½ and no later than 70½—the IRS comes a knockin' for its share. Remember, the money that you originally put into your

401(k) was pretax dollars, and those pretax dollars grew, tax-deferred, in the account. But a 401(k) never promised to be tax-free. When you make withdrawals from your 401(k), you will be required to pay taxes on the money that you take out, at whatever your income tax bracket is at that time.

## THE PENALTY BOX

To get all the tax breaks of a 401(k), you have to give something up in return: freedom. Once you invest in a 401(k), you basically don't want to touch the money until you are at least 59½. If you make a withdrawal before then, in most cases you will owe income tax on all the money that you withdraw, plus a 10 percent early-withdrawal penalty. So if you make an early withdrawal of $10,000 and you are in the 15 percent tax bracket, you will pay $1,500 in tax and another $1,000 penalty, leaving you with just $7,500. That's the stick that goes with the carrot. When Congress came up with this plan, they wanted to make sure you not only invested for your retirement, but that you didn't raid it when you were forty for a midlife-crisis blowout vacation. The 10 percent penalty is to keep you in line with investing for your retirement.

## BORROWING FROM YOURSELF

There is one way you can get at your money before 59½ and not pay the penalty: Take a loan from your 401(k) account. You can take a loan for any reason that you want, as long as it is for more than $1,000 but not more than $50,000; at the same time, your loan cannot exceed 50 percent of your account's value. You can also get hit with some fees on the loan—say, $50 to $100. On a large loan of more than $10,000, that's not a big deal, but realize that if you pay $100 on a $2,000 loan, you've just spent 5 percent of your loan amount. That's not smart.

Once you take out a loan on your 401(k), you must commit to a periodic repayment plan—monthly or quarterly—and you typically have five years to get the loan paid off. The one exception is if the money is used for a down payment on a home, in which case your repayment period can be longer. There are plenty of risks with taking out a loan on your 401(k), but if you can't see another way to make a down payment, it can be a viable option. I cover this in more detail on page 198.

## TAKE A TRIAL RUN

I know you are already stressed out about living on your paycheck, even before you have signed up for the 401(k), so you're not exactly thrilling to my idea that you should shrink your paycheck by starting to make 401(k) contributions just to get your employer's match. But I am not going to back down. It is that important. Just try making the contributions for a few months and see if you can live with them. I respect that this is a big step for you to take, all I ask is that you try it for six months and see if you can manage. My experience is that once people sign up and have the money deducted, they don't even miss it. Their expenses usually adjust to their lower paycheck. And remember that not only will you be investing, you'll also be lowering your tax bill; because your 401(k) contributions come out of your paycheck before taxes, they reduce the amount of income that Uncle Sam gets to take a take bite from.

## ROTH AND ROLL

Are you with me so far? If you get a company match on your 401(k), you are to go for it, full force ahead. But then, at the point that you get the maximum company match, I want you to turn your attention to a **Roth IRA**. As far as I am concerned, a Roth IRA is the best financial friend a YF&Ber could ever have. It is my favorite type of investment account for you. Let me explain my Roth crush.

Unlike a 401(k), where your contributions are made with pretax dollars, a Roth offers you no up-front tax break. Your contribution comes from money that you have already paid taxes on. Let's make sure that computed; I know this is the financial equivalent of mastering a new language. With a 401(k) plan, your money comes straight out of your salary, before taxes are deducted. That's why your contributions are called pretax. With a Roth, your contributions are made with money that you have already paid taxes on. Your Roth is funded with after-tax dollars.

So you're wondering why I would say that a Roth is better than a 401(k), right? Well, as with most things in life, it's not where you start but where you end up. And a Roth offers a better tax deal on the back end. Remember, your 401(k) withdrawals that you will make are going to get hit with income tax. How much income tax? Well, whatever the rates are at the time that you withdraw your money. But with a Roth, the money that you contributed is not going to be taxed (it already was taxed before you contributed it, remember?), and all the money that you earn on those contributions—what's known as your investment gain—is not going to be taxed, either, as long as you have owned the Roth for a minimum of five years and you are at least 59½ at the time that you make the withdrawal. That's the big tax break with a Roth: There's no tax at the end. None. Nada. Forever.

That makes a Roth an incredibly smart investment, and that's why I am offering up some unconventional wisdom. The standard advice says that you should contribute as much as you can into a 401(k) to get the tax break. I disagree. I think you should contribute only if you can get a company match. If you don't get a match, and even for any contributions beyond what you need for the match, I want you to concentrate on a Roth; they are a far better deal than 401(k)s.

## ROTH VS. TRADITIONAL IRA

Before we go on with my love affair with Roths, I just have to tell you about one more type of retirement plan that may come into play in your life. It is known as a traditional IRA. I like Roths better than traditional IRAs. A traditional IRA used to be the only IRA in town, until Roths were created in 1997. The maximum contribution in a traditional IRA is the same as for a Roth: $4,000 in 2005. And just like a 401(k), with a traditional IRA, the money grows tax-deferred, but you must pay income tax on your withdrawals.

If you don't have a 401(k) at work, you can invest in a traditional IRA no matter what your income is, and your contribution is tax-deductible. For example, if you invest $4,000 and you are in the 15 percent tax bracket, your tax bill will be reduced by $600 ($4,000 x 15 percent). But if you have a 401(k), you are eligible for the full tax break on the traditional IRA only if you are single and your modified adjusted gross income (MAGI) is below $50,000 in 2005. For married couples filing a joint tax return, the limit in 2005 is $70,000. Between $50,000 and $60,000, single filers can get a partial deduction; for married couples filing a joint tax return, the partial deduction cuts off after your MAGI exceeds $80,000.

If your income exceeds those limits, you can still invest in a traditional IRA, but you won't get the tax break on your contributions; you must contribute with after-tax money.

Even if you get the full tax break on a traditional IRA, the Roth is the smarter IRA move. With tax rates so low right now, I don't think the deduction is anything to write home about, especially when you are in your YF&B years and are in the lowest tax brackets anyway.

## FOCUS ON THE FINISH LINE

The fact that the traditional IRA (and your 401(k)) gets smacked with income tax when you make withdrawals is why I think a Roth is a much better deal. I hope you're with me on the notion that right now the up-front tax breaks on a 401(k) or traditional IRA aren't the be all and end all, given that your broke status means that you are in a low tax bracket.

But let's just jump forward thirty or forty years and check in on you at the point that you start to make the withdrawals from the 401(k) or traditional IRA. I'm going to presume that you have indeed had much career and financial success, which means you are in a much higher tax bracket. And I have to tell you that I think the odds are that tax brackets in general could be a lot higher in the future than they are right now, given the high deficits that we have to finance. So what sense does it make to get a tax write-off right now, when rates are the lowest they have ever been and you are in the lowest brackets anyway, considering that you will probably be stuck with higher tax rates when it is time to take your money out? I think it makes a lot more sense to invest in a Roth today and never have to worry about the tax bill down the line.

Let's do the numbers so you can see what I am talking about. Let's say you start investing $4,000 a year in a Roth in 2005, when you are thirty, and you make the same $4,000 investment in 2006 and 2007. Then we'll take the simple route and assume that all your subsequent annual investments will total a steady $5,000 per year beginning in 2008. You'll keep up your Rothing for twenty-nine years, and once again we will assume an 8 percent average annual return on your investment. That will give you $535,480. If for some reason when you reach the

59½ threshold, you decide to take all the money out, your tax bill will be zero. You'll get all $535,480.

But if you were to withdraw the same amount from a 401(k), that hefty sum would bounce you into a high tax bracket. I am going to be generous and use a reasonable 30 percent rate. That means your $535,480 would be reduced by about $160,000, leaving you with about $375,000. I think it makes sense to give up a little tax break now and be better off in the long run.

Now, the truth is, many of you may not be able to invest in a Roth every year for thirty years, because there may come a point when your income disqualifies you. (Remember, the cutoff is $95,000 for an individual and $150,000 for a married couple filing a joint tax return.) I sure hope you have that problem down the line, but that makes it so crucial that you do everything possible to sock money into your Roth while you can.

## ROTH RULES

Now that I've got you sold on a Roth, we just need to make sure you meet the income eligibility rules. Given that you are a YF&Ber, I'm guessing that you're good to go, but let's take a look at the modified adjusted gross income (MAGI) requirements:

| 2005 ROTH ELIGIBILITY FOR FULL $4,000 CONTRIBUTION | |
| --- | --- |
| Single Tax Filer with MAGI Below | Married, Filing Joint Tax Return |
| $95,000 | $150,000 |

Single filers with MAGIs that fall between $95,000 and $110,000, and joint filers with combined income between $150,000 and $160,000, will be able to make only partial contributions. If you are married, you both can make the full contribution ($8,000) to a Roth (assuming that your joint income is below the cutoff). Even a spouse who is working full-time raising the kids or does not work can make a contribution. In a nonworking spousal Roth IRA, all the same rules apply. The maximum annual contribution limit is:

**2005–2007:** $4,000

**2008:** $5,000

**2009 and beyond:** Inflation adjustments will be made in $500 increments.

Please realize that those are simply the maximums. If you can rustle up only $500, many mutual fund companies will be happy to let you open up a Roth IRA. And if you can't come up with that in one big check, you may be able to sign up for a plan where you invest $50 or so a month. I'll explain more about automatic investing plans in the next section. I also just want you to be clear that the current law that governs the limits of how much you can contribute to a Roth is set to expire after 2010, and the contribution limits could be rolled back to their 2001 level of $2,000 per year. It would be a big shocker if Congress didn't extend the higher contribution limits. Given the Social Security problems that lie ahead, can you imagine that they would encourage you to save less, not more? But even the remote possibility that the limits could be reduced is a great reason to contribute as much as you can right now.

I also want to be super-clear about that annual limit. It is $4,000 per year in Roths, period. Not $4,000 for every Roth that you might want to open. Got it? So if you want to, you can invest that $4,000 in any number of different Roth accounts (but make sure you read on, because I think this approach is just a waste of money). But the absolute maximum that you can invest in all your Roths in 2005 is $4,000. Then, in 2006, you can invest another $4,000, in 2007 another $4,000, and so on. Once you are over the limit, you can make no new contributions, period.

## FEWER STRINGS ATTACHED

Another great advantage of a Roth over a 401(k) plan is that if you get into financial trouble, you can withdraw the money that you originally invested in the Roth (your contribution) at any time, without paying income tax or a penalty tax. Remember, your contributions are made with money that's already been taxed, so there will be no punishment for taking it out.

So let's say that you are twenty-eight years old and you contribute $4,000 a year to your Roth for the next three years. When you turn thirty-one, you will have contributed $12,000 to your Roth. You can withdraw any amount up to that entire $12,000 without taxes or the usual 10 percent penalty. It's only the *earnings* on those contributions that you can't take out without the penalty and tax. So let's say over those three years your $12,000 grew to $14,000. The only money you can't touch without incurring taxes and penalty is the $2,000.

I never want you to consider raiding your retirement accounts for just any old indulgence, but I am also sensitive to the fact that emergencies are a part of life. A Roth IRA does double duty as a great retirement investment and an emergency cash fund.

## WHERE TO ROTH

A Roth is just a type of account. You must choose where you are going to open this account and what you are going to fill it up with. Much like a suitcase, which is just a holder of your clothes, a Roth IRA is simply a container for your retirement money. In the next section, we will talk about which types of investments are good Roth choices, but first things first: We need to discuss where you can open up a Roth account. I recommend either a discount brokerage or a no-load mutual fund company. The terms "discount" and "no load" mean that these companies charge lower fees than other firms. As I will explain in the next chapter, lowering your cost of investing plays a huge role in how large your account will be decades from now.

Some of the most highly rated discount brokerages are Muriel Siebert (800-872-0444, www.msiebert.com), Scottrade (800-619-7283, www.scottrade.com), and

Fidelity Brokerage (800-343-3548, www.fidelity.com). Vanguard (877-662-7447, www.vanguard.com) and T. Rowe Price (800-225-5132, www.troweprice.com) are terrific fund companies.

## CHOICES, CHOICES

If your head is spinning right about now, don't worry. I know that's a lot of info, and you're probably ready to kill me. When we started this section, you weren't even sure you could afford to invest in a retirement account, and now I am throwing all sorts of options at you. Let's review:

If your 401(k) offers a company match, and you plan to stay at the company long enough for your match to vest, you must invest in your 401(k) to get the max company match. It does not matter what else is going on in your financial life; you can have credit card debt up to your ears. I still want you to find the money to invest in your 401(k) so you can get the maximum company match.

After you max out on your company match (or if you don't get a company match in the first place), and if you are a cash-strapped YF&Ber, you are to stop your 401(k) contributions for the rest of the year. Just contact your HR or employee benefits department and request that your contributions be suspended for the rest of the year. But make it clear that you want to start the contributions in time for the next year, when you once again want to invest enough to get the maximum company match.

Once you suspend your 401(k) contributions, you need to decide what to do with the money that would normally go into your 401(k). Find the scenario that best fits your life in the chart on pages 194 and 195, and then work your way through the recommended steps. You are to complete A before moving to B, and B must be finished before you move on to C. Got it? Some of you may be able to rip through everything in a year, but most of you will probably need a few years to get through one step, let alone your entire game plan. That's fine. Just remember that you need to make sure you rejoin your 401(k) each year to get the maximum company match. Then, once you take care of that, you can again suspend your contributions and pick up where you left off on the chart.

You have credit card, student loan, or car loan debt, and the interest rates you pay are more than 8 percent. Your FICO score is low, and you want to buy a home.

A. Boost your debt payments as much as possible to get your balances down. Timely payments and lower balances will boost your FICO score.

B. Once your FICO score rises, tell your credit card companies to reduce your interest rate, or do a balance transfer.

C. When the interest rates on your debts are less than 8 percent, save for a home down payment using a money-market deposit account or money-market mutual fund.

D. After you buy your home, open a savings account to build an eight-month emergency fund.

E. When the emergency fund is in place, fund a Roth IRA to the annual max.

F. Go back and fund your 401(k) to the annual max.

You have credit card, student loan, or car loan debt, and the interest rates you pay are less than 8 percent. Your FICO score is high and you want to buy a home.

A. Pay the minimum amount due each month on every debt.

B. Save for a home down payment using a money-market deposit account or money-market mutual fund.

C. After you buy your home, open a savings account to build an eight-month emergency fund.

D. When the emergency fund is in place, fund a Roth IRA to the annual max.

E. Continue to make your monthly debt payments.

F. Go back and fund your 401(k) to the annual max.

You already own a home, or you have no desire to own a home. You have credit card, student loan, or car loan debt, and the interest rates you pay are more than 8 percent.

A. Try to get your interest rates lowered.

B. If you can't lower your interest rate to less than 8 percent, use your extra money to pay down your debts. The debt with the highest interest rate is to be paid off first.

C. Once your debt is paid off, or the interest rates you pay are less than 8 percent, open a savings account to build an eight-month emergency fund.

D. When the emergency fund is in place, fund a Roth IRA to the annual max.

E. Continue to make your monthly debt payments.

F. Go back and fund your 401(k) to the max.

You already own a home, or you have no desire to own a home. You have credit card, student loan, or car loan debt, and the interest rates you pay are less than 8 percent.

A. Pay the minimum amount due each month on every debt.

B. Open a savings account to build an eight-month emergency fund.

C. Fund a Roth IRA to the annual max.

D. Go back and fund your 401(k) to the annual max.

You have no credit card, student loan, or car loan debt, and you want to buy a home.

A. Save for a home down payment using a money-market deposit account or money-market mutual fund.

B. After you buy your home, open a savings account to build an eight-month emergency fund.

C. When the emergency fund is in place, fund a Roth IRA to the annual max.

D. Go back and fund your 401(k) to the annual max.

You have no credit card, student loan, or car loan debt, and you already own a home or do not want to own a home.

A. Open a savings account to build an eight-month emergency fund.

B. Fund a Roth IRA to the annual max.

C. Go back and fund your 401(k) to the max.

## DON'T FORGET TO REJOIN YEARLY FOR YOUR 401(K) MATCH!

If your company offers a matching contribution on the 401(k), make sure you "rejoin" your 401(k) plan in time to start your contributions again when the new year rolls around. You want to start up again so you can get your maximum company match each and every year. Check with your HR or employee benefits department to find out when you need to make the request; you might need to alert them a few months before the new year.

Because there are so many variables in deciding when it makes sense to invest for your retirement (and in which type of account) and when to tackle other financial goals, go to my website and use the Action Planner tool, which will tell you what to tackle first: debt or investing for retirement.

# STRATEGY SESSIONS

**PROBLEM:**

I am thirty years old, and the thought of putting away my money and not being able to touch it for another thirty years is so unappealing. Besides, I barely have enough to pay my bills right now.

**SOLUTION:**

All I can tell you is, if you don't start now, you'll be in worse shape later on.

I know it's tough for you to make ends meet, but if you don't save now, how are you going to be able to afford the bills when you retire? You'll be up that proverbial creek. So my honest advice is that you need to do everything you can to start socking away money for your retirement now.

Besides, if you followed my advice, you aren't investing a ton of money in your 401(k)—just enough to get the company match. You shouldn't sweat about your lack of control over that money. (As I explained earlier, when you invest in any 401(k) retirement account, you must leave the money untouched until you are at least 59½. Make a grab for it before you reach that age, and in most cases, you will be hit with a 10 percent penalty along with having to pay the usual income tax on the withdrawn amount.) The money that your company is giving you through the match is free, so it seems to me that it's worth a loss of freedom. Besides, those restrictions are there to help keep you from making a short-term move (that is, pulling out the money) that can mess up your retirement plans.

That said, emergencies do indeed happen, and I understand the anxiety that you won't have any available cash to deal with the unexpected. Once again, the Roth will come to your rescue. Remember, with a Roth, all your contributions are yours to take out, penalty-free, 24/7/365. Your Roth doubles as an emergency cash fund.

**PROBLEM:**
I have credit card debt that I am paying 18 percent interest on. I wonder if I should borrow money from my 401(k) to pay off that debt.

**SOLUTION:**
Loans against your 401(k) are downright dangerous. Work on boosting your FICO score so you can transfer to a low-rate card, before you consider a 401(k) loan.

Raiding your 401(k) to loan money to yourself is absolutely the wrong move to make for paying off credit card debt. You will be tempted to think it's a good idea because all of your friends (who probably know less about money than you do) will tell you that you can take a loan on your 401(k), and that you will have five years to pay it back. They'll rave to you about the cool fact that you repay the loan at a nice, low rate—say, 8 percent—and that you're actually paying the interest back to yourself. You think this sounds like heaven: raid your 401(k) to pay off your credit card debt, which costs you 18 percent interest, and all you'll need to do is pay 8 percent interest on the 401(k)—back to yourself!

Don't fall into this alluring trap. You are going to trigger a lousy tax situation if you take out a 401(k) loan. Remember, you contributed to your 401(k) with pretax money (that is, money that you have never paid taxes on). But when you start to repay the loan, you will have to repay it with after-tax money—that's money that has already been taxed. But that's just going to be Uncle Sam's first tax bite.

When you eventually start withdrawing that money after you retire, it is going to get taxed all over again. You will have paid Uncle Sam twice on the same money. Call me crazy, but I think paying a tax once is enough.

Need more convincing? Well, you need to understand that 401(k) loans are good only as long as you stay at your company. If you decide to leave, or if you are laid off, in most companies, the balance of what you owe on that loan is due at the time you leave. If you needed the loan in the first place, I'm guessing that you don't have cash sitting around to repay it ASAP. So if you do not have the money, your loan becomes a withdrawal. And it's going to be an early withdrawal, so you will pay income tax, plus the 10 percent penalty. Ouch. Don't have the money to cover the tax and penalty? No problem, it will be deducted from your 401(k) account. Got it? There is no escaping.

I also hate the whole loan bit because you risk having your money "out of the market" at just the time when stocks have a big rally. Remember, the way the markets behave is highly unpredictable. Some years you get big gains, some years you get big losses. If you have removed money from your 401(k) and the market has a big upswing, you have just lost out on the opportunity to have your money grow.

I also can't resist pointing out that if you ever get into huge financial trouble and file for bankruptcy, your 401(k) assets will not be touched. They are not an asset that can be tapped to pay off your debts, though interestingly, your Roth assets *could* be used to pay your debts. Now, the whole purpose of this book is to make sure you live a financially strong life, so I am not suggesting that you favor a 401(k) over a Roth, but it's just one of those odd quirks that I thought was worth mentioning.

Bottom line: Just say no to anyone who suggests that you take out a loan on your 401(k) to pay off credit card debt.

Your employer merely "sponsors" your plan but has absolutely no control over the management of the plan. Your company hires another firm to run the plan, which includes holding your money "in trust" for you. That third party is a brokerage firm or a fund company, or perhaps an insurance company. Check out your latest 401(k) statement; it didn't come from your employer. It came from a firm that your company hired to "administer" the plan.

In concrete terms, this means that your 401(k) money doesn't stay at your company. It is physically transferred to an outside firm that handles your plan and invests the money for you, based on the choices you have made. Your 401(k) investment is never part of your company's finances. So if your company goes belly-up, it won't affect your 401(k) contributions or the gains on those contributions, unless some of the money in your 401(k) plan is invested in the stock of your employer (more on that in a sec). The only other possible impact is that you may not receive any unvested portion of your 401(k) matches.

If you are a Nervous Nellie, then by all means periodically check up to make sure that your company has transferred your contributions to the 401(k) plan administrator. Your quarterly statement should show the contributions that have been credited to your account. Or if that's too infrequent, call up the plan administrator—or use the online account service—after each scheduled contribution to make sure that everything is where it should be. Check with your employee benefits department to learn what the usual time frame is between the money being deducted from your paycheck and it being deposited in your 401(k) account. There is some bookkeeping involved, so it can take a few days. The plans are required to make the move as quickly as possible, but the rule is that they have until fifteen business days after the end of the month in which the contribution was made. If for some reason you feel your employer is slow to make the deposits, or if you feel like something is going wrong with the accounting of your money, talk to your employee benefits department. If that doesn't get you the answers you want, you can contact the Employee Benefits Security Administration at the U.S. Department of Labor: http://www.dol.gov/ebsa/ or 1-866-444-3272.

Now, there is one scenario where your 401(k) can be in serious danger if your company goes bankrupt, à la Enron. When that high-flying company collapsed because of management malfeasance, thousands of employees saw their 401(k)s collapse, too—not because Enron execs did anything illegal with the money, but because the Enron employees made the tragic mistake of having their 401(k)s invested in Enron stock. That was just really poor judgment.

You never want more than 5 percent of your investment money to be riding on one stock, whether or not it is stock of your employer. If your employer insists on giving you your match using company stock, I have to tell you that you and your colleagues should be screaming for a change in policy. Enron should be all you need to mention.

That's not being pessimistic about your company. That's just spreading your risks—diversifying. You want to protect against the risk of being financially crippled if anything bad happened to your company. Let's think through all the ways that you already have a lot riding on your company. You rely on it for current income. You may have stock options. You may also be able to invest in an employee stock-ownership plan. So why would you want to ratchet up your financial dependence in this one company by also investing your 401(k) assets in it? If you are forced to have the match in company stock, then do what you can to reduce any other investments in the company stock to get your overall exposure down. Exercise options when they become vested, sell the stock, and reinvest in another stock or a mutual fund.

**PROBLEM:**
I got a new job, and now my old employer is telling me that I have to move my 401(k).

**SOLUTION:**
When you change jobs, be happy that you can take your 401(k) with you by doing an IRA rollover. You keep your money growing, tax-deferred, and greatly expand your investment options. It's win-win.

Most likely, the reason that your old employer is telling you that you have to take the money out of the 401(k) plan is that you have less than $5,000 in the plan. But it is no big deal, for even if you were not asked to move your money, I would tell you to move it no matter what.

When you contribute to your company's 401(k), you are captive to the investment options offered in the plan. Typically, you have a bunch of mutual funds to choose from. Some of those funds may be great, and some may not be so great. But the bottom line is that you are stuck with what the plan offers.

However, once you leave that job, you suddenly have plenty of options. I want to run through them from least appealing to most appealing:

- Cash out.

- Leave it at your old employer (assuming it is at least $5,000).

- Move it to your new employer's 401(k) plan.

- Do an **IRA rollover**.

The cash-out is a colossal mistake, and one that so many YF&Bers make when they job-hop. I know the allure: It's so tempting to take the money to live off of, or to pay off credit card debt. But when I hear about anyone who has cashed out of their 401(k), it just makes me sick to my stomach.

I do not care how small your 401(k) account is, please don't do a cash-out when you leave your job. You will pay income tax on the withdrawal, plus a 10 percent penalty, and, most important, you will no longer have that money growing for your retirement days.

Let's say you have $5,000 in your 401(k) right now, and you desperately need money, so you cash it out. First, there's going to be a $500 penalty owed to the IRS (10 percent of the withdrawn amount). And if we assume you are in the 15 percent federal income tax bracket, that's another $750 that will go to the IRS. So you're left with just $3,750. As if that's not bad enough, your real loss is more to the tune of $45,313. For if you simply kept the $5,000 invested for thirty years and earned an average annual return of 8 percent, you would end up with $50,313. Case closed: no cash-outs.

Nor do I want you to leave it where it is. Again, why be hemmed in by the funds offered in the plan? It makes a lot more sense to take your money and invest it in anything you want. You can do this with an IRA rollover, which I will explain in a sec. There's the same issue with rolling it into your new employer's 401(k). You're going from one straitjacket to another. (The only exception is if you absolutely love the funds offered in your old 401(k); in that case, you might want to sit tight.)

That leaves us with the last option: an IRA rollover. This is your best move, hands down. With a rollover, you simply transfer your 401(k) balance out of your old employer's plan and into an IRA account that you set up at a discount brokerage firm or no-load mutual-fund company that has low expenses. You will literally "roll" the money "over" into a traditional IRA.

When you do this, you will owe no taxes or penalties. As far as the IRS is concerned, you are simply moving your money from one tax-deferred retirement plan to another.

And you will now have maximum flexibility in how you can invest your retirement money. You are no longer limited by the choices in your company's plan. In the next chapter, I will tell you some great investments for your IRA. Rollovers are also a great move if you have multiple 401(k)s from many old jobs. You can move all those separate accounts into one IRA rollover account; talk about simplifying your life!

The best part of a rollover is that if you meet the income rules, you can then convert your rollover account into a Roth IRA. And you know how much I love Roths.

**PROBLEM:**
I am doing an IRA rollover and was told I can't use a Roth IRA.

**SOLUTION:**
You can't move your money directly from a 401(k) to a Roth, but you can move it to a rollover IRA, and then convert that into a Roth. At your age, that can be a really smart move.

To get your 401(k) into a Roth, you first need to transfer the money into a rollover IRA, which really is just a traditional IRA. Once you have that rollover done, you can then convert it to a Roth IRA. Now, many of you may think I am speaking Greek, but just stick with me here, because this is a great thing for you to know about. The basic rule is that when you invest in retirement accounts, the IRS is going to make sure it gets its share at some point. Remember that with a 401(k), you contribute pretax dollars, so the tax bite is on the withdrawal. With the Roth, the tax bite comes at the beginning, when you contribute with after-tax dollars.

Which brings us to why you can't roll over money directly from a 401(k) to a Roth. If you did this, you would be cutting out the IRS completely, because you didn't pay tax when you contributed to the 401(k), and you won't pay tax when you withdraw money from the Roth. So to make sure that you pay the tax, you must first do the rollover into a traditional IRA. Then you can do a Roth conversion, where you convert or transfer all or any amount of money in that rollover account into a Roth. What you need to know is that you will have to pay ordinary income tax on the amount that you convert.

I know the thought of paying tax right now doesn't sound too appealing, but a little pain now can produce great pleasure down the line. Because you are so young, I am guessing that you don't yet have a ton of money invested in any 401(k)s that you want to convert. So the tax bite isn't going to go too deep; and with tax rates near historical lows, the federal government is really bending over backward to make this as painless as possible.

But the payoff can be huge. You probably have thirty-five years or so until retirement (or at least until the IRS will allow you to start withdrawing money from these accounts without a penalty). By paying the tax now on the amount that you convert to a Roth, you are giving your money all those years to grow tax-free. Not tax-deferred, but tax-free. That's a huge advantage when you are investing over the long term.

Let me walk you through this.

Let's say you have $10,000 in your 401(k) plan. You do a standard rollover and then you decide to take that account and do a Roth conversion. To make the conversion, you must first pay tax (in the year that you convert) on whatever money is being transferred from the IRA rollover to the Roth.

If you convert all $10,000 at once, you could end up in a higher income tax bracket that year. But you've got a great option: You can do partial conversions over a number of years. You can convert $5,000 a year for the next two years, or $2,000 a year for the next five years, or whatever combination makes sense for you, tax-wise. After your money has been in the converted Roth IRA for at least five years, you can take out any of the money that you originally converted, regardless how old you are, without any tax or penalty. It is the earnings, or the growth, of your money that you converted that has got to stay in there until you are 59½ years of age.

There is one catch to be aware of: Your modified adjusted gross income (MAGI) must be less than $100,000 in the year that you convert. Your spouse's income will be included, too, if you are married. So whether you are married filing jointly or single, you are not allowed to do a Roth IRA conversion if that return has more than $100,000 of MAGI showing. This is one great move custom-tailored for your YF&B years.

**YF&B**
More details on the rules and regulations for conversions (and a tricky move called a recharacterization) are provided on my website.

---

**PROBLEM:**
I took money out of my 401(k) when I left my job, to do an IRA rollover, but I ended up being hit with income tax plus a 10 percent penalty on the money.

**SOLUTION:**
To avoid that mess in the future, always choose a direct rollover where the money is transferred without you touching a penny of it.

---

Never have your old 401(k) plan send you the rollover check, because then it becomes your responsibility to get the money invested in a rollover IRA. This will create a huge tax headache if you slip up. If you don't get the rollover done in sixty days, you are going to be hit with income tax plus the 10 percent penalty. To make sure you avoid this, the only type of rollover I want you to consider is a **direct rollover**, where the firm that has your existing 401(k) sends the money directly to the firm where you are going to set up your new IRA.

A quick aside: If you ever get caught holding the money and you unintentionally miss the sixty-day window, you might want to hire a certified public accountant to write a letter on your behalf. If you can prove to the IRS that you intended to get the money invested inside the sixty-day window but you inadvertently hit a snag, you might be able to get a special ruling to have the tax and penalty waived.

Opting for a direct rollover also helps you steer clear of the ugly 20 percent withholding rule. In this lovely IRS setup, if your old employer cuts the check to you, they are required to withhold 20 percent of your account value for taxes. So let's say you have $10,000 in your 401(k) account. If you have the money sent to you, $2,000 will be withheld for taxes, so you'll get $8,000. Now you have only sixty days from the date that you receive the check to get it into an IRA rollover account at a brokerage or mutual fund company. If day sixty-one rolls around and you haven't done the rollover, you will have to pay ordinary income tax on the $10,000, plus a 10 percent penalty tax. So be careful. (If you do the rollover in time, the money withheld will come back to you as a tax refund or be credited toward any other income tax you owe for the year.)

Even if you are conscientious and are ready to do the rollover within the sixty-day window, you are still in for some hurt. You got that $8,000 check from your old 401(k) plan, but the IRS insists that your rollover be for the entire $10,000 that was withdrawn from your 401(k). So unless you have $2,000 lying around to make up for the amount that was withheld for taxes, you've got yourself another rollover hangover. If you don't get the extra $2,000 invested in the rollover within sixty days, it will be treated as a withdrawal, so you will be forced to pay both income tax and the 10 percent penalty. And remember, if you don't have the cash for the tax and penalty, the IRS will take the money for it out of your retirement account.

So please just take the direct rollover route.

Discount brokerages and mutual fund companies will be downright ecstatic to help you do a direct rollover. Realize that this is their dream: You call and tell them that you have money that you want to invest with them. They have entire staffs dedicated to making this process absolutely painless for you. All you'll need to do is fill out a simple IRA rollover form, and they will contact your 401(k) plan directly and get the rollover done.

A regular taxable account for your retirement savings makes a lot of sense if you've maxed out on the Roth and don't have a 401(k) at work—but only once you've taken care of some more pressing financial business. I want you to pay off high-rate credit card debt, save up for a down payment, and build an eight-month emergency cash fund. If you've got that all in place, then by all means, let's talk about why taxable accounts can be your best move after you max out on your Roth contribution.

When you invest in a taxable account, there is obviously no up-front tax break. You invest with money that has already been taxed. But when you withdraw your money, you can have a much smaller tax bill than you would with your 401(k) or a traditional IRA. That's because "regular" accounts aren't necessarily hit with income tax. Instead, you can pay the capital gains tax rate if you have held the investment for more than one year.

Here's a breakdown of the capital gains rates:

|  | If you are in the 15 percent income tax bracket | If your tax bracket is above 15 percent |
| --- | --- | --- |
| If you own your investment for less than one year | 15 percent | Your ordinary income tax rate; anywhere from 25 percent to 35 percent |
| If you own your investment for more than one year | 5 percent | 15 percent |

As you can see, if you own an investment for at least one year, your capital gains tax will be either 5 percent or 15 percent; meanwhile, your 401(k) investments will be taxed at your income tax rate, which can be as high as 35 percent.

The one big catch here is that you can get caught paying tax every year that you are invested in a regular account. Any trades you make that trigger a gain will be taxed. And mutual funds can hit you with a tax bill each year, even if you didn't make one trade. But there's an easy solution to this. As I will explain in the section coming up on investing, you can invest in index mutual funds and exchange-traded funds; if you buy them and hold them—meaning you don't trade them—you are going to either eliminate your tax bill (for the ETF) or keep it super-low (for the index fund). This way, you can pretty much mimic tax-deferred investing with your taxable account. And when the time comes to cash out, you get to pay the lower capital gains tax rates rather than income tax rates. You will also give yourself some nice flexibility if the market has one of its intermittent swoons; investments in taxable accounts that are sold at a loss can be claimed as a deduction on your taxes.

**PROBLEM:**
I have four different IRA accounts, and it is
becoming a pain to keep track of all of them.

**SOLUTION:**
Consolidate. It makes monitoring easier, and it
reduces your costs, too.

With all the broad choices offered by discount brokerages and large mutual fund companies, you should have just one mega-IRA account where you consolidate all your existing IRA accounts. This doesn't mean that you have to put all the money into one fund or stock. You can take all the money from the multiple accounts and move it into one account where you invest in as many funds and stocks as you want. The upside is that all your money is in one place, so there's just one statement to keep track of. Even better, you will be hit with just one custodial fee. This is an administration fee of $10 to $40 or so a year that some financial institutions charge on IRA accounts. You may not think that is a lot of money, but look at it this way: If you are able to scrounge up $500 for a Roth but end up paying a $40 maintenance fee, you're losing nearly 10 percent of your investment. That is just way too expensive for a YF&Ber. If you have four different accounts, you could easily be paying more than $100 a year in custodial fees. That's nuts. Pay just one fee, and you'll free up more money to invest! Besides, many financial institutions will completely waive your IRA maintenance fees once your account rises to $25,000 or $50,000. By having all your money in one place, you will get to that nice break point even faster and have no fee to pay. And in about thirty or forty years, you are going to love having all your IRA money in one place; it will make dealing with your withdrawals so much easier.

**PROBLEM:**
I don't have the money for a home down payment, so I'm considering withdrawing money from my Roth or 401(k), since I heard I won't get hit with the typical 10 percent early-withdrawal penalty.

**SOLUTION:**
Raiding your retirement funds comes with plenty of trade-offs. If you insist on doing this, go for the Roth first, then a loan from your 401(k).

I know those of you in expensive real estate markets can't imagine how you will ever be able to save up for a home down payment, so raiding your retirement accounts seems like a smart move. But it's not nearly as smart as you think. That said, I know you can't live in a retirement fund; you need a home to live in. So I am going to walk through your best options if you insist on taking money out of your retirement accounts for a down payment. But I want to be very clear that I am not advocating this as a slam-dunk great move. Ideally, you would spend a few years saving on your own, so you would not need to rely on your retirement money, or so you could at least reduce the amount of money that you will take out of your retirement funds for a home down payment.

When it comes to being able to withdraw money from a 401(k) plan, I'll admit there is a nice deal for folks who haven't owned a home for at least two years: The federal government will allow you to withdraw up to $10,000 penalty-free from your 401(k) to use for your down payment. But it's just the 10 percent penalty on early withdrawals that gets waived. You'll still have to pay income tax. If you are in the 25 percent tax bracket, you will have your $10K reduced to $7,500. That's a mighty big haircut.

That might be a haircut you're willing to get, if owning a home is your biggest priority. But if you make this move, I want you to be strategic. Here are your best options, from best to worst:

- **Take a withdrawal from a Roth IRA.**

- **Take a loan from your 401(k).**

- **Take a hardship withdrawal from your 401(k).**

Let's talk about the Roth first. Remember that your original contributions to your Roth were made with after-tax money, so you are free to withdraw the money that you put into your Roth at any time for any use whatsoever. You can also withdraw up to $10,000 in *earnings* penalty-free if the money is used for a down payment. The only catch is if your Roth is less than five years old—day one is the first day you opened the account—you will be hit with income tax on the earnings withdrawal. (That's a great reason to open a Roth today, even if it is a small amount. It will start your five-year clock ticking immediately.) If you haven't hit the five-year mark but want the money for a down payment right now, I would recommend using your Roth contributions, but do not touch the Roth earnings.

Okay, let's say you don't have a Roth, or there's not much money in your Roth account. That brings us to option two: a loan from your 401(k). The good news is that when you borrow money from your 401(k) for a home down payment, you get a few nice breaks.

Normally, you have just five years to repay a 401(k) loan, but when the money is used for a home down payment, you may be able to pay back the loan over the entire length of your mortgage, so that can be up to thirty years. Not bad, eh? But I need you to focus on the big risk you will be taking here. If you are laid off from your job, or if you decide to take a new job, you will need to repay that loan pretty darn quick—typically within sixty days. If you can't get it repaid, then the loan is treated as a withdrawal and you will be hit with income tax, plus the 10 percent penalty.

If you do go the loan route, I want you to take out a home equity line of credit (HELOC) the minute you have enough equity in the home. Do not use the HELOC. Just keep it handy for an emergency. And the emergency we are talking about here is that you do leave your job—voluntarily or involuntarily—and need to repay the 401(k) loan ASAP. For more info on HELOCs, see Chapter 9, Big-Ticket Purchase: Home.

Your last option is to take a hardship withdrawal from your 401(k). The IRS does indeed consider a home down payment a "hardship," so you will not have to pay the typical 10 percent penalty that is levied on withdrawals before you are $59\frac{1}{2}$. But you will still be required to pay income tax on the amount that you withdraw.

In a perfect world, I would never suggest that anyone should short-circuit their retirement savings for any reason. But I know that many of you are hell-bent on owning a home. While using your retirement assets can be a solution, you need to think long and hard about the trade-offs you will be making.

# QUICK
# PLAYBACK

A company match on a 401(k) is free money that you are not to pass up. Contribute enough to qualify for the max match each year.

You get a tax break when you invest in a 401(k), but when you make withdrawals, you must pay income tax on all the money.

Always invest enough each year in a 401(k) to get the max company match. Then suspend your contributions and pay off any high-rate credit card debt or invest in a Roth IRA.

Roth IRAs don't give you a tax break when you invest, but they are the only retirement investment where your withdrawals will not be taxed. Contribute to a Roth each year if you are eligible: Individuals who file a single tax return and have adjusted gross income of less than $95,000, and couples filing a joint tax return with combined adjusted gross income of less than $150,000, are eligible to make the full Roth contribution.

The best investment tool is the power of compounding; small investments made today have time to grow into large investments by the time you retire.

The more money you have riding on your company stock, the greater your investment risk. Diversification is the smarter move.

A direct rollover is the best option for your 401(k) when you leave a job. Never take the money in cash, and never have the rollover money sent to you.

Once you move your old 401(k) to a rollover IRA, you can then convert the account to a Roth IRA if your adjusted gross income is less than $100,000. This move can save you from a big tax bill when you make withdrawals in a few decades. But you will owe tax now on the amount you convert, so you may want to convert only a portion of your total IRA every year so you aren't hit with one huge tax bill.

# investing

## made
## easy

chapter **7**

You will never
truly be powerful
in life until you are
powerful with
your own money.

## THE LOWDOWN

As I write this section, I am sitting in my south Florida home, staring out at the Atlantic Ocean. Yet what keeps popping into my mind is the Ford Econoline van I lived in when I first arrived in Berkeley, California, in the mid-1970s. Yes, yours truly lived in a van because I couldn't afford to rent an apartment, or even a room. I couldn't even afford the van; my brother loaned me the money for it.

I know why that memory is so vivid right now. I want you to understand that I was not born with money, I did not inherit money, and I have not married money. I spent the first seven years after college waiting tables at the Buttercup Café in Berkeley, earning about $400 a month—not your typical career training for a financial adviser.

I was the original poster girl for the YF&B. Fast-forward thirty years, and I still *think* I am young and fabulous. Hey, you can argue with me, but a girl's gotta dream. Thankfully, I am no longer broke. But my path from van to beachfront property took plenty of detours; I had to learn some hard lessons about investing. The advice in this section is the product of all my experiences; my hope is that I can put you on a straighter line out of broke.

# THE MONEY GAME DEMYSTIFIED

This section is titled Investing Made Easy, because I truly believe it can be. The so-called "money experts" just want you to think it is hard. It's a head game; if they can convince you that you don't have the aptitude or training to manage your money, then you will seek out their advice. They make a living off your fear of handling your own money.

But I am here to tell you that in most cases, you don't need them. No one will ever care more about your money than you will. You can lean on others for help, but ultimately you must take full responsibility for every money move you make. I figured this out quite painfully. I entrusted a stockbroker with $50,000 that a bunch of Buttercup patrons loaned me to start my own business, and within months the money was gone, because I didn't understand what the broker was doing with my money. That's when I realized why they called them brokers—they just make you broker.

Here is the bottom line: What happens to your money affects the quality of *your* life—not mine, not some financial adviser's life, but yours. And you will never truly be powerful in life until you are powerful with your own money. How you feel about it, think about it, and how you invest it.

The most important lesson that I want you to learn is that brokers—or "financial advisers," as they like to call themselves these days—can be some of the most well-intentioned people in the world, but many (not all) are nothing more than salespeople who have been trained to sell you investments. Many financial advisers will offer you free financial advice, because they count on getting paid when you actually buy the investment they suggest. Their mortgage payment, their car payment, their student loan payment, and their vacation funds are all dependent on what their clients—that's *you*—buy and sell from them. That creates a conflict of interest. Do you really think that commission-based financial advisers never have it in the back of their mind exactly how much money they will make if you follow their suggestions?

However, there is a breed of planners I love. They are called fee-based advisers. Rather than living off your commissions, they charge you a flat fee for basic services, or to manage your assets. They make no money off commission, so they have no incentive to suggest that you buy something that really doesn't make sense for you.

Fee-based advisers are indeed a viable option for you, but to tell you the truth, you probably don't yet have the assets to make this a financially smart move. Besides, I am not backing down from my position that you can do this on your own, and do it as well as anyone else.

## SAVING VS. INVESTING

Before we dive into the wonderful world of investing your money so it can grow, I want to double-check that we're on the same page about something very important. When I refer to investing, I am talking about investing in stocks or mutual funds to meet your long-term goals. If you are saving up for a short-term goal, such as a down payment on a home that you'll want to buy in a few years, paying off your debts, or saving to buy a car or to make a home improvement, that money should never be invested in stocks or mutual funds.

It's all about risk. When you've got a short time frame, which is anything less than five years, you can't afford the risk that your money could lose value and won't have time to rebound before you need it. Let me explain. Let's say you had an investment that went from $100 to $50: a 50 percent decline. Guess how much you need to gain to get back to break-even?

A. 25 percent

B. 50 percent

C. 100 percent

# It's all

# about risk.

I'm afraid it's C. You lost 50 percent, but it's going to take a 100 percent gain to get from $50 back to $100. That'll take some time, my friend. And that's actually a pretty mild example, compared to the real-life experience many investors suffered just a few years ago. A popular index of tech stocks (I'll explain indexes in a sec) fell 78 percent from its March 2000 high through its October 2002 low. It will take more than a 350 percent gain for the index to just get back to where it was in March 2000; that works out to about a 7.8 percent average annual gain. Yikes. If you had invested in that index to finance a home down payment, you'd be renting for a whole lot longer.

You get my point. Stocks and mutual funds are not the right investment for short-term goals. Head back to page 164 in Chapter 5, Save Up, for a discussion of the right places to put money that you will need in five years or less.

## INVESTING 101

When you are YF&B, I know you don't have a ton of money to invest, so we are going to focus on two basic moves: what to invest in your 401(k), and what to invest in a Roth IRA or an IRA rollover of an old 401(k).

As I explained in Retirement Rules, if your 401(k) plan comes with a company match, you'd better sign up and contribute enough to get the maximum match. No YF&Ber is to ever turn down free money.

Once you sign up, you've got to decide how to invest your money. Most plans offer you a variety of options known as mutual funds. What normally happens is that when you look at all your options, you go blank. Your colleagues are most likely just as clueless. So you just make a wild guess on which investments you should choose. I think we can do better than guessing.

I am going to move nice and slow through here. If you don't need an intro to stocks and mutual funds, head on down to A Little Goes a Long Way on page 232.

## STOCK EXCHANGE

Let's talk about stocks first. When a company needs money to fund its future business activities, it often "goes public"—the company sells shares in itself. Those shares are called stock. When you buy a share of stock, in essence, you become an owner of a tiny bit of the company. The technical term is that you have equity in the firm. Shares of stock can be bought or sold five days a week on what is known as a *stock exchange*. If the company does well—the business is thriving, people are buying their products and services, and the future for the company looks bright—then the stock price usually will rise as more investors are willing to pay a higher price to own the stock. Of course, if the business tanks, so will the stock. For most of you, the only individual stocks you can own within your 401(k) plan are shares of the company that you work for. Within a Roth, you can own any stock that you so choose, if you have opened an account with a brokerage firm.

Remember what we discussed back in Retirement Rules: The most important investing rule for anyone, at any age, is to diversify your money. That means you hold stocks from a bunch of companies rather than loading up on just one stock. You want your diversified stock portfolio to include stocks from different industries, large companies, small companies, companies here in the United States, foreign companies, new companies, and old companies. You get the idea. Mix it up. If you own dozens of stocks, you will minimize the chance that any single problem will sink your ship. And since you are YF&B and likely do not have a lot of money to invest in dozens of stocks, it is important that you invest in a way that allows you to be diversified. That brings us to mutual funds.

## FUND-AMENTALS

I'm going to use my good old suitcase metaphor one more time: A mutual fund is like a suitcase that holds dozens—and often hundreds—of individual stocks. If you like what is packed inside the suitcase, then you simply purchase shares of that mutual fund and, voilà, you are the proud owner of a small fraction of each one of the holdings in that suitcase. This gives you instant diversification, even though you bought just one mutual fund.

What has probably been a big turnoff to you, especially within your 401(k), is trying to figure out which type of mutual fund to choose. I think it might help if we switch our example to jeans for a moment. You know how you walk into the clothing store and there are all sorts of jeans to choose from? Different brands, different styles, different sizes. But they all are essentially the same product; they are jeans. And rather than get stressed out by your choices, you love it. I want you to look at mutual funds in the same way. All those mind-numbing fund categories and investment objectives that you see in the fund literature do nothing more than describe the difference in the funds—like the difference between straight-leg and boot-cut jeans.

So I am going to walk through the main fund styles and brands that I think you need to know, and then I will tell you what you should own in your fund wardrobe.

## STYLE POINTS

The stocks in a mutual fund generally break down into three broad styles: growth, value, and blend.

Growth stocks are shares of companies whose earnings (profits) and revenues are, well, growing fast. Investors who buy growth stocks are convinced that the growth of the company will also cause the price of the stock to go up. The Internet bubble a few years back happened when growth stocks took off and reached dizzying valuations before crashing back to Earth.

Value stocks are less flashy. Their share price is believed to be lower than the true value of the company. They are basically an unloved stock. Sometimes that can be because the company has hit a rough patch, or just because "the market" has soured on the industry. Value investors use patience to their advantage. They look at the underlying fundamentals of the company. If they feel that the stock price is wrongly "undervalued," they will buy and then hold on to it until others in the market take notice that the stock is undervalued and start to buy in.

There's a saying that you buy a growth stock at a good price and hope it rises to a great price. With a value stock, you buy in at a great price (meaning cheap) with the hope that it will merely rise to a good price.

Mutual funds that own stocks that share both growth and value characteristics are called blend funds.

## SIZE MATTERS

Each mutual fund typically concentrates on stocks that fall into one of three size categories: small-cap, mid-cap, or large-cap. Small-cap funds own stocks of, no surprise, smaller companies. Quite often, these are newer, fast-growing firms. So small-caps can offer a great chance of big gains if the company continues to grow and grow; but there is also the risk that it will hit turbulence as it tries to grow into a more mature firm. Mid-caps are next up the size ladder. Think of these stocks as having graduated from grade school to middle school. The companies are still in their faster-growth stage, but they have more stability than small-caps. Many people think that mid-cap stocks offer the best of all worlds. And, finally, we have the large-caps. They are considered the least "risky" in that these firms are big, established multinational companies that are entrenched in their industries. That doesn't mean they can't implode, but the idea is that they are not the unknown, unproven type of companies that typify small-caps.

## ACTIVE OR AUTOPILOT

The last characteristic you need to understand is whether your fund is actively managed or unmanaged.

Most mutual funds come fully equipped with a professional money manager whose full-time job is to figure out the best investments for the fund. Think of your portfolio manager as your professional suitcase packer. This person, or team of managers, decides what to put in the suitcase and what to get rid of; portfolio managers decide what to sell and what to buy within the mutual fund. Funds with a money pro making the decisions are called actively managed funds. Some managers are really good, and some aren't. So when you buy a mutual fund, it is important to know about the portfolio manager. We'll talk about how to size up a fund and manager in a few minutes.

Index funds are typically called unmanaged funds, because there is no manager making ongoing buy and sell decisions. An index fund simply tracks an existing market index. A market index is made up of a number of stocks that represent a slice of the market. There is no human judgment at play with an index fund.

The most well-known index is the Dow Jones Industrial Average, which I am sure you have heard of. The Dow Jones Index is composed of just thirty stocks. When those thirty stocks move up or down, the Dow Jones Index moves up or down accordingly. So by looking at one number, you know what the overall market did for that day—just like tracking a ballplayer's batting average. Another popular market index is the Standard & Poor's 500 stock index. It comprises five hundred stocks of big established companies. The NASDAQ Composite tracks all the stocks traded on the NASDAQ exchange; typically, these are smaller, new companies and stocks in fast-growing industries such as technology.

What is important for you to know is that over the years, index funds have out-performed the majority of actively managed mutual funds. A big part of the reason is that they charge investors less in fees, which boosts their net return. Index funds are the best way for a YF&Ber to invest; it's simple and well diversified, and over the long term, there's a good chance you will outperform the majority of actively managed mutual funds.

## TAKE EXPENSES INTO ACCOUNT

Let's talk about those fees I just referred to. Whether the funds you are looking at are actively managed or index funds, your next step is to figure out which funds are worthy investments.

Some of the most important things to look for when checking underneath a fund's hood are its fees. All funds charge annual fees to cover their operating costs. This is known as the expense ratio. The average expense ratio for an actively managed stock fund is about 1.5 percent. What this means is that a fund with a 1.5 percent expense ratio deducts 1.5 percent off its performance each year to pay the manager and various fees.

Every little amount you fork over in annual fees has a huge impact on your overall gains. One of the reasons I like index funds is that they tend to have low expenses. One of my favorites, Vanguard 500 Index, charges just 0.18 percent a year. Can't get too heated up about the difference between 1.5 percent and 0.18 percent? Well, let me put it in terms that matter to you: If you invest $3,000 a year for thirty years and you earn an 8 percent average rate of return (before expenses are deducted), the fund with the 1.5 percent expense ratio would give you a net return (after expenses are deducted) of $276,000. The fund with the 0.18 percent expense ratio would be worth more than $354,000. I can get worked up about $78,000—how about you?

## LONG-TERM PERFORMANCE

After expenses, I want you to check out the long-term performance of the fund. You should not care what your fund has done for the past month, quarter, or even year. Funds are long-term investments. You don't want some flash in the pan that does well for a nanosecond and then tanks. It is far more important that your fund has performed well over three years, five years, and ten years.

If you are evaluating an actively managed fund, you'll also want to check out how long the manager has been running the show. You may have a fund with a terrific ten-year performance, but if the current manager was hired just a year ago, that long-term performance is useless, because the brain who produced it isn't in charge anymore. That said, don't dismiss the fund outright. See what you can learn about the new manager. If you visit the fund's website, you can usually get the manager's background. Hey, your new manager may have just been promoted from another fund where he had an incredible record. In that case, you can be cautiously optimistic; make the investment, but keep a close eye on the fund to see if over the next year or two the newbie has the same touch with your fund.

When you size up a fund's performance, you want to see how it rates compared to its peers. Each fund is thrown into a fund category. Large-cap value funds are one category, large-cap growth is another. Large-cap blend is a third. You get the idea here? There are actually dozens of categories, but I don't want you to get bogged down with a list of all the different types. All you need to concentrate on is how a fund in your 401(k) plan or one you are considering for a Roth rates among its category peers. If you are sizing up a large-cap growth fund that had an average annual gain of 8 percent over the past three years, and the average large-cap growth fund was up 6 percent, you know that your fund did better than average.

Here's how you can find that information. Head on over to http://finance.yahoo.com, where you can input a fund's ticker symbol in the search box. (The ticker is five letters that end in X, and is shorthand for a fund's name. You can find the ticker symbol in any fund literature you get in the mail or online.) If you click over to the performance info on a fund, you will be able to see its performance relative to both its category and a pertinent index fund.

If you are in a 401(k), I realize that you are confined to the funds that are offered in your plan. By doing the evaluation, you can at least find the best options within your plan. And if you find some dogs, get some coworkers together and give your HR department a tough time. If enough of you express displeasure with your choices, changes can be made. Don't be shy. The law is clear that a 401(k) is to be run solely for the benefit of the participants (that's you). If the participants aren't happy, the folks sponsoring the plan (that would be your employer) should be receptive to hearing your opinion.

If you are really lost, you can always call your HR department and have someone sit down with you and explain everything that you need to know. That is why they are there, so use them.

## LOADED — OR NOT

Next, you need to look out for sales loads that are charged on many funds. A load is a sales commission that is used to pay the adviser who sold you the fund. It is different than the expense ratio. All funds have expense ratios, but not all funds have a load. You should never buy a mutual fund that has a load, in my opinion. Let me explain why.

There are basically three main fee structures for mutual funds that you can invest in — what are known as A-share funds, B-share funds, and no-load funds.

Funds with an "A" at the end of their name charge a load, or sales commission, when you invest. It can be as much as 5 percent. So if you invested $1,000 today, really only $950 is going to be invested for you, since 5 percent went to pay the adviser. That means the fund has to go up more than 5 percent in value for you to just break even. You call that a deal?

Funds with a "B" at the end of their name are sold to you under the guise that if you just stay in the fund for a certain period—typically at least five years—you will not pay a load. These funds came about as a way to compete with real no-load funds that never charge a fee, no matter if you leave after one year or five years. To stay competitive, fund firms came up with a way to hide the load by not charging it when you invest but when you leave. There are two catches with B-share funds. Even though you aren't paying a load when you invest, the fund company will still pay the adviser who sold you the fund. And you'd better believe the fund company is now going to figure out a way to get you to pay, with the hope that you won't understand what is happening. The way the mutual-fund company gets paid back for fronting the commission to the adviser is to charge you a super-fat expense rate that includes a hefty 12b-1 fee. And you are stuck paying that higher expense ratio *every year*. The other whammy is that if you try to leave the fund before they get all their money back (usually five years), you will be hit with a back-end load, or what is also called a deferred-sales load or surrender charge. A surrender charge can start at 5 percent or higher the first year and then decline one percentage point a year until it disappears. The idea is that if you leave early, the fund company still has a way of making back the money it gave your adviser when you first invested. Even worse is if you buy B shares in a 401(k); no adviser "helped" you out, but you're still stuck with the high fees. In my opinion, A shares are not a good way to go, and all B shares are the absolute pits. Avoid both!

Funds that are true no-loads are the only kinds of funds you should consider buying. A true no-load fund never charges a fee to buy, and charges no fee to sell, no matter when you want to exit. And, of course, you want your no-load to have a low annual expense ratio. Now, what is important for you to understand is that commission-based financial advisers cannot sell you a no-load fund, because they make no money that way. So if you go to a full-service brokerage and an adviser suggests a fund, you can be pretty sure it is a load fund. That's why I don't want you to work with a commission-based adviser.

If you have a 401(k) plan that has A-share or B-share funds, I would start an uproar among the employees and demand that they give you a 401(k) plan that offers you true no-load funds. But if you are currently stuck with A and B shares, please just invest in your 401(k) up to the point that you get the maximum company match. Then stop investing in the plan and buy some true no-loads for an IRA or a Roth IRA.

If you want to find out if a fund has any kind of load on it, just call customer service—every fund has an 800 number—and ask. You can make it really clear what you are talking about with this spiel: "So, hypothetically, if I invest three thousand dollars today, and if the markets didn't change and I wanted all my money back tonight and I sold, would I get all three thousand dollars back?" If the answer is yes, you have a no-load fund.

**YF&B** On my website is a list of recommended index funds, as well as some of my favorite actively managed funds. Yes, there are indeed some managers who do a terrific job and can be a great complement to your index funds.

## A LITTLE GOES A LONG WAY

Alrighty, you're now hip to how to find the right fund. Now it's time to get crackin' on actually investing. Don't worry, you don't need the big bucks. You can start with small sums and let the power of compounding work its magic. And you don't have to go after the big returns. Consistency is a lot better than an investment that goes sky-high one year and craters the next.

Quiz time: I give you $10,000 and offer you two investing options:

A. Your $10K rises 80 percent in the first year and then falls 50 percent in the second year.

B. Your $10K rises 5 percent in the first year and then rises another 5 percent in the second year.

What's your choice?

A is the popular answer, because you think that after an 80 percent gain a 50 percent loss is still going to leave you 30 percent in the win column. Wrong, wrong, wrong.

The correct answer is B. A quick math review will make it all clear. If your $10,000 rises 80 percent you will have $18,000 after one year. Then, if that $18,000 loses 50 percent, your account will fall to $9,000. You started with $10,000 but you are now $1,000 underwater, my friend. If your $10,000 instead gains a modest 5 percent in each of those two years, your original $10,000 would be worth $11,025. That's a gain of $1,025. Yeah, it's not as sexy, but it is more profitable. And that is all you should care about.

So please don't fall into thinking that you need to invest in high-flying risky stocks to be successful. When you are YF&B, steady is the way to go. Investing in a broad market index fund, or top-notch actively managed fund, is going to give you a smart diversified approach to investing. And by forking over small amounts (for that is all you really have to invest) every few weeks, or monthly, you are going to latch on to one of the coolest investing tricks. You will be a YF&Ber who's into DCA—**dollar cost averaging**.

Let me explain.

## THE TORTOISE APPROACH

When you make periodic investments, such as having money deducted from your paycheck every two weeks and deposited in your 401(k) account—or making periodic investments into a Roth account—the amount you invest probably doesn't change. But the price of the funds will change. When the fund share price is lower, your dollars buy more shares. When the fund share price rises, your dollars buy fewer shares. If you commit to your steady periodic investment, the idea is that over time, you will buy more shares at a lower cost than if you simply plunked all your money into the market in a onetime lump-sum investment (as if you actually have a lump sum handy). This process is known as dollar cost averaging.

I bet an example would help here. Let's say you have $250 a month taken out of your paycheck and deposited in your 401(k). In your first purchase, the share price for your fund is $10. So with your $250, you can buy twenty-five shares. One month later, the share price is $11, so your $250 buys you just 22.7 shares.

Now look at the chart below to see how this would work out over an entire year.

| | Purchase Amount | Purchase Price | Shares Purchased |
|---|---|---|---|
| First Purchase | $250 | $10 | 25 |
| Second Purchase | $250 | $11 | 22.7 |
| Third Purchase | $250 | $9 | 27.8 |
| Fourth Purchase | $250 | $8 | 31.3 |
| Fifth Purchase | $250 | $8.50 | 29.4 |
| Sixth Purchase | $250 | $8 | 31.3 |
| Seventh Purchase | $250 | $8 | 31.3 |
| Eighth Purchase | $250 | $7.50 | 33.3 |
| Ninth Purchase | $250 | $8 | 31.3 |
| Tenth Purchase | $250 | $8 | 31.3 |
| Eleventh Purchase | $250 | $7.75 | 32.3 |
| Twelfth Purchase | $250 | $8 | 31.3 |
| Totals | $3,000 | $8.48* | 358.3 |

*Average

So can you see that at the end of the year, you have invested $3,000, and you now own 358.3 shares of this mutual fund. The price of the mutual fund at the end of the year is $8. Multiply the 358.3 shares by $8 and you have $2,866.40. That's a 4.5 percent loss from the $3,000 you invested. But don't freak just yet. Stick with me. Let's say that you get fed up and you stop your investing (big mistake, but it helps with this example) but you keep your mutual-fund shares. The market starts to rise again, and one year later, the mutual fund is back at $10 a share—right where it was when you started to invest. You might think you're glad to be back to even. But you're not just even. You're way ahead of the game. Remember, you kept buying as the mutual fund went down, so you were able to accumulate 358 shares. If you now multiply 358 by $10, you get $3,580. Yet you only invested $3,000, so you now have a profit of $580, or 19.3 percent on your original investment. Divide that over the two years that your money was invested, and you now have made more than 9 percent on your money per year. By comparison, if you had left your money in savings account for two years, you would be lucky to have $3,100.

I want to be really clear about this, though; the example I gave you does not mean that DCA works every year. There will indeed be years when the price rises throughout the year, so you are buying fewer shares. The whole takeaway from this is that if you stick to DCA over many years, you will eventually end up making a nice return on your investment, as long as you are in good stocks or mutual funds.

DCA is a built-in feature of 401(k) investing, but I also want you to consider it for all your other investments, such as Roths, rollovers, and even regular taxable accounts. A handful of mutual funds love to encourage DCA by offering special deals if you agree to make a direct deposit from your bank account into a mutual fund account every two weeks, monthly, or even quarterly. Instead of requiring you to start with an investment of $1,000, you often can start with as little as $50 if you agree that your periodic investments will be at least $50. Both the T. Rowe Price mutual funds (800-638-5660, www.troweprice.com) and the TIAA-CREF funds (800-223-1200, www.tiaa-cref.org) let you sign up for a DCA plan with just a $50 minimum. The Oakmark funds (800-625-6275, www.oakmark.com) will let you get started for just $100, and $100 in each subsequent investment.

# YOUR ACTION PLAN

I wouldn't call this Investing Made Easy without giving you a simple game plan for choosing the right funds for your 401(k) or Roth. The easiest one-stop-shopping move is to put your money in what is known as a total stock market index fund. This index mimics the **Wilshire 5000**, which is the kitchen sink of stock indexes; it includes large-cap, mid-cap, small-cap, growth, value, and blend stocks—all in one investment. I think it is a great core investment.

Below is a chart that shows how you might construct your 401(k) and Roth IRA investments. Because many 401(k) plans do not offer index funds, I have given you other strategies if your hands are tied by available options.

|  | Your best choice for allocating among funds in your 401(k) | Your best choice among Roth IRAs at a discount brokerage firm or fund company |
|---|---|---|
| **First Choice** | 85 percent in an index fund that tracks the entire market (these are typically called total market index funds); 15 percent in a foreign stock fund | 85 percent in an index fund that tracks the entire market (these are typically called total market index funds); 15 percent in a foreign stock fund |
| **Second Choice** | 60 percent in an S&P 500 index fund; 15 percent in a mid-cap fund; 10 percent in a small-cap fund; 15 percent in a foreign stock fund |  |
| **Third Choice** | 30 percent in a large-cap growth fund; 30 percent in a large-cap value fund; 15 percent in a mid-cap fund; 15 percent in a foreign stock fund; 10 percent in a small-cap fund |  |

You can branch out from here. Just remember, diversification is key. You want to make sure you have many different types of stock funds (large-, mid-, and small-cap, as well as growth and value) represented. And hey, if you love researching funds and think you can find the managers who beat the indexes, then by all means reduce your index allocation and add some actively managed funds to your mix. But please make sure you read my advice on when to sell a fund (see page 239). When you have active managers, you really need to keep an eye on what is happening and be ready to pull the plug.

I also want to stress that these allocation recommendations are targeted to your YF&B years. Eventually, as you slide into your late forties and into your fifties, you are going to want to tweak your portfolio a bit; typically, as we age, adding a portion of **bond**s to your portfolio helps provide a bit of stability as you get nearer to retirement. But while you are in your twenties and thirties you want to be leaning heavily on stocks; you've got the time to ride out the bumps in pursuit of higher returns than bonds deliver.

**YF&B** On my website, you'll find a list of recommended index funds and actively managed funds that you can choose for your Roth IRA.

# STRATEGY SESSIONS

**PROBLEM:**
I get sick when my 401(k) goes down; I don't want to invest anymore.

**SOLUTION:**
Your investing horizon is so long that you've got plenty of time to weather the dips and enjoy the gains that only stock funds can deliver.

Why in the world, when you are so young and cannot use this money now anyway, would you want the markets to go up? The more the markets go up, the more expensive the shares in your fund will be. The more expensive the price of a fund share, the fewer shares your money will buy. With dollar cost averaging, you want the share price to be lower, not higher. So take a deep breath and keep investing. As long as you are in a good mutual fund, you will be just fine in the long run. Remember, the goal is to accumulate as many shares as you can. If you have one thousand shares of a fund, every time its share price rises $1, you make $1,000. But if you own two thousand shares, every time the share price rises $1, you will make $2,000. While you are YF&B, you actually are better off if the markets go down during these years.

**PROBLEM:**
A mutual fund I invested in five years ago is down 30 percent from my purchase price; I don't want to sell it until I break even.

**SOLUTION:**
That is the most expensive investing trap you can fall into. If you wouldn't buy the stock today, you shouldn't continue to own it.

Saying you want to hold on until you get back to your purchase price is a purely emotional response. You don't want to have to admit you made a mistake. Don't feel too bad; a few years ago, the Nobel Prize in Economics was awarded to a Princeton professor who studies this odd investor behavior. In economic wonkland, it's known as the disposition effect. We hold on to our losers and sell our winners. Read that again slowly. It is absolutely the wrong thing to do. You want to get rid of your losers and let your winners run.

You must focus on what you have, not what you had. Investing is about what will happen in the future, not where you started in the past. If you have a stock (or fund) that is down 30 percent, you need to ask yourself if it is still a good investment. If it is, stick with it. If it isn't, get out and find yourself a better investment for the long run.

Let me be extra-clear here: I am in no way implying that any investment that is down should be sold. As I explained in The Lowdown, the DCA strategy works best when you can buy more shares of a stock or fund when prices are low. But it must be an investment that makes sense. If you have no faith in the fund, then you need to get out ASAP. Read the next problem/solution and learn how to get out with your shirt on.

One of the benefits of owning an index fund is that you don't have to worry that a manager has left the fund or lost his magic touch. An index fund is going to give you the return of that index (minus the fund's expenses).

It gets trickier once you are relying on a manager to make buy and sell decisions for a fund. At least twice a year, I want you to check the fund's performance relative to its category peers and the index fund that it most closely resembles (see page 229). Again, don't stress over the monthly or quarterly performance. You are looking to see that your fund is keeping ahead of its peers over periods of three years or more. That does not mean it has to be in the top 10 percent every time period you check. That's a level of perfection that is hard for any manager to attain. What you want to see is that the fund's performance is consistently above average. Trust me, funds that are consistently in the top 30, 40, or 50 percent of their category over longer periods are going to provide you with index-beating returns. But if your fund's long-term performance is consistently below average, it's time to move.

Next, you need to check for musical chairs. If a new manager has taken over, you need to go to the firm's website and see what the new manager's background is. You may be getting a terrific manager with a stellar record at another fund. But if you are getting a complete unknown, you need to be circumspect. You can either bail immediately or just keep a close eye on the fund over the next year or two to see how the rookie fares. If it's a popular fund, you might also check some investing websites, such as www.morningstar.com, which will give an analysis of whether the change is something to worry about.

And keep an eye on the news. If you ever hear that your fund company is accused of improper activity, you are to move your money immediately—especially if your investment is in a Roth IRA or 401(k); you can sell your shares and invest in a new fund without triggering a tax bill. I know I am supposed to believe that people are innocent until proven guilty, but that just doesn't fly when it comes to your money. The minute there is a whiff of scandal—which happened to more than a few fund companies in 2003—that firm is going to see a lot of money flow out. And that's just not good for your investment. It makes it harder for the manager to maneuver, and it can lead to a rise in fund expenses.

**PROBLEM:**
I am thirty years old and don't know how I should divide my money between stock funds and bond funds.

**SOLUTION:**
At thirty you have another thirty or forty years of investing ahead of you. Keep the bulk of your money in stock funds, and don't use bond funds at all.

As you may have noticed, I did not mention **bond**s in The Lowdown.

Let me explain my problem with bonds, which first requires us to walk through what a bond is.

When a company needs to raise money to fund its growth, or to pay expenses, it has two ways to do it. The first way is to sell shares of the company, which are known as **stock**. The second way to raise funds is to simply borrow the money. That's where bonds come in.

A bond is debt that a company or government takes on to finance its operations. And it's no different than the debt you have for a car loan or student loan. When a company or government borrows money, it issues what is known as a bond. When you buy a bond, the money you pay is your **principal** investment. The folks who borrow the money (the bond issuer) agree to pay you **interest** on that principal. And they also agree that on a certain end date, known as the **maturity date**, you will get your **principal** returned. The further out the maturity date, the higher the interest rate you will be paid.

Basically, what you are doing with a bond is giving out a loan, getting paid interest while the loan exists, and then getting your money back when the loan reaches its end date. Nice and simple.

The only risk you have with a direct investment in a bond is that the entity you lent your money to might go belly-up. That would mean it stops making interest payments and can't even repay you your principal. That's called a **default**. But you don't have to worry about that too much; every bond comes with a "credit quality" rating. That rating tells you how risky the bond is, and most bonds are so-called "high-quality" bonds.

Bonds are sold not only by companies, but also by the federal government, as well as state and city governments. One thing I never want you to forget is that if you buy a bond from the U.S. government, there is a "guarantee" that you will be repaid—that's why U.S. Treasury bonds are considered the safest bond investment.

**YF&B** For more information on bond ratings, please go to my website.

That brings us to bond funds, which own a bunch of individual bonds. I don't like bond funds, because there isn't a set maturity date when you are guaranteed to get your principal investment back. Also, in a bond fund, you are going to have to pay those expense ratios that we talked about on page 228, and that cuts into your return. Given that bonds (and bond funds) return far less than stocks—the average annual return over the long term is about 5 percent—having 1 percent or more shaved off to pay expenses is just way too pricey.

That's why I do not recommend investing in bond funds. The only possible time I will bend for those of you in 401(k) plans where your choices are limited is when interest rates are very high and are expected to start falling. Bonds are odd birds;

when interest rates fall, the value (or price) of bonds rises. So when you have a high-rate scenario, you can make a nice gain if you hold bonds or bond funds and rates fall. But that is not what we have happening right now. As I write this in the fall of 2004, interest rates are at near-historic lows. If anything, the outlook is for rates to rise, not fall. And in that situation, the last place you want to be is in a bond fund.

Besides, at the age of thirty, you have so much time until you retire that I believe stocks are your best investment. Bonds usually are for safety and to generate income as you get older. And if you are a true YF&Ber, income is not what you need. You need growth now, but not income to live off of. There's no need to start adding bonds to your portfolio for another ten or fifteen years.

Now, I know that after the hurt of the bubble bursting a few years ago, many of you fled to the safety of bonds or bond funds. I realize that those big declines in the stock market were hard to stomach, but I need to stress that you can't afford to be out of the stock market. It's all about being patient over the long term so you are in the market when it does well. If you are sitting in bonds, you will not participate in those upswings.

## PROBLEM:
My colleagues keep talking about the "lifestage" fund in our 401(k). I don't know if it's a good investment for me.

## SOLUTION:
Lifestage funds are just an okay choice if you want a quick and easy solution. But you can do a lot better without too much extra effort.

The brains behind the 401(k) plans began to realize a few years ago that all the funds offered in 401(k)s were turning folks off. It was just too confusing for employees to figure out which funds to invest in. So the brains started rolling out so-called "lifestage funds." You invest in just one fund that is geared toward the types of investments that the "experts" believe make the most sense, given how long you have until you will retire and need the money.

These funds are designed for different age groups. There's typically one fund if you are under thirty-five or forty, another fund if you are in the forty-to-fifty age range, and another fund for when you are near retirement. The funds become progressively more conservative as you get older, piling on more bond funds and even cash.

There is nothing horribly wrong with lifestage funds. If the only way you are going to invest is to go for this one-stop solution, then I won't give you a hard time. But I don't think they are the ideal way to go. If the lifestage fund owns bond funds, I think you are shortchanging yourself. Before you opt for the lifestage option, check out the investing strategy I laid out in the chart on page 236. Without much elbow grease, I think you can build yourself a better fund portfolio.

**PROBLEM:**

I have stock options that I can exercise. When I exercise them, should I hold on to the stock to see if its price goes higher, or just sell it immediately?

**SOLUTION:**

When you exercise your options, I insist that you sell right away.

For those of you who may not know what we are talking about, let's have a quick lesson. Stock options are the big carrot that some companies love to dangle in front of employees. It is an incentive to stick around, and to work hard so the stock goes up. Stock options give you the right to purchase company stock at a future date, once your shares have vested. When you purchase the stock, the technical term is that you are *exercising your options*. The price you will pay for the stock is determined on the day you are given your options; this is known as the **exercise price**. And there is usually a pre-set date as to when you are legally allowed to exercise those options.

Now, the whole allure of options is that by the time you are allowed to exercise them, the current stock price will be higher than your exercise price (you hope). The difference between the exercise price (what you will pay) and the market price on the day you sell is your realized profit.

There are two basic types of options; I am going to assume that YF&Bs have the most popular type, which are known as non-qualified stock options (NQSOs). It's just a technical name that refers to the way you get taxed on your options.

Here's my general thinking on stock options: If they're vested and you have a nice gain, why not exercise the option, get the cash, and reinvest the profit in another investment? My theory is: If you are doing well at the company, you are probably going to get additional options periodically, so it makes sense not to have all your "paper" wealth tied up in this one stock. It is better to take some profits off the table from time to time and move them into other investments.

So, when you exercise NQSOs, I want you to sell the shares immediately and diversify into other investments.

**YF&B** There's an important tax reason why you should exercise and sell immediately. For more details, go to my website.

## PROBLEM:

I tried to sell my mutual fund and was told I could not sell it till the end of the day. I thought stock funds could be sold right away.

## SOLUTION:

Exchange-traded funds can be a good fund alternative if you are concerned about "liquidity."

All mutual funds have a quirk that I want you to be aware of. They really don't trade during the day. When the stock market opens at 9:30 A.M. (Eastern time), the prices of all the stocks within a fund start to go up and down. But if you called your fund at 10:08, there's no way that that the fund could figure out the value of all the stocks in the portfolio at that very moment to give you a sale price for your fund shares. So funds simply wait until the end of the day to price all their holdings, based on the closing price of stocks for that day. (The market closes at 4 P.M. Eastern time.) That means you can't buy or sell fund shares during the day. You can place an order at any time of the day, but it will not go through until the close of the market, when the fund is priced. Because a fund can be priced only once a day, you're at a slight disadvantage.

Let's say the indexes are having a very bad day. At 10 A.M., the S&P 500 is down 5 percent. You want to get out of your index fund, so you call your fund company and place a sell order. They are happy to take your order, but it's just going to sit around until 4 P.M. Between the time you call and the end of the trading day (4 P.M.), the index falls another 5 percent. You are out of luck. Your sell order is going to go through at the closing price, even though you placed the order when the index was down just 5 percent.

As much as I love index funds, exchange-traded funds can be even better. ETFs are index funds with one added benefit: They trade like a stock, not like a fund. So that means that if you call at 10 A.M. and ask to sell your ETF shares, the trade will be conducted at the current price—no waiting around for the market to close and your fund to be priced. That's what's known as liquidity; an ETF is much more liquid than a fund. And ETFs can have even lower expenses; a popular ETF that tracks the S&P 500 is the iShares 500 index and has an expense ratio of 0.09. You can research ETFs at the American Stock Exchange website, www.amex.com, as well as at Yahoo! Finance.

**YF&B** At my website, you will find a list of recommended ETFs.

But remember that investing for retirement is a long-term goal, and you probably shouldn't sweat the fact that funds are less liquid than stocks. You don't want to be trading your funds all the time. Simply buying and holding can be the best move. Yes, you will have to live through some downdrafts, but that also means that your money will be invested when the market goes up, and that is the only way to make money. If you are constantly moving your money in and out of the market, you may miss the upswings.

And ETFs don't make sense if you use the dollar cost averaging method of investing. ETFs are sold only through brokerages, so you will need to pay a commission. If you invest just once a year, paying $10 or so to make the purchase isn't too big a problem. But paying that $10 if you are investing every two weeks or every month just doesn't make sense. So stick with a no-load fund if you DCA.

**PROBLEM:**
I was told by an adviser to buy a variable annuity for my Roth IRA, but I am not sure if this is the right move.

**SOLUTION:**
Fire your adviser.

A variable annuity is basically a mutual fund with tax breaks. You get no tax deduction on your contributions, but while your money is invested, you will pay no taxes, no matter how often you buy and sell the funds within your variable annuity. There is also typically a guarantee that you or your heirs will be assured of getting back at least what you originally invested, even if the current value at the time of withdrawal is below the original purchase price. But just like a 401(k) or IRA, those withdrawals are taxed at your ordinary income-tax rate.

I could bend your ear for a while on why I really don't like VAs. Actually, I don't dislike VAs—I hate them. Here's why: They are really expensive. In addition to the regular expense ratio of the fund, you'll also have some insurance-type charges that can run more than 1.3 percent a year. Add that to a 1.5 percent expense ratio, and you are pushing 3 percent a year in various fees. That's ridiculous.

And a VA within a Roth IRA is financial insanity. You already have tax deferral in a Roth, so why are you paying for an expensive VA when you don't need its tax deferral? Even worse, most VAs have a surrender charge. That makes no sense. The beauty of a Roth IRA is that you eventually will be able to withdraw your money tax-free. Don't let some salesperson make money off of you by trying to sell you a VA for a Roth. Walk away.

The most important investing rule for anyone, at any age, is to diversify your money. That means you hold stocks from a bunch of companies rather than loading up on just one stock.

# QUICK PLAYBACK

⇨ Stocks are only for long-term investments where you don't need the money for at least five years.

⇨ Diversification is key when investing; you never want all your money riding on one or two stocks; if they implode, you will be in big trouble.

⇨ On a limited budget, mutual funds are better than stocks. You can own shares in dozens of companies, rather than have your money riding on just one or two stocks. This is instant diversification.

⇨ Periodic small investments—dollar cost averaging— is the secret to long-term success.

⇨ Expenses are often the difference between good and bad funds. Aim for funds with low annual expense ratios—below 1 percent—and never pay a front-end or back-end load.

⮕ Low-cost index funds often outperform actively managed funds.

⮕ When you are YF&B, there is little reason to invest in bond funds.

⮕ When you exercise your stock options—assuming they are nonqualified stock options (NQSOs)— you should sell immediately and reinvest in another vehicle to diversify your holdings.

big-ticket
purchase:

car

If you were raking in the big bucks and had money to throw around on indulgences, I'd let you be. But come on, that's not your story.

**THE LOWDOWN**

When it comes to buying a car, I think a lot of YF&Bers must be inhaling exhaust fumes. I am your biggest fan, but my goodness, your car sense is non-sense. I see so many of you shelling out big bucks for tricked-out cars that you can't afford because of some insane need to impress people you don't even know who pull up alongside you at red lights.

If you were raking in the big bucks and had money to throw around on indulgences, I'd let you be. But come on, that's not your story—at least not yet. Right now, you need to make sure every dollar you spend is spent wisely.

And a car is flat-out the worst investment you will ever make. Actually, you shouldn't even look at your car as an investment. The moment you drive a new car off the lot, it loses about 20 percent of its value; within three years, its value will decline by at least one-third. The technical term is that a car is a depreciating asset. Not appreciating. Got it?

So why shovel what little you do have down a financial sinkhole? Sure, I know it's a necessary sinkhole. Unless you live in a big city with reliable public transportation, you need a car in order to function, and hey, they sure make the weekends more fun. But if you look at your car as a sinkhole, I am hoping you will be less inclined to throw so much money at it. At the risk of sounding, well, practical, doesn't it make more sense to drive a less flashy car and use the money you save to fund a Roth IRA, reduce your credit card balance, or work on whittling down your student loans?

# TAKE THE PATH OF LEASE RESISTANCE

I don't blame you for your car fetish. The auto industry has perfected the art of playing to your ego. They roll out super-expensive luxury cars that you can't afford to buy, and then wait for you to start salivating. Then they hit you with the great news that you can indeed afford to drive the car of your dreams. Instead of buying it, you'll just borrow it for three years, with what is known as a lease. It's such a seductive sell. Rather than settling for buying a boring car that you can actually afford, you get to slide into the smooth leather seat of a much nicer car that you merely borrow for a couple of years.

Seductive but stupid. When you lease, you are stepping into a hamster wheel that you may never be able to get off of. Every three years or so, when your lease period ends, you basically have three choices: You can buy the car outright at a pre-negotiated price, which is usually higher than the actual value of the car; you can walk away and look into buying another car altogether; or you can simply lease another car. That last one is what most people do, and that means starting a new three-year cycle of car payments. Because you are in a cycle of leasing a car every few years, you are always going to be making monthly payments. They never end.

That's why I would prefer that you take out a loan to buy a car. After you finish paying off the loan in three, four, or five years, you will own the car outright. Now, I realize that's just about when you start to think, *Time for a new car.* But let's slow down here. Will you need a new car, or will you just want a new car? I know it's not as fun, but hey, you can definitely keep driving the car you own. I know it is tempting to trade in every few years, but you can't afford to when you're YF&B. Forget about what your parents or your friends with better cash flow can afford. The money-smart move for you is to keep your car longer. If you hold on to it for a few more years after you have the loan paid off, that means you'll have a few years during which you'll owe no payments—just the insurance and gas. And don't try to hit me with the complaint that older cars cost too much to repair. Spending $1,000 or so a year for maintenance is still a lot better than spending $20,000 or more for a new car. I recently had to explain this to a YF&B friend.

Katie was so excited to tell me about the new Mercedes Benz C-Class she was leasing for "just" $385 a month. I sat her down with my trusty calculator and put a flat tire in her car story. We pulled up some auto loan info on the Web; the going rate in the fall of 2004 for a five-year loan was 5.9 percent. That meant I could buy a $22,000 car with a $2,000 down payment and finance the remaining $20,000 with a loan that would work out to about $385 a month. Katie gave me a playful chuckle; she had a sleek Benz for her $385 a month, but I was going to be far less flashy in a $22,000 car.

Less flashy but a lot better off financially. Five years later, my car loan would be paid off. In year six, I no longer would have car payments to make. I told Katie I would keep paying that $385 a month—but into my own bank account, while she, the Loser with a Lease, would still be making her monthly lease payments. And since her original lease was good for only three years, by the third year, she would have already taken out a new lease and probably have to put some money down up front. And, given the way car prices rise, I wouldn't be surprised if her next four-wheel splurge would cost $420 a month.

Then I let the calculator do the talking. In that sixth year, Katie's lease payments will total $5,040. My car payments will be nada; I'll have paid off my loan. Oh, by the way, I'll also be able to save up $4,060 in my bank account by continuing to pay my $385 monthly car payment—to me.

After year six, it will be time for Katie to get another new car lease, and it will no doubt be even more expensive. We agreed on a 10 percent increase, so that would bring her payments to about $460 a month. That means that over the next three years, Katie will shell out more than $16,500 in lease payments. Me? I haven't had a penny in car payments, and my bank account is now close to $14,000. Even if we assume that my old car will require a few thousand dollars in repairs and maintenance, I'll still be thousands of dollars ahead of Katie. I'll also make at least a few thousand dollars when I sell the car; I had to explain to Katie that when you lease, you can often get stuck owing money when you sell. The trade-in price you agreed to pay when you first took out the lease—what's called the residual value—can be quite high. It's a common way for the leasing company to get your monthly payments low enough for you to say yes to the deal. And then there are the hidden costs of leasing.

When you turn in the leased car, if it has a few dents, your wallet is also going to be dinged; the leasing company can charge you for wear and tear. And don't ever exceed your allotted mileage limit; you could be stuck paying 15 cents for each additional mile. A 12,000 limit might sound great when you are just driving six miles a day to work, but what if you take a new job and your daily round-trip commute runs to fifty miles? That's about 12,000 miles per year right there.

## WHAT YOU AUTO DO

Okay, so I've convinced you to buy rather than lease. Your next step is to think through your financing options. Because you are YF&B, I am going to assume that you will need a loan to buy the car. In case you missed this nugget from Chapter 1, here's how your car loan rate can be affected by your FICO score:

| | 720–850 | 690–719 | 660–689 | 625–659 | 590–624 |
|---|---|---|---|---|---|
| Percent of interest on a four-year auto loan | 5.1% | 5.9% | 8.0% | 10.5% | 14.4% |

Rates as of Fall 2004

If you have a sparkling FICO score, you might qualify for the zero-percent-financing deal some lenders are offering these days. But as I will explain on page 266, there's typically a tradeoff between the zero-percent deal and getting the dealer to offer you a cash rebate. As alluring as the zero-percent deal sounds, it actually can make more sense to take the cash back on a lower-priced car and finance the rest of the purchase with a regular loan.

If you are going to go for a loan that charges interest, shop around. The dealer doesn't necessarily give you the best deal. Banks and credit unions may have a better offer. And also check out websites such as www.lendingtree.com and www.eloan.com, which provide auto loans. You want to know what your options are before you walk into the car dealership.

Next, let's have a chat about what type of car you should set your sights on.

I think it's insane to buy a new car when you are a cash-strapped YF&Ber. I recommend shopping for my favorite oxymoron, a new used car. There are plenty of cars that are just a year or two old and have less than 10,000 miles on their odometers. They are in great shape, but because they don't have the new-car smell, you will get a great deal. Remember, the minute a new car is driven off the lot, it loses 20 percent of its value; if you buy a new used car, you won't be paying for that.

Now, I know you're not thrilling to the used-car approach because you don't want to run the risk of getting stuck with a clunker. I'm with you. But I've got a solution. I want you to look into Certified Pre-Owned cars (CPOs). These are relatively young cars with limited mileage that the car dealer will sell to you and back up with a warranty. You want the "certified" part to come from the car manufacturer, not the car dealer. That way, your warranty will be backed by the manufacturer, which is a heck of a lot better than something a used-car dealer is going to offer.

Even with the manufacturer's warranty, you can't have blind faith. This is still a used car. Here's what you need to check out:

- Spend $100 or so for an independent mechanic to inspect the car.

- Ask the dealer for the car's inspection history. If they won't give it to you, consider that a red flag.

- Run the car's vehicle identification number (VIN) through a national database to check for any record of accidents. When you find a car that interests you, ask the dealer for its vehicle identification number. This is like your car's Social Security number; no matter how many times it has been bought and sold, its VIN doesn't change. At www.carfax.com, for about $20, you can get a report on the car's background. The service searches public and private records for reports of whether the car has been in a wreck, whether the odometer has been tampered with, whether it was used as a rental car or even a police cruiser in a previous life, and if it was sold at a salvage auction or returned to a dealer as a "lemon." For about $25, you can get unlimited reports.

- Read the warranty carefully so you understand what is and what is not covered.

The manufacturer's warranty on a CPO makes this option more expensive than buying your used car without a warranty, but the extra $500 to $1,000 or so can be worth it for peace of mind alone—besides, it's still going to run you thousands less than a new car. You can shop for CPO cars at websites such as www.carmax.com and www.autotrader.com, or check out a car manufacturer's website for information about their CPO offerings.

You can reduce your costs even more by shopping for a car that's not popular with car thieves. The "hotter" your car, the higher your insurance premium will be. The Insurance Institute for Highway Safety (www.iihs.org) has a list of cars with the "highest theft claim frequency." Stick with a car that's not on the list (or one that's low on the list), and you can reduce your cost of ownership by snagging a less expensive insurance policy.

**YF&B** On my website, you will find links to online resources that explain in more detail the ins and outs of CPOs and used-car buying, and how to negotiate the best deal.

## WHEN IT'S GOT TO BE NEW

I know that for some of you, no amount of financial reasoning will get you to budge from buying a new car. If you are absolutely stuck on a new car, you'd better buckle up and commit yourself to learning how to negotiate a good deal. About fifty-one cards in the deck are stacked against you; the more confused you are, the better chance the auto salesperson has at making a fat profit off of you. Auto dealers are kings of creating confusion.

Let's start by deciphering the sticker on the window.

The salesperson will do everything to get you to focus on the manufacturer's suggested retail price (MSRP) that is listed on the sticker. Don't fall for it. Unless the car you want is super-popular and on back order, there's plenty of room for negotiating a price that is closer to the invoice price that is listed on the same sticker. This is the price the dealer paid to get the car from the manufacturer. So the MSRP might be $18,000, but the invoice price is $15,000. But don't stop at the invoice price. The real cost to the dealer can be even lower if there are any manufacturer incentives. These are the cash-back deals—also known as hold-backs—the manufacturer will give the dealer if they sell the car. I'm not talking about the advertised cash-back deals that are offered to the buyers. These are incentives the manufacturer pays the dealer if you buy the car. So if there's a $1,000 incentive, you want to make sure you don't let the dealer have all of it. Ideally, you want to walk into the dealership, take a look at the invoice price, and say: "Hey, we both know you've got a $1,000 holdback that knocks the invoice price from $15,000 to $14,000, so I'll pay you $14,500, and we can split that." That shows you know what you're doing and won't be some uninformed pushover for the salesperson.

Now, it's not like the auto manufacturers and dealers are advertising these deals, so you need to do some research. Websites such as www.carsdirect.com or www.edmunds.com provide info on dealer incentives.

Do not talk about financing options with the car salesperson until after you have agreed on the price. When you are negotiating the price, keep asking for the "out-the-door" price. This is some insider lingo that makes it clear that you are going to have no patience for all the hidden costs that will turn up on your deal when the paperwork is done.

**YF&B** For more information about how to negotiate a deal and get the best loan, go to my website.

Once the price is set, you can discuss financing options that the dealer will give you; compare that to what you have already researched on your own, and decide how you want to proceed.

The more confused you are, the better chance the auto salesperson has at making a fat profit off of you. Auto dealers are kings of creating confusion.

# CAR INSURANCE 101

I bet a lot of you with cars opted for the cheapest insurance policy you could get that would meet your state's requirements. This is one area where you are nuts to pinch pennies. You want to make sure you have ample coverage to protect you in the case of an accident; what good does it do to have a policy that won't take care of you—and others—in the event of a serious accident?

Let's do a quick spin through the basic parts of your coverage. You must have bodily injury liability to provide coverage if you or anyone else is injured, as well as property liability coverage if you damage another car or piece of property. Collision insurance is an important option for more expensive cars, since it provides coverage no matter who is at fault. Comprehensive coverage covers repairs—and replacement—if your car gets damaged in a non-car-related mishap, such as a collision with a deer.

A typical minimum amount of mandatory coverage is often expressed as 30/50/20. This means you have $30,000 worth of bodily injury liability coverage for each person, with a $50,000 limit per accident, and then $20,000 in coverage for property damage. My advice is that you are better off going for 100/300/50 if you own your home or have started building up some investment assets. (If you get into an accident and you don't have enough insurance to cover the damage, the other party can seek payment from your assets.)

Now that I've told you to splurge and get more coverage than you probably have, let me change topics and help you save some money.

Your good old FICO score is at play again. Some insurers use a version of your score, known as an insurance score, to figure out what sort of risk you are. Their logic goes like this: Folks who pay their credit card bills on time are also less likely to have car accidents or make a lot of claims. So, once more in unison: Get your FICO score as high as possible to put youself in line for the best auto insurance rate.

You also want to double-check that your record at the DMV is in good shape. Contact the DMV to make sure you don't have any dings on your record that aren't yours, and that any points that should have expired are in fact wiped off your record. Any smudges on your record are going to be a reason for an insurer to sock you with a higher premium.

If you own a home, check with your insurer about coupling that policy with an auto policy; using one company for both policies can cut your premiums—the annual cost of your policy—by 10 percent or more. If you don't have an agent, the Internet can be a great place to shop for insurance: www.insure.com gets you premium quotes from multiple lenders; www.geico.com and www.21stcentury.com are two low-cost auto insurers.

You'll also want to go for a high deductible. Your deductible is what you agree to pay out of your own pocket for repairs after an accident, before your insurer kicks in and covers the rest. I know it is tempting to have a low deductible of $250 or so, but that's going to end up costing you more in the long run. Let me explain: If you have a low deductible and make a lot of claims, your insurer is not going to be amused. You're bad business as far as they are concerned. So they might cancel your policy outright, or when you are up for renewal, they may boost your premium up the wazoo. Look, insurance is meant to protect you against big-ticket accidents—not little dings. You'll want to raise your deductible to $1,000. It will reduce your premium by 15 to 30 percent and keep you from annoying your insurer. Ideally, you will have an emergency cash fund that will cover having to pay a $1,000 deductible. But remember, if you followed the advice in Chapter 3, Give Yourself Credit, you've also got a low-interest credit card. If you need to finance paying a deductible on a low-rate card, that's worth it.

You can reduce your premium even more by dropping the collision coverage on an old car. Just check the book value of the car; that's typically what the insurance company is going to be willing to pay you if the car gets banged up. The Kelley Blue Book (www.kbb.com) has free estimates of what your car is worth based on its make, model, mileage, and condition. This is known as a car's book value. If your car has a book value of just a few thousand dollars, and you'd have to pay a $1,000 deductible before your coverage kicks in, it doesn't make sense to pay for the collision coverage, which can run hundreds of dollars a year.

**PROBLEM:**

I don't know if I should take the zero-percent-financing deal on a car or go for the $3,000 cash back.

**SOLUTION:**

It depends on the price of the car.

You need to realize that not everyone qualifies for the zero-percent offer. Only a dealer's favorite customers get the zero-percent deal. And when it comes to loaning you money, favoritism is all about your FICO score. Yep, here we go again: With a FICO score of 720 or better, you have a good chance of landing the zero-interest-rate deal.

But I am going to think positive. You've read Chapter 1, Know the Score, and are now doing everything you can so your score will soon be in that upper tier of 720+. That means you've got an interesting choice. The dealer is probably going to offer you an either/or deal: You can either have the zero-percent deal or you can get the $3,000 cash back, but then you'll have to pay interest on the remaining balance that you need to finance. You're not going to hit the jackpot and get them to give you both breaks.

My advice is to take the cash back if you are buying a car that costs less than $20,000, and opt for the zero-percent financing if the car price is above $20,000. Let's say you are in the market for an $18,000 car. If you take the zero-percent deal on a five-year loan, your monthly payment would be $300. (For simplicity's sake, we're assuming no down payment here.) But if you took the $3,000 cash back, you would reduce your price to $15,000. And, given your great FICO score, I know you're going to qualify for a good interest rate. In late fall of 2004, that was

5.9 percent. That works out to $289 a month, or $11 less a month than if you took the zero-interest loan. That comes to a savings of $660 over the life of the loan.

But for more expensive cars, the zero-percent financing works to your advantage. Let's say you're looking at a $25,000 car. A zero-percent financing deal over five years comes to $417 a month. Now if you got $3,000 back and paid 5.9 percent interest on the remaining $22,000, your monthly cost would be $424. That $7 monthly differential comes to $420 over the full term of the loan. And the more expensive the car, the more you will end up saving by going for the zero-percent-financing deal.

**PROBLEM:**
I can only get a 10 percent interest rate on a car loan because my FICO score is so low.

**SOLUTION:**
Improve your score and then refinance your auto loan.

Those tantalizing offers of low- (and no-) interest-rate car loans are eye candy to lure you into the showroom. But there's no guarantee you will actually get such a good deal. At the risk of annoying you with this one more time: The only shot you have is if your FICO score is at least 720. As the chart on page 258 shows, the lower your score, the higher your car loan interest rate will be.

Obviously, you want to do everything you can to boost your score before you apply for a car loan. But if you really need a new car ASAP, take out the higher-rate loan and keep working to improve your FICO score. When your score improves, check to see if it makes sense to refinance to a new car loan at a lower interest rate. The trick is to make sure that the money you would save in lower interest payments will offset any costs of getting a new loan. And please, if you do refinance, do not extend the term of the loan. For example, if you took out a four-year loan and it's now down to three years, you do not want your refinanced loan to be longer than three years. You never want to extend your payback time, because all that does is increase your total interest costs to get your car paid off. And you'll need to check what the current book value of your car is at the point that you want to refinance. Lenders will only give you a new loan for the current market value of the car; if your existing loan is for more than that, you won't be able to refinance.

## PROBLEM:
I use my car 50 percent of the time for business. Even with the drawbacks of leasing, I figure the tax break makes it a good deal for me.

## SOLUTION:
Owning and keeping a car for more than three years still makes more sense than leasing.

You get the business tax break whether you lease or own; and owning is going to be less expensive in the long run. Besides, we need to break down this Pavlovian response to the term "tax break." It causes so many people to make bad financial moves. Let's do the math. You have a $400 monthly car-lease payment. If you use the car for business half the time, $200 is eligible for a tax break. Next, let's assume you are in the 25 percent federal tax bracket. That means that for every dollar of your lease that is eligible for the deduction, you will get back 25 cents. By my math, $200 x 0.25 = $50. You are eligible for a $50 break, which means you've only reduced your after-tax cost of leasing to $350 a month. That's still pretty steep. And as I just explained on page 256, you are always going to be making those payments, because leasing is like a drug—it's really hard to stop once you start. That's why I don't like leasing; with today's low income tax rates, the tax break isn't to die for, especially when you are YF&B and in a lower tax bracket.

Even if you are using the car for business 100 percent of the time and are in the 35 percent tax bracket, I would still question your reasoning. Buy a car with a loan. You still get the tax break, and the day will come when you will own it outright—that's when the car will really pay off. The longer you drive it without having to fork over monthly payments, the more value you will get from your purchase. When you become a lease junkie, chances are that you will never get to the point where you stop making car payments.

**PROBLEM:**

I cannot afford to make my lease payments anymore, so I gave back the car. Now I don't have a car and I just got a bill showing that I owe thousands of dollars on a car that I do not even have.

**SOLUTION:**

Sorry to say, this is completely legit … and yet another example of why I think leasing is such a dangerous ride.

You signed a contract when you leased the car, and just because you can't keep up with the payments, the leasing company has every right to demand that you keep up your end of the deal. So let's say when you turned over the car you still owed $15,000 in lease payments. The leasing company will try to sell the car, but they have no incentive to get top dollar for it, because they know you are going to have to come up with the $15,000 regardless. So they end up selling your car for $10,000 and hit you up for the remaining $5,000. It is absolutely legal. And it could get even worse: The dealer could sell the car at auction to its own used-car-lot division for even less than $10,000. Let's say they sell it for $8,000. So now you are technically on the hook for the $7,000 difference between the auction price and what you still owe ($15,000). Then the smart used-car folks take that car they just paid $8,000 for and sell it for $12,000. So they made $7,000 off of you, and $4,000 off of selling the car to themselves at an auction before reselling. That's $11,000 that they made off your misfortune.

So rather than just give the car back to the lease company and wait for their bill after they sell it, I want you to sell the car on your own before you give it back. You are motivated to get the highest price possible, whereas the leasing company isn't. The more you get for the car, the more you will have to put toward repaying the leasing company for the amount you still owe. If you get $11,000 for the car, you can use that $11,000 to repay the leasing company. That leaves you with just $4,000 that you will need to come up with to give the leasing company their $15,000. That's better than if they sell it for $8,000 and stick you for $7,000.

**PROBLEM:**
I bought a car from a used-car lot, and it constantly needs repairs. I don't have the $3,000 it will cost to fix it properly.

**SOLUTION:**
Each state has so-called "lemon laws" to help consumers deal with used cars that suck.

When you buy a used car, you are taking on a whole lot of risk. At a minimum, you need to pay $100 or so to have a mechanic give the car a thorough checkup. Do not rely on the folks at the used-car lot for a mechanic recommendation. Ask friends if they have a car shop that they trust. Check with your local American Automobile Association (AAA) chapter to see if they offer a diagnostic service for used cars.

If you still end up with a clunker, you'll need to check with your State Attorney General's office; each state has its own consumer-protection laws for car buyers, which are known as "lemon laws." You can find the AG number listed in your phone book's government section.

Whether you can get the used-car dealer to fix the problem or reimburse you depends on how tight your state's laws are. If you bought the used car from a franchise dealer, you should check out whether you can get mediation help through the AUTOCAP program run by many state Automobile Dealers Associations. To locate your state association, you can contact the National Automobile Dealers Association (NADA) at 800-252-6232.

**YF&B** On my website, you will find a list of all Attorney General phone numbers and website addresses, as well as a list with each state's lemon law.

**PROBLEM:**
I cosigned for a car loan for a friend, and now my friend has defaulted on the payments.

**SOLUTION:**
Get the loan paid off ASAP if you don't want your credit record to become mud.

As far as I am concerned, friends don't ask friends to cosign loans. Look, if your friend can't get a loan on her own, that means there is something funky going on. If a lender doesn't trust your pal enough to give her a loan on her own, don't you think you should be worried, too?

And once you cosign, you are on the hook for everything. Cosigning a loan authorizes the lender to use you as the backup insurance policy. Your name is going to be on the title of the loan; you may not have contributed a penny to the purchase of the car, but you're essentially seen by the lender as a co-owner. If your friend falls behind on the payments, you are promising to come to her rescue. If you don't make the payments, the car is going to get repossessed, meaning the lender will take it back. The lender will sell it, and if the price is less than what your buddy (and you) still owe on the loan, you'll have to make up the difference.

If you don't, the lender can take you to court to get the money back. And during that time, you will absolutely ruin your FICO score. Oh, sure, you're super-responsible with your own debt, but guess what? Because you cosigned that loan, your pal's bad history with the car loan will show up on your credit profile. Your friend's financial car wreck can make it impossible for you to get your own loan, because lenders are going to take one look at your FICO score and brand you a really bad risk.

Your only out is to get the car paid off as fast as you can. Short of forcing your pal to sell all her worldly possessions to repay the lender, you are probably going to have to reach into your own wallet to resolve this problem. And, by the way, once you've gotten the car paid off, check your record with the DMV and local parking authority; you could also be on the hook for any unpaid parking tickets your buddy (or ex-buddy) ran up.

The "hotter" your car,
the higher your insurance
premium will be.

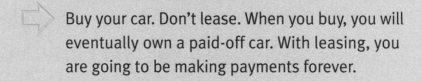 Buy your car. Don't lease. When you buy, you will eventually own a paid-off car. With leasing, you are going to be making payments forever.

Buy a car you can afford, not a status symbol that puts you in the poorhouse. Remember, cars are the worst investment you will ever make.

If the car costs less than $20,000, take a cash-back offer. If it is more than $20,000, a zero-percent-financing deal is better.

Go for the higher deductible on your car insurance; it will reduce your cost by as much as 30 percent, and will keep you in the insurance company's good graces.

Keep the car for as long as possible. When you own it free and clear, you will have more cash handy for better investments, such as saving for your retirement or paying down your credit card balance.

# big-ticket purchase:

# home

A home is flat-out the best big-ticket purchase you will ever make.

**THE LOWDOWN**

As much as I love stocks and mutual funds for your long-term investing goals within your retirement accounts, I have to admit that I am a two-timer. I also think that after you've maxed out on the company match in your 401(k), and after you have your credit card debt either paid off or declining, it's smart to focus on buying a home. As lousy an investment as your car is, a home is flat-out the best big-ticket purchase you will ever make. Just like your student loans, mortgage debt is truly good debt.

Let me tell you why. You have probably noticed that the real estate market in the first four years of the new millennium has been on fire, with prices in many areas climbing more than 50 percent or more since 2000. That's a 50 percent return during a time when the stock market couldn't manage to stay above water. Now, I am not saying that real estate is always up during the periods when stocks are down, or that real estate will ever see returns like these again. But even if real estate values come down to a more normal average annual return of about 4 percent, you'd still be a very happy camper if you got into the game.

I'm going to use a $100,000 home as an example. Those of you living in areas where you can't even buy a garage for $100,000, settle down. This is just an example. Besides, there are indeed plenty of areas in the country where you can get a great starter home for $100,000. And this example works just fine no matter what amount you plug in.

When you buy a house for $100,000, you must come up with a percentage of the purchase price in cash, and the rest can be financed with a loan—what is known as a mortgage. The cash is your down payment, and it typically ranges from 3 percent to 20 percent or more. Let's say you decide to make a 10 percent down payment on the $100,000 home. That's $10,000 of your own cash that you are putting toward the purchase of the home. Now pay attention, here's where it gets fun. If your home's value rises 4 percent, your $100,000 home is now worth $104,000. You made $4,000. But your real return is a lot better than 4 percent. Remember, you only invested $10,000. And you just "made" $4,000. That's a 40 percent return on your money. That's better than the stock market, the gold market, and any market that I know of. Now, I can't guarantee that real estate values will never go down, but the long-term trend is positive, and there's no reason to think that will change.

You'll also be in line for a nice tax break when you go from renter to owner. The interest you pay on your mortgage is tax-deductible. Most important, the home is yours, not your landlord's. Ask anyone who owns, and they will be happy to gush that even with all the upkeep that's required, it feels great to no longer be living in a home that isn't really your own.

Add that all up, and you can see why owning a home is such a smart move—but only if you do it right. A home is the ultimate big-ticket purchase, so you really need to make sure you don't let your heart rule your head. If you move too hastily, without carefully weighing your best choices, you could find yourself in a home that is financial quicksand.

I want you to understand how mortgages work, what the best deal is for you, and which booby traps to avoid, *before* you look at a single house. If you take a few minutes to wrap your head around some essential rules of housing, you are going to end up buying a home that you can enjoy. It will be affordable, not a huge financial stress. And you will save yourself tens of thousands of dollars by making only the right moves. Seems to me that's worth a few minutes of homeschooling.

**YF&B**

In this chapter, I focus on the buying process. I'm proceeding from the assumption that as a YF&Ber, you probably have yet to take the housing plunge. But if you are already a homeowner and are pondering your first home sale, please visit my website for advice on how to make sure you snag the best possible deal for your home.

Before we launch into strategies for home loans, we need to go back to the beginning. Your FICO score is a big factor in what kind of deal you can get on a mortgage. If FICO is a foreign term, do not pass go. You are to hightail it back to Chapter 1, Know the Score, to learn why your credit rating is all-important.

I also want to talk to you about your credit card balance. I know that in Chapter 3, Give Yourself Credit, I gave you the green light to run up a credit card balance early in your adult life so you can "afford" to follow your career dreams. But when you reach the point when you are serious about buying a home, you want to start paying down that card balance. First, if you can get your balance paid off or at least reduced, you will have a higher FICO score. And that lower debt level is also going to make a lender more eager to work with you.

## BRINGING CASH TO THE TABLE

As I described earlier, mortgage lenders are happy to do most of the heavy lifting; you can get your lender to finance 90 percent or more of the purchase price of a home. But you still need to have a hefty stash of cash to make the deal a go—cash for the down payment, cash for a pesky charge known as private mortgage insurance (PMI), and cash for all the fees that come with the mortgage, what are known as points and closing costs.

Let's start with the down payment. The more money that you invest in the house up front, the happier your mortgage lender will be. There's no rocket science at work here; the theory is that the more skin you have in the game, the more likely you will be to stay in the game. You will be less likely to default on the loan (meaning stop making monthly mortgage payments to the lender) if you have more of your money invested in the home.

The magic number with down payments is 20 percent. That's the amount at which lenders are most comfortable working with you. But don't worry, that doesn't mean you must show up with 20 percent. Lenders aren't clueless. They know the YF&B aren't sitting around with $40,000 to put down on a $200,000 home, or $80,000 for a down payment on a $400,000 condo in New York City. So they have come up with all sorts of mortgages where you can make a down payment of just 3 percent. There are even lenders who will offer you a zero-down option. No matter how cash-strapped you are, I think zero down is the wrong way to go. If you haven't been able to save up even the smallest down payment, I don't think you are ready to take on the responsibility of a large loan.

I am not saying you must save up for a 20 percent down payment, but come on, you have to be able to come up with at least 3 percent. It is a self-administered litmus test to prove that you are financially responsible.

When your down payment is less than 20 percent, the lender will require you to pay for private mortgage insurance (PMI). This is insurance you pay to make the lender feel more comfortable loaning money to you. If you put down 10 percent, PMI will cost about $43 a month for every $100,000 that you borrow. If you put down less than 10 percent, the PMI cost will go up. On a $150,000 mortgage where you made a 10 percent down payment, you are looking at paying about $65 a month in PMI. Typically, you make that payment separately from your mortgage. But on page 308, I explain a neat way to save a bundle by rolling your PMI cost into your mortgage.

Your other big cash outlay is for closing costs, which are all the fees that the lender charges to get the deal done. Fees vary from lender to lender, but figure that your closing costs will run about 2 to 3 percent of the cost of your mortgage. Sometimes those closing costs include what are known as "origination points"; one point equals 1 percent of your mortgage amount. Lenders are required to give you a good-faith estimate of your closing costs when you apply for the loan.

So let's see how painful this is going to be. On a $150,000 mortgage, you will need to show up at the closing (when you sign the documents and become the homeowner) with more than $3,000 in cash, or you may be able to add those costs to your mortgage amount.

The magic number with down

payments is 20 percent.

Here are some national averages for typical closing costs on a $180,000 home:

| Lender/Broker Fees | Average | | | |
|---|---|---|---|---|
| Points in $ | $1,234 | | Credit report | $22 |
| Administration fee | $267 | | Flood certification | $14 |
| Application fee | $234 | | Pest & other inspections | $62 |
| Commitment fee | $218 | | Postage/courier | $40 |
| Document preparation | $221 | | Survey | $174 |
| Funding fee | $231 | | Title insurance | $718 |
| Mortgage broker or lender fee | $1,037 | | Title work | $164 |
| Processing | $360 | | **Government Fees** | **Average** |
| Tax service | $68 | | Recording fee | $74 |
| Underwriting | $253 | | City/county/state tax stamps/intangible tax | $1,734 |
| Wire transfer | $30 | | | |
| **Third-Party Fees** | **Average** | | **Total Fees** | **Average** |
| Appraisal | $317 | | All fees of all types | $3,652 |
| Attorney or settlement fees | $451 | | | |

Source: Bankrate, Inc., Spring 2004 survey

And remember that those are just averages. Depending on where you live, and the price of your home, you could see these figures double.

If you don't have a lot of cash handy, you can set your sights on a lower down payment or spend some time saving up more. For some ideas on how to come up with cash for your housing fund, head on back to Chapter 5, Save Up.

No matter how cash-squeezed you are, I don't want you to raid your 401(k) to cover the down payment and closing costs. As I explained earlier, it is best to keep your retirement savings growing. Keep what you have saved in your 401(k) accounts untouched, and continue to invest up to the point of the company match each year. But then you can stop your contributions into the 401(k) for the rest of the year and redirect it into your own savings account for a down payment and closing costs.

Your family could also be a source for your down payment cash. Lenders are happy to have your relatives chip in for the down payment, but it needs to be an outright gift, not a loan. Again, it's all about the lender's comfort zone. If your down payment is actually money that you need to repay, that makes lenders a bit nervous. But if it's a no-strings-attached gift, the lender will relax. If you do hit up family members for a gift, the lender will require a formal letter documenting that the dough is in fact not a loan.

## NAVIGATING THE MORTGAGE MAZE

The mortgage market today reminds me of the wine list at swank restaurants. Instead of having your choice of the house white or the house red, you are presented with dozens, if not hundreds, of different wines and vintages from which to choose. That can be a bit daunting. Same with mortgages; it can get frustrating trying to choose from among all the different types. But it's really not that hard once you understand that just like wine, all mortgages have the same basic ingredients. You just have to decide which one fits your taste.

Let's run through some mortgage basics.

All mortgages are for a finite period of time, known as the term. You are required to pay back the loan by the end of the term. Most mortgages last thirty years, though there are also fifteen-year and twenty-year options. Everyone loves longer terms, because you have to pay less each month. Let's keep things simple for a moment and see how this works if you hit up a friend for a $1,000 loan where you don't even have to pay interest. If your friend wants the money repaid in monthly payments over a five-year period, that's going to work out to about $16 a month. But if your friend wants it back in just one year—a shorter term—you are going to have to come up with about $83 a month.

Obviously, the longer term is a lot easier to deal with. But if we switch to the world of mortgages, we are faced with a big tradeoff. Unlike your friend, the mortgage lender is going to charge you interest on the amount that you borrow. That original loan amount is called the principal. On a $150,000 mortgage, your principal is $150,000 and the interest payments are the additional payment you are going to give the lender for being kind enough to loan you the principal amount. Let's look at an example.

On a $150,000, thirty-year fixed-rate mortgage where the interest is 6 percent, you will pay a total of nearly $174,000 in interest over the life of the loan. Remember, this $174,000 is above and beyond the $150,000 principal that you also have to pay back. But if you take out a fifteen-year mortgage for the same $150,000, your total interest charges would be just $78,000, assuming the same 6 percent interest rate. (A fifteen-year mortgage actually would have a half percent lower interest rate than a thirty-year mortgage, but for this example, let's keep the interest rates the same to compare apples to apples.) That said, your monthly costs are going to be higher on the fifteen-year mortgage because you have half the time to repay the money. Ideally, if you can afford the higher monthly payments on a fifteen-year mortgage, it makes a lot of sense to choose that option, given how much you will save on the interest payments. But the reality is that when you are YF&B, a thirty-year term will give you a monthly payment that you can live with. That's more than okay. I just want you to understand what your options are, and how everything works. But I also want you to check out the table on page 314; at the point when more cash starts to flow into your life, paying off your mortgage in fifteen years is simply a great investment. That said, paying off your loan faster only makes sense if you expect to live there for a long time. If you think you will trade up to another house in the future, don't rush to pay off your current mortgage.

Okay, back to our mortgage basics. When you get the mortgage, your lender will give you an amortization schedule. This shows how much of your monthly payment will go toward paying off the principal and how much will be for interest. In the early years of your loan, the vast majority of your payments go for interest. That's because lenders figure that you won't actually stay in the house for thirty years, so they want to collect as much interest (that's their profit) in the early years, before you move on. Just so you know, after fifteen years of making payments on a thirty-year loan, you will have paid off just 30 percent or so of the principal.

**YF&B**
On my website, the mortgage calculator will show you how a different term affects your monthly payments, and what your personal amortization schedule will look like.

## THE MORTGAGE MENU

Now we need to talk about the fact that different mortgages have different interest rates. Basically, we've got three different types to choose from here: fixed, adjustable, or hybrid. For most of you, especially first-time buyers who will trade up soon, a hybrid is your best deal.

With a fixed-rate mortgage, the interest rate you get when you close the deal will never change, and therefore your required monthly payments for the entire payback period will never change. No surprises, no fluctuations—ever. That's quite different from an adjustable-rate mortgage (ARM). The initial interest rate on an ARM is going to be much lower than that of a fixed-rate mortgage—typically more than 1.5 percentage points, but you need to respect the word "adjustable." The interest rate can be changed—adjusted up or down—based on whether the general direction of interest rates in the economy has changed. A typical adjustment occurs once a year—what is known as a one-year ARM—with an annual max change of two percentage points. Over the entire life of the loan, the rate can only change—again, up or down—a total of six percentage points from your original rate. Obviously, if you get hit with a big upward adjustment, your payments are going to skyrocket. What looked great in the first year can become a nightmare soon after.

Which brings us to the Goldilocks option for the YF&B: a hybrid mortgage. With a hybrid, the initial interest rate on your mortgage is fixed for a period of three, five, seven, or even ten years. After that period, the loan converts to an ARM. The initial rate on a hybrid is going to be lower than the interest charge on a thirty-year fixed-rate mortgage, and more than the rate offered on an ARM that starts adjusting after just one year. For example, a 5/1 hybrid has a fixed rate for the first five years and then becomes an ARM that is adjusted every year.

Here are the rates for the three types of mortgages, as of Fall 2004.

| | |
|---|---|
| Fixed-Rate Mortgage | 6.0 percent |
| 5/1 Hybrid Mortgage | 5.0 percent |
| One-Year ARM | 4.2 percent |

The hybrid seems custom-tailored for the YF&B. Chances are that given your age, your first home isn't going to be your last home. In fact, homeowners typically stay put for only five to seven years. So if you don't plan to stay in the house for thirty years, why pay more (in the higher interest rate) for the assurance that your rate won't change for thirty years? Pick a hybrid (three, five, seven, or ten years) that gibes with how long you expect to stay in the home. You'll get a lower rate than with a fixed mortgage, but without the annual rate risk of an ARM.

In an effort to talk you out of jumping at the super-low initial rates on an ARM, please spend just a minute or two casing the table below, which shows how payments on a $150,000 mortgage vary based on the type of loan you choose.

| | Current rate* | Monthly payment at current rate | Monthly payment after one year, if interest rates rise one percentage point | Monthly payment after two years, if interest rates rise two percentage points | Monthly payment after three years, if interest rates rise three percentage points | Monthly payment after five years, if interest rates rise four percentage points | Monthly payment if maximum six-percentage-point hike is imposed on adjustable and hybrid |
|---|---|---|---|---|---|---|---|
| Thirty-Year Fixed-Rate Mortgage | 6.0 | $899 | $899 | $899 | $899 | $899 | $899 |
| Hybrid Mortgage with a Fixed Rate for Five Years | 5.0 | $805 | $805 | $805 | $805 | $998** | $1,428 |
| One-Year Adjustable-Rate Mortgage | 4.2 | $734 | $824 | $919 | $1,018 | $1,122 | $1,339 |

*As of Fall 2004

**Even though interest rates have risen four percentage points, the maximum annual hike for the hybrid is two percentage points.

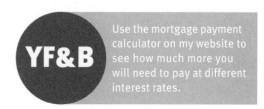

YF&B

Use the mortgage payment calculator on my website to see how much more you will need to pay at different interest rates.

Here's a quick cheat sheet that shows which mortgage can make the most sense for you.

| Your Situation | Best Mortgage | The Rationale |
| --- | --- | --- |
| You plan to move in five years. | three-year or five-year hybrid | If getting the initial payment as low as possible is important, the three-year mortgage will at least start at an interest rate well below that of the thirty-year mortgage, and you will probably be hit with only one adjustment (a max of two percentage points) before you move. For less stress, the five-year hybrid will cost you more at the start, but you don't have to worry about any adjustments before you move on or refinance. |
| You plan to move in seven to ten years. | seven-year or ten-year hybrid | Same concept as above; the seven-year mortgage will have a lower initial rate, but the ten-year mortgage will give you maximum security, and is still going to have a rate lower than that of the thirty-year fixed mortgage. |
| You have found the home of your dreams, and you don't ever plan on moving from it. | thirty-year fixed-rate or fifteen-year fixed-rate mortgage | You are staying put, so the goal is not to get hit with "interest-rate shock" anytime in the future. Lock in a fixed rate now, and you'll never have to worry about your payments ever changing. |

# HOW LOW CAN YOUR INTEREST SAFELY GO?

I also want you to know that you can pay discount points to get an even lower interest rate. Remember, a point equals 1 percent of your mortgage amount. If you have some extra cash handy, each discount point that you pay the lender when you are taking out the loan will reduce your interest rate by $\frac{1}{8}$ to $\frac{1}{4}$ of a percent. So if you paid two points on a $150,000 mortgage, that would be $3,000 to reduce your interest rate from 6 percent to possibly as low as 5.5 percent.

Sure, a super-low interest rate sounds great, but I don't think "buying down" your interest rate makes sense for most YF&Bers. First of all, who's got the cash for it? If you've got extra cash, it should go toward the down payment, so you are closer to the magic 20 percent that will free you of having to pay PMI. And I don't want you to use every last penny to get your home; at the point that you become a homeowner, it becomes even more important to have an emergency cash fund. So I would love for you to build up an emergency fund before you use all your cash to pay points to reduce your mortgage rate.

Now, if you happen to have a whole lot of cash handy for a 20 percent down payment and all the closing costs, then you can entertain whether it also makes sense to buy yourself a lower interest rate. The biggest factor is how long you intend to stay in the house; if you are paying cash to get the rate lower, you want to stay in the house long enough that you will recoup the points with your lower mortgage payments. If you plan to move in five years or so, you probably don't want to pay any discount points.

When you are checking out interest rates, make sure that you ask the lender if you will be required to set up an escrow impound account to get that interest rate. This is where the lender makes you fork over all the money for your annual property tax and insurance costs up front. I don't like this setup at all; you are to shop around for a mortgage where you can handle those payments yourself. First, I have heard too many stories of the lender "forgetting" to make the payment, and then your FICO score is ruined. Besides, why should you give your lender a lot of money up front so they can earn interest on it? I want it to stay in your savings account, where you earn the interest till those bills are due. We'll talk more about this in a bit.

One last point. When you look for a mortgage, lenders must show you two numbers: the interest rate, and what is known as the APR. So you may see this on the front of your mortgage document: 6 percent interest, 6.5 percent APR. APR stands for annual percentage rate. While you may think that the best deal out there for you is one where the APR is the least expensive, that's a common trap that you are not to fall for. APR is a calculation that includes the cost of any points and many of your closing costs, and then averages those costs over the term of the loan. If it is a thirty-year term, then those costs are averaged over thirty years. But what if you do not stay in that house for thirty years? What if you plan to sell it after five years? Then the APR means nothing to you. Just stick to the interest rate in your comparison shopping.

## ASSEMBLING YOUR TEAM

It takes a village to buy a house. A qualified mortgage broker is a crucial member of your team. A mortgage broker is going to shop around at different lenders for your best deal, and quite often your broker can get you a lower interest rate than you would get sitting down with the bank loan officer on your own. Besides, who has the time to talk to a bunch of bankers? The best resource is the least high-tech: Ask friends for referrals. You want to work with someone who not only gets you the best terms but also sticks with you through the entire process, from qualifying for the loan to the closing. Having a conscientious mortgage broker by your side can make the process less stressful. However, if you feel confident that you know the ins and outs of mortgages, you can instead look into using online lender services such as www.lendingtree.com or www.eloan.com.

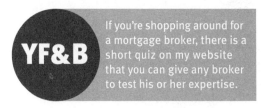

**YF&B** If you're shopping around for a mortgage broker, there is a short quiz on my website that you can give any broker to test his or her expertise.

Once you find a broker that you want to work with, ask for a prequalification; this is where you get a professional assessment (based on your income, FICO score, etc.) of how big a mortgage you will be able to get. I am not saying you should go for that limit (more on this in a minute), but it is important to confirm that you will indeed be able to get a loan for the amount you want. However, the prequalification is not a guarantee that the lender will give you that exact same deal when you come back in a few weeks or months and apply for a mortgage. To get that rate guaranteed, you need a "lock-in" rate; that's your lender's guarantee of the mortgage rate you'll get. Typically, the lock-in is good for only sixty days. If you don't buy a home within that period, you lose your rate guarantee. A lock-in is great when there is an indication that rates might rise between the time you start home shopping and the time you actually close on (that is, buy) the house. If rates are predicted to remain stable or fall, you can hold off on locking in the rate.

And here's just a friendly reminder, in case you didn't catch this the forty-two other times I have brought it up: Your mortgage broker is going to be very interested in your FICO score. The best way you can help the broker get you a great rate is by bringing a FICO score above 720 to the game. Remember this table from Chapter 1, Know the Score?

| | 720–850 | 700–719 | 675–699 | 620–674 | 560–619 | 500–559 |
|---|---|---|---|---|---|---|
| thirty-year fixed-rate mortgage | 6.0% | 6.1% | 6.7% | 7.8% | 8.9% | 9.5% |

The difference between being in the top FICO range (you get a 6 percent mortgage rate) and the lowest range (you get a 9.5 percent mortgage rate) means that you will pay $362 less a month on a $150,000 mortgage ($899 v. $1,261). That's $4,344 a year that you can save by having a great FICO score rather than a lousy one. Over a thirty-year mortgage, you would pay a ridiculous $130,000 more if you had the higher interest rate.

Your broker will also take a hard look at your debt-income ratio: how much your monthly mortgage payments will be, compared to your pretax income. As a general rule, the mortgage you are hoping to get should not equal more than 28 percent of your gross monthly income (that is, before taxes are deducted). So if you make

$3,000 a month, your mortgage shouldn't be more than $1,000. And all your debts—the mortgage, the credit card balances, the car loan—shouldn't equal more than 36 percent of your gross monthly income.

The income-debt ratio is only a guideline used by lenders, but it's a good exercise to compute your percentages before you apply. If you are way over the limits, you still may be able to get a mortgage, but you'll be hit with some trade-offs. You might be required to make a bigger down payment. Or the interest rate you are offered might be higher than the best rate.

In addition to having a mortgage pro on your home-buying staff, you will want someone to help with the actual house shopping. That person is a real estate agent. It's super-important to understand how real estate agents work. Typically, the seller has an agent and the buyer has a different agent. The home seller is on the hook to pay both of them. The typical commission is 6 percent of the home's sale price. The selling agent gets the 6 percent and works out an agreement on how much goes to the buyer's agent. Typically, it's a basic split. But do you see how the deck is stacked against you, the buyer? You're not paying the commission, the seller is. So who do you think is going to command the agents' attention? And it's a commission based on the sale price. The more you pay, the more the agent makes. Even if it's your agent.

Don't get me wrong, I think real estate agents play a crucial role on your team. But you have to understand how they get compensated. The more you spend, the more they make.

Real estate agents, rich friends, and maybe even your parents are going to try to talk you into stretching to buy a bigger house than you can afford right now. Their well-intentioned philosophy is that your income will grow in the coming years, and so the mortgage payments will become easier to handle. Un-uh. That's just way too much pressure. Besides, you've got other things you need to work on. (Have I mentioned lately how much I want you to fund your 401(k) to the max match and then contribute as much as you can to a Roth?) Go for a house that leaves you room to breathe. If in five years your career has taken off and you can afford a bigger place, then that's the right time to buy it—not now, when you really can't afford it.

Agents will want you to sign an "exclusive" deal where you agree to work with only them for ninety days or more. Before you sign on, ask the agent how long it takes for the average house to sell in your market. If the answer is one month, then why are you signing on to work with them for three months? Tell them you will work with them for one month and then be happy to extend your agreement beyond that period if you are pleased with their work and you still haven't found a home.

## SET YOUR OWN BUDGET

Knowing how much lenders will let you borrow is simply not the same as knowing how much you can afford. You need to make sure that you can truly afford the total costs of owning a home. Let's start by having you figure out your basic mortgage cost. On page 298 is a table that you can use to match your general purchase range with an interest rate that you are likely to get on an ARM, hybrid, or fixed-rate mortgage. That will lead you to an estimate of your monthly basic mortgage cost.

**YF&B**
If you don't know the current interest rates, you can get an updated rate check on my website. You can also use the mortgage calculator to determine your costs based on a specific purchase price you have in mind.

## MONTHLY MORTGAGE COST

### AMOUNT OF MORTGAGE

| INTEREST RATE | $100,000 | $150,000 | $175,000 | $200,000 | $300,000 |
|---|---|---|---|---|---|
| 4.0 | $477 | $716 | $836 | $955 | $1,432 |
| 5.0 | $537 | $805 | $939 | $1,074 | $1,610 |
| 5.5 | $568 | $852 | $994 | $1,136 | $1,703 |
| 6.0 | $600 | $899 | $1,049 | $1,199 | $1,799 |
| 6.5 | $632 | $948 | $1,106 | $1,264 | $1,896 |
| 7.0 | $665 | $998 | $1,164 | $1,330 | $1,995 |
| 8.0 | $734 | $1,101 | $1,284 | $1,467 | $2,201 |

Think of the chart above as merely telling you the going price for the pizza dough. To make a complete housing pizza, we need to add on the cost of tomato, cheese, and any "extra" toppings. And we're not talking about chump change. Those ingredients are going to add at least 40 percent to your basic mortgage cost.

Here are the main "extras" you need to factor into your housing budget. You will pay property tax, which varies from less than 1 percent to more than 3 percent of your home's value, depending on where you live. I am going to use a middle ground of 1 percent. You also need home insurance—that can run about $25 a month per $100,000 of value. And since we're pretty sure that you are not going to be able to make a 20 percent down payment, you could get hit with that private mortgage insurance we mentioned earlier, which runs about $43 per $100,000 of your mortgage. We also need to figure on paying at least $125 a month to cover any unexpected repairs. Hey, if anything goes kerflooey with your home, you're on the hook. No more landlords and supers to bug—you are wearing both of those hats now.

On a $150,000 home, if you make a 10 percent down payment, you could face the following costs:

| | |
|---|---|
| Base Monthly Mortgage Payment | $855 |
| Monthly Property Tax | $156 |
| Monthly Homeowner's Insurance | $38 |
| Monthly PMI | $65 |
| Home Repairs | $125 |
| **Total Monthly Payments** | $1,239 |

Suddenly our $855 is now $1,239. And you will probably have plenty more "new" costs that you didn't need to deal with as a renter. All the utilities are now your responsibility (heat, air-conditioning, water, garbage collection, etc.); and if you have a yard but lack a green thumb, are you going to need to hire a gardener? Do you plan to dig yourself out in the winter, or will you hire a snow-removal firm? Add it all up, and you're looking at adding more than 40 percent to the basic mortgage cost.

But let's not get all slump-shouldered and depressed. How about I throw in some good news? You get a neat tax break when you own, which will reduce your real housing costs. The interest you pay on your mortgage is tax-deductible. If you are in the 25 percent tax bracket, that means that for every $1 you pay in interest, you will get 25 cents back. In the early years of a mortgage, the bulk of your payment to the lender will indeed be interest, so you're going to get some nice relief. That said, I don't want you to base how much house you can afford on the size of the mortgage interest deduction you will receive. If the only way you can afford the house is with the tax break, then I think you are cutting it really close. You should view that tax break as a nice bonus, but not a necessity. You can use it to pay for all the unplanned repairs on the house, or to make an extra mortgage payment each year (more on this soon).

# PLAY HOUSE BEFORE YOU BUY A HOUSE

Given all the extra costs of owning, you need to be plenty sure you can handle the bills before you take the housing plunge. Put yourself through my six-month "play house" test.

- Figure out the cost of homes in your area. Use the table on page 298, or the calculator on my website, to estimate your basic mortgage cost.

- Add 40 percent to that sum. That is your home ownership cost.

- Subtract your current monthly rent from your home ownership cost.

- Set up a new bank account and deposit that difference in the account on the first day of every month for six months.

If you pay $1,000 in rent but your home ownership cost (including all the extras) is $1,271, you need to deposit $271 a month into your test account. If you miss one payment, or if you are consistently late in making the payments, you are not ready to buy a home. If you can handle the extra payments, then you've got the thumbs-up to start looking for a home to buy. By the way, in playing house, you've also helped to beef up your down-payment fund. In the previous example, you would have saved up $1,626 in six months.

## SHOPPING TIPS

Okay, now we're ready for the fun stuff: shopping for a home. Finally! Before you head out to see any homes with your agent, I want you two to have a serious chat. You are not to be shown any home that is above your target purchase price. It's just too tempting and too frustrating. It reminds me of when I was YF&B; I wouldn't allow myself to walk down this particular block in town, because there was a designer shoe store where every pair was at least 50 percent of my monthly take-home pay. I had (and have) a serious thing for shoes, and I knew I couldn't afford to tease myself by even window shopping. It would tempt me to blow my limited budget, and even if I didn't buy a pair, it would make the affordable shoes that I owned seem boring by comparison. Why allow yourself to see a home that you can't afford, when all it will do is make the homes in your price range seem so blah?

When you see a house that you love, please don't lose your head. So often I see people get so emotionally attached to a home that they forget it is the biggest expenditure of their life. Instead of bargaining hard, they become total softies and agree to pay the seller's asking price. Slow down, there. This is business, not dating.

I totally understand that for the past few years most of the country has been a seller's market, meaning sellers have had the upper hand. Homes sell fast, and often above their asking price. In many markets, you have five or ten people putting in competing bids on the same home and getting into bidding wars. But that's beginning to change. In many parts of the country, you can now make an offer that is below the asking price and not have to worry that you will be outbid by four other people.

The best offer strategy for you depends on what is going on right now in your particular market. To make an informed offer, you need to start keeping track of what real estate is doing in your area long before you are ready to house shop. Become an avid reader of the real estate section in your local paper. Check out the list of homes that have sold recently, and start your own housing spreadsheet. Here's what you want to track:

- How many weeks are homes in your area on the market before they sell?

- If homes are selling above or below their asking price, then by how much above or below?

Now, here is the key. If homes are selling faster and faster, and are selling for more and more above the asking price in your area, you are still in a seller's market, and you may have to pay full price or even above the asking price to get a home.

However, if homes are staying on the market for longer before they sell, and if they are also selling below their asking price, you are in a buyer's market. Therefore, you most likely will not have to pay full asking price to get the house you want.

| You know you're in a... | Buyer's Market | Seller's Market |
|---|---|---|
| When the time it takes for a house to sell is... | On the rise | Falling |
| When the final sales price for a home is... | Below the original asking price | Above the original asking price |

## GET A BIO OF YOUR HOUSE

When you find a home you like, get at least two "comps" from your agent. This is shorthand for comparable sales. You want to know how much similar homes have sold for recently, and use that as a guide in figuring out what your bid should be. A comp from a year ago is not nearly as good as a comp from a few weeks ago. If two similar homes sold for 10 percent less than the asking price and they were on the market for two months, you know you don't need to come in with an offer that is above the asking price. You might make an offer that is 15 or 20 percent or so below the asking price. That leaves you some negotiating room.

You also want to know all the particulars of the house that you are going to bid on. How long has it been on the market? When did the seller buy the home? That helps you understand what they paid for the house, which is no doubt a prime factor in determining how low they will go on the sale. Has the seller already bought a new home? Have they been relocated by their employer to a new area? Is this an "estate" sale, meaning the homeowner recently passed away and the heirs are now selling? All of those are great bits of insider info.

Someone whose firm has paid for a relocation is probably getting help from the company to sell the home. That can make it easier for you to get a lower bid accepted. An estate sale can also work to your advantage. If the heirs are 600 miles away, they might just want to make a deal as fast as possible to avoid the hassle of holding on to the home. Besides, if the deceased homeowner had lived in the house for thirty years, the heirs are going to make a good profit on the sale. They might be more flexible in negotiating with you than someone who is selling a home that they bought three years ago and haven't seen rise in value too much.

## HOW TO BID

If you are in a hot seller's market, please remain calm and strong. Do not get swept into a bidding war. Before you make your first bid on a house, have in mind a set dollar limit of how high you will go. Write it down. Consult it every time your agent calls to say that someone else just offered $5,000 more. If the price goes beyond your budget, you are to walk away. I know this is excruciatingly difficult, but what sense does it make to buy a house that you can't afford? You are asking for trouble. One work-around for a hot market is to look at less expensive houses; that way, if you have to raise your bid to beat out other potential buyers, you won't run outside of your financial comfort zone.

Keeping your cool is especially important when you consider that someday you may want to sell the house that you are now trying to buy. If you overpay to buy, you could end up losing when you sell. Selling is expensive; remember, you typically pay a 6 percent commission to your agent. So let's say a house is valued at $150,000, but you get caught in a bidding war and pay $160,000. Then, three years later, you want to sell, but the market has slowed down and you can only get $163,000 for the house. You figure, *Okay, at least I made $3,000.* No you didn't. After you pay a 6 percent commission on the $163,000, you will net just $153,220. That leaves you nearly $7,000 in the hole from your purchase price.

## THE INSPECTION

Every bid that you make on a house should include a contingency clause that the home must pass a structural inspection. You are to hire a professional home inspector (ask friends, rather than the real estate agent, for a referral), who will give the house a thorough checkup. If you find any major problems, you can either walk away from the house or negotiate with the seller; get an estimate of the cost of the repairs and have it deducted from the sale price. I also recommend that you arrange to go along on the home inspection. It's a great opportunity to have a pro walk you through the general state of the house. The roof may pass inspection, but your inspector might also point out an area where a little repair work right now could save you from a major overhaul down the line.

The inspector should run through all of the items below, but it doesn't hurt for you to bring along this list and make sure your house checks out.

- Run the bath and shower to make sure the water pressure is good.

- Check how long it takes for the water to run hot in the bathrooms and kitchen.

- Run the heating and air conditioner. Make sure they work and are easy on your ears. Find out when they were installed.

- If there is a fireplace, light some paper to make sure the smoke runs up the flue and not into the house.

- Flush all the toilets.

- Check behind pictures for any cracks or water damage.

- If there are storm screens or regular screens for the windows, check their condition.

- Turn all the light switches on and off.

The website www.realestate.com has useful information and resources for smart homebuying, including search engines for homes, real estate agents, and home inspectors.

## CLOSING THE DEAL

Once your bid on a house has been accepted, you will set a closing date with the seller and your lender. When this date rolls around, get ready to be signing a whole bunch of checks. This is the due date for all the closing costs that you haven't yet paid. And you'll also need to bring proof of insurance (more on this in a minute) to the meeting.

Before you show up at the closing, I want you and your agent to arrange a final walk-through of the house, so you can make sure everything is in good shape. If the seller scraped the walls while moving out, you need to get them to cover the cost of that repair. And if they agreed to include the dishwasher, washing machine, and dryer in the purchase price, you want to make sure those appliances are still there. Same goes for the cool dining-room chandelier that you fell in love with and asked to be part of the sale.

You also need to decide how you are going to take title to the house. If you are a single homeowner, it's pretty easy; you're the owner, so the house is in your name. But if you are married or buying the home with a partner, you've got two basic choices: **joint tenancy with right of survivorship (JTWROS)** and tenancy in common (TIC). With JTWROS, you are agreeing that when one of you dies, the other person becomes the sole owner of the home. With TIC, you are saying that you want someone else—a parent, a sibling, a charity, etc.—to inherit your share of the property. How you take title will be stipulated in one of the documents signed at the closing.

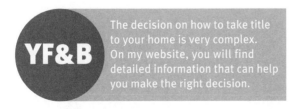

YF&B

The decision on how to take title to your home is very complex. On my website, you will find detailed information that can help you make the right decision.

# PROTECTING YOUR PALACE

You won't be able to close on your house without proof that you have insurance. But don't rely on your lender to tell you how much you need. All the lender cares about is that they get paid for the outstanding amount of the mortgage if something is to happen. But you have a bigger concern: If something were to happen to your home, would the insurer pay for you to replace whatever was damaged—perhaps the entire house—based on the current cost of making those repairs and renovations? You also want to make sure that you have enough coverage for the contents of your home. A standard policy typically offers contents coverage that is 50 percent of the insured value of the home. So if you insured your home for $150,000, then your contents would be covered, up to $75,000. You can always buy additional coverage if necessary. You also want to make sure that your policy has a built-in inflation guard; this will increase your coverage automatically, to keep pace with the rising cost of replacing your home.

The only policy that is acceptable is one that provides replacement cost coverage. Do not take out a policy that provides actual cash value coverage. Let's say you didn't listen to me in the Give Yourself Credit chapter, and you charged $3,000 on your credit card for a flat-screen TV. A year later, your home is robbed and you lose the TV. If you have actual cash value coverage, your insurer is going to give you money only for the depreciated value of the TV. Let's say that's 25 percent less than what you paid. So you get a check for $2,250. But it's still going to cost you $3,000 to buy another flat-screen TV. That's your problem, not the insurer's. If you want your insurer to fork over what it will actually take for you to go out and buy a new TV, you need replacement cost coverage.

Insurers are tightening the screws on even replacement coverage; to make sure your coverage stays up-to-date with rising construction costs and home values, make sure you and your insurer review the policy annually.

You also want to have the insurer walk you through which specific items are not covered in your basic policy. For example, there typically is a low limit on jewelry coverage. If you have a few heirlooms or a fancy engagement ring, you will probably want to buy additional coverage; this is known as an endorsement, or floater, to your standard policy.

And make sure you save enough to pay your premium in full once a year. If you opt for the monthly, quarterly, or semiannual payment, the insurance company is going to tack on a service charge. That can be $5 or $10 for every payment. Let's say you have a $400 premium. If you pay a $10 service fee on your four quarterly payments ($40), you've just boosted your premium cost 10 percent.

You can comparison-shop for home insurance coverage at www.insure.com and www.insweb.com.

**PROBLEM:**
I have only $10,000 to put toward a $200,000 home, so I am being told that I need to pay something called PMI.

**SOLUTION:**
Roll the PMI cost into the mortgage.

When you can't make a 20 percent down payment, lenders get nervous. To ease their nerves, you need to take out private mortgage insurance (PMI). This is an added monthly charge—typically, $43 for every $100,000 of your loan, assuming a 10 percent down payment—that buys insurance for the lender, not you. It's insurance that even if you flake out on the mortgage, the lender will get repaid.

You must continue to pay this fee until your equity in the home reaches 20 percent. Equity is the percent of the home's value that you own outright; that is, it isn't part of your mortgage. For instance, if you make a $15,000 down payment on a $150,000 home, you have 10 percent equity. The other 90 percent ($135,000) is debt, the size of your loan. Now let's say the value of the house rises to $165,000 and you've paid down your mortgage to a balance of $130,000. So you now have $35,000 in equity, not just the $15,000 down payment. Your equity ($35,000) is now 27 percent of your mortgage value, not 10 percent.

PMI typically comes out of your pocket, as a separate cost from the mortgage. And that can be a huge hassle when you are YF&B. One option is to agree to have the total PMI costs rolled into the mortgage. Yes, it boosts the cost of your mortgage, but you are now essentially paying off the PMI over thirty years, so your monthly out-of-pocket expenses are going to be lower. And with the PMI in your mortgage, it becomes part of your payments that are tax-deductible.

If you want to roll the PMI into your mortgage, it will typically cost you 1 percent of your mortgage amount. On a $150,000 mortgage, that will run you an  additional $1,500, so your new mortgage total would be $151,500. On a thirty-year fixed-rate mortgage, that will boost your monthly cost from $899 to $908—just an extra $9 a month. Not bad, eh? Instead of the $64 you would pay if the PMI were simply a separate fee, you are paying an extra $9 a month on your mortgage. And remember, straight PMI that you pay separately is not tax-deductible. When it's wrapped inside your mortgage, it is.

Ask your lender to work up your mortgage if you pay the PMI separately and also if you have it rolled into your mortgage, and compare.

But if you choose to pay PMI the old-fashioned way, as a separate monthly cost that you write a check for, I want you to stay super-alert. When your equity gets to 20 percent, you can get rid of the PMI. Lenders are legally required to drop the charge once you have 22 percent equity, but you should keep an eye on property values in your area. At the point that you think you're at 20 percent equity, call the lender and ask them which appraiser they will approve to check the value of your home. You don't want to hire just any appraiser. Make sure it is one that the bank will listen to. If that appraiser comes back and says you're at 20 percent equity, your lender must stop the PMI charge.

**PROBLEM:**
A starter home where I live costs at least $330,000. The only way I can afford that is to take out an interest-only loan.

**SOLUTION:**
Then you can't really afford it—at least not right now, when the housing market is cooling down a bit.

Interest-only loans are the fast food of mortgages. There's always someone willing to sell them to you, but that doesn't mean they're good for you.

The problem is that the spiel sure is tasty. Rather than pay both principal and interest each month, for an interest-only loan, you are required to pay just the interest component for as long as ten or fifteen years. On a $300,000 five-year hybrid interest-only mortgage with a 5 percent interest rate, your monthly tab is $1,250 compared to $1,610 if you were paying principal along with the interest. That's a huge difference if you are currently cash-strapped.

I totally respect that this can make the difference between renting and buying for a YF&Ber. But homes are not casinos. And taking an interest-only loan is no better than a roll of the roulette wheel. At some point, you'll need to pay back the principal. When that kicks in, your payments are going to be much higher; if you took out a thirty-year loan and just paid interest for the first ten years, after that you'd have to pay off all the principal in the remaining twenty years, rather than spreading the cost out over the full thirty years. How can you be sure that you will be able to handle the higher payments in year eleven?

And don't try the old refinance angle with me. I know you think your home will appreciate enough in the next few years that you will have built up at least 20 percent equity and will be able to switch to a conventional loan. But are you positive that's how it is going to play out? As I write this book in the fall of 2004, real estate is beginning to slow down after a torrid pace. That doesn't change my opinion about a home being a great long-term investment, but I don't want you to rely on your home's value being 20 percent higher five years from now. It may just run in place for a while or appreciate modestly where you live. It's a natural breather—but it's one that you can't afford if you need to build up equity really fast so that you can get out of an interest-only loan.

**PROBLEM:**
My best friend and I can't afford homes of our own, so we want to buy a home together.

**SOLUTION:**
As tempting as this is, I want you to wait till you can afford something on your own.

I've been hearing this one a lot the past few years, as home prices have gone up, salaries haven't, and many YF&Bers are in no rush to partner up with the love of their life. Yet at the same time, you don't want to be paying rent for another ten years before you do settle down or can afford a place on your own. So going dutch on a house with a friend sounds great.

I don't think so. Let's do a time trip forward—say, two years. Your best friend, with whom you bought a house, is now madly in love with Ms. Right. They are ready to move in together. And you're not part of their picture. No hard feelings, right? It's just that things change, and your buddy is ready to move on. So what happens to the house? He wants to sell it so he can pocket his half of the proceeds and use it for his new place with Ms. Right. But you don't want to sell, because you love living there—it is your home, too. Do you expect to have the money to buy him out of the house?

Or let's roll out a morose but not impossible scenario: Your housing pal gets into a fatal accident, and in his will he leaves everything to his sister. That means you now own the home with the sister. What if you can't stand her? What if she lives 300 miles away and has no interest in the house? She can force you to sell it so she can get her half of the proceeds.

Look, when you are young and fabulous, your entire life is about change—exciting, fun change. Locking yourself into home ownership with someone who is not a life partner is pretty much a guarantee for future stress. My advice is just to sit tight; continue to rent, and see what progress you can make saving up for your own down payment. In the meantime, you may just find that special someone who you want to build your life with. That's a good person to go in on a house with.

**PROBLEM:**
We have $20,000 in credit card debt, but thanks to strong appreciation rates in our area, we have built up a lot of equity in our house. We are wondering if we should take out a home equity line to pay off the credit card debt.

**SOLUTION:**
You need to understand the risks before you put your home on the line.

Okay, this is downright scary to me. A home is not a four-sided credit card! When it comes to taking money out of your home, you have two choices: a home equity loan or a home equity line of credit. With a home equity loan (HEL), also known as a second mortgage, you get a pile of cash up front from the lender, and you start paying interest on the loan immediately. With a home equity line of credit (HELOC), you open up an account with the lender, with which you can borrow money in the future; you won't need to pay interest until you actually withdraw money from the HELOC. It works just like a credit card. The one big difference is that a HEL comes with a fixed interest rate, while a HELOC has an adjustable rate that is tied to an underlying index (similar to the way an adjustable-rate mortgage works).

Given their flexibility, HELOCs are more popular with consumers. Too popular, if you ask me. You need to understand that if you mess up and use a HELOC that you then can't make the payments on, the lender is not going to be amused. If you fall way behind on your HELOC payment, you could be forced to sell your home.

So let's think this through: Put your house at risk to pay off credit card debt? As I explained on page 85, credit card debt is unsecured, which means that if you can't pay it off, the card company can't force you to sell anything to make the payment, including your house. So why put your home at risk to pay off a debt that is unsecured?

I think a far better move is to see if you can get your credit card interest rate lowered. As we discussed in Chapter 3, Give Yourself Credit, with a good FICO score, you can qualify for a zero-interest-rate balance transfer, or a card with a lower interest rate. That reduces the amount of interest charges that you will run up, which means you should have an easier time coming up with some extra money each month to slowly get the balance paid off (see page 99 for a strategy) without having to put your house at risk.

All that said, I do think HELOCs can be good emergency cash funds. But let's make sure we agree on what constitutes an emergency. Your one and only car breaks down, or you have a big medical bill that isn't covered by insurance — those are emergencies. A trip to Cabo to decompress after a big project at work is not an emergency. You are to open the HELOC now; don't wait for the emergency. But I do not want you to touch it unless a real emergency pops up.

If you are in a home that you intend to stay in, I think it makes a lot of sense to pay off the mortgage as fast as possible to avoid paying years and years of interest — but only if you've got everything else checked off your financial to-do list. If you have any credit card debt at a high interest rate, that comes first. As does investing in your 401(k) to get the company match, as well as funding your own Roth IRA or other retirement account.

If you've got all that taken care of (in which case you are Y&F, but not B), let's talk about the fifteen-year mortgage option compared to the thirty-year option. With a term that is half as long, your payments are going to be a lot higher, but you get a break in that the interest rate is typically half a percentage point lower than with a thirty-year loan. Let's take a look at how the payments pan out on a $150,000 mortgage:

| | Interest Rate | Monthly Payment | Total Interest Payments over Life of the Loan |
|---|---|---|---|
| Thirty-year fixed-rate | 6.0 | $899 | $173,757 |
| Fifteen-year fixed-rate | 5.5 | $1,226 | $70,613 |

As of Fall 2004

You are saving more than $103,000 in interest charges by committing to the faster payback schedule, and you also will have your home paid off well before you reach retirement age. Let's say you are thirty-two today. That would mean you would be mortgage-free no later than age forty-seven. That's an awfully sweet setup.

But having said all that, I am not convinced that a YF&Ber should be taking out a fifteen-year loan. Once you commit to the new mortgage, you are obligated to keep at it every month. You can't suddenly say, "Oh, we decided to send our kid to private school, so we'd like to go back to the $899 monthly cost of the thirty-year mortgage, rather than pay the $1,226 on our fifteen-year mortgage." Or you get laid off. Or you decide that one of you is going to become a stay-at-home parent. Catch my drift? Your life changes, and you no longer want to make the higher payments. But getting back to the lower monthly cost will require refinancing, and refinancing assumes that rates will not be going higher.

So here's the best-of-both-worlds solution: Keep your existing thirty-year mortgage, and just add extra payments each month. You can use the calculator on my website to see what you would need to add to your current monthly mortgage payment to get it polished off in fifteen years. Yes, I know that if you took out a real fifteen-year mortgage, you would get a slightly lower interest rate, but I don't think it's worth boxing yourself into the commitment of always making those payments. I would much rather see you keep the flexibility to change your mind if another financial need pops up that is more urgent than paying off the mortgage. And by the way, if you're interested: Paying off a thirty-year fixed-rate at 6 percent in fifteen years would require sending in an extra $375 a month to your $899 payment.

I am a huge fan of paying off your mortgage as quickly as possible, given that it will reduce your total interest costs. But only a flake would go for a biweekly mortgage.

Let's first lay out the basic lender pitch: Rather than pay your mortgage once a month, you can reduce the time it takes to get your mortgage completely paid off by splitting the mortgage cost into two payments a month (every two weeks). With a $1,000 mortgage, you would pay $500 every two weeks, rather than $1,000 monthly. If you did this, you would reduce the payback time on a 6 percent thirty-year mortgage by about 5.3 years. That's going to reduce your total interest costs a ton.

But here's the hitch. Paying $500 every two weeks is not the same as paying $1,000 a month. Given that there are 52 weeks in a year, paying half your mortgage every two weeks works out to 26 payments a year. So that means that at $500 every two weeks, you will pay $13,000 for the year. If you stick with the monthly $1,000, you're only going to pay $12,000 a year. That's why you pay off the mortgage faster; you're paying $1,000 more each year!

If you are in a house that you plan on staying in for a long time, this can be a smart move. But please don't throw away money by signing up for your lender's biweekly mortgage. You will probably get hit with a start-up fee ($300 to $500 or more) and service fees ($4 or so per payment, or $104 a year). I can't resist pointing out that if you instead invested that $500 and added $104 to the pot every year, you would have $6,905 after twenty-five years, assuming a return of just 5 percent.

That sounds a whole lot smarter than paying those lender fees—especially when you consider that you can achieve the same goal without the biweekly mortgage. Yep, you can create your own free plan for paying off your mortgage ahead of schedule.

All you need to do is send in one extra mortgage payment per year and tell the lender to apply all of the payment to the loan principal, not the interest. If that sounds too daunting, take your monthly mortgage cost and divide it by twelve. Then add that sum to your regular monthly payment. Let's say you have a $1,000-a-month mortgage. If we divide $1,000 by twelve we get about $83. So you can plan to send in your $1,000 mortgage payment each month, plus an extra $83. Keep this up and your $150,000 thirty-year mortgage will be paid off in less than twenty-five years, and you will save about $40,000 in interest.

Most lenders will let you send in the extra payments without a charge. If you do have a prepayment penalty, you need to calculate if your interest savings will be more than the prepayment fee.

**YF&B** At my website, you can calculate with a prepayment calculator how much you will save by paying off your mortgage.

The basic mortgage cost for a home is deceptive. You must add at least 40 percent to a basic monthly mortgage to account for all the extra costs that come with ownership: property tax, higher home insurance costs, maintenance, and possibly private mortgage insurance.

Family gifts can be a great down payment source, but it must be a gift, not a loan, to make the lender happy.

Closing costs can run to 2 to 3 percent of your mortgage costs. These costs are paid in cash or can be rolled into the mortgage. Either way, be prepared to cover the closing costs.

When you make a down payment of less than 20 percent, ask for the private mortage insurance to be rolled into the mortgage to save you money.

A mortgage broker will shop around for the best loan deals for you; get prequalified before you house hunt to make sure you will be able to get a loan in your price range.

➡ A hybrid mortgage is smarter than a thirty-year fixed-rate mortgage if you intend to move within the next ten years.

➡ In a seller's market, houses sell fast and at prices that can be higher than the asking price. In a buyer's market, homes are staying on the market longer and are selling at prices below their asking price. The type of market you are in determines how you should price your initial bid on a home. Track sales info in your local newspaper to get a sense of your market.

➡ Set a price limit before you make an initial bid on a home. If a bidding war develops, walk away once the price exceeds your limit.

➡ A home purchase must be contingent on the property passing a home inspection.

➡ Replacement cost coverage is better than actual cost coverage for your home insurance. Check with your agent annually to make sure your policy is updated to cover rising construction and material costs in your area.

I know you love each other, I know you're committed to each other, but are you really in sync financially?

THE
LOWDOWN

Ask anyone what first attracted them to their partner and what keeps them so connected, and you're not going to hear "I fell in love the moment I learned her FICO score," or "He had me when he told me about his emergency cash fund." Nor have I ever seen a wedding announcement mention a shared passion for dollar cost averaging.

Don't get me wrong, I'm big on romance. The emotional and physical intimacy we create with our partners is the foundation for our connection. But a lasting relationship also requires financial intimacy. A big part of staying together is having an appreciation and mission for making the right financial moves together.

Opposites may attract, but I wouldn't put my money on a relationship of financial opposites. Look, there are many factors that contribute to a national divorce rate of 50 percent, but I can tell you from listening to thousands of people over the years that money issues are near the top of the list. And that makes perfect sense to me. Money decisions are with you every day of every week for the rest of your life. If you aren't in sync, you will have constant stress in your relationship.

And I am not talking about whether you both make the same amount of money or have identical credit card balances. Financial intimacy is when you understand that you have different financial personalities and you work to come up with a shared approach to spending, saving, and investing. How good you are at that process is one of the clearest signs of how much you truly love and respect each other.

Yet I know that finances are just about the last thing couples want to talk about. A heart-to-heart on contributing to a 401(k) up to the point of the company match isn't exactly great conversation. Yet those of you who have been in a relationship for many years know all too well that if you don't talk about money stuff before you move in together or get married, you're just delaying inevitable problems. And it is especially important when you are YF&B; when you don't have much money, you need to be sure you agree on how to handle what little you have.

Andrew and Kim met in their early twenties and knew within weeks that this was "it." They were a great match in all those typically inexplicable ways—perfect complements to each other. When they moved in together six months later, they decided to keep it simple and just divide the various costs in half and keep their checking and credit card accounts separate. Andrew was such a romantic that he was constantly surprising Kim with weekend getaways at extravagant hotels that he insisted on paying for, even though he was an underpaid high-school teacher. Three years later, when they were married, they decided to buy a house. That's when their lack of financial intimacy hit hard. Andrew's romantic inclinations had created a $12,000 credit card balance that simply overwhelmed him. But he didn't let Kim in on the fact that some months he didn't pay his bill, and a few times he had exceeded his credit limit. But it all became quite clear to Kim when they went mortgage shopping and Andrew's FICO score was 150 points below hers; there was no way they could get a good interest rate if they applied together for a mortgage, but Kim knew she wasn't going to qualify for a loan on her own. That's when the arguments began.

Kim was so angry with Andrew for being irresponsible and creating this problem for them. But from my vantage point, Kim is just as culpable. It is irrelevant who had the debt. What matters is that they were sharing their lives but not their finances. Deep down, she had to know that his finances weren't adding up, yet she didn't want to face reality. That's a sham relationship. It doesn't matter who makes more or who makes less, it's all about complete openness. You both must share every nook and cranny of your financial lives and be open to asking and answering any questions. From that intimacy, you can build a shared plan for handling the finances in your relationship.

# THE MONEY CONNECTION

Whether you are in the throes of a hot new relationship or ten years into a marriage, how financially compatible are you and your partner? Yeah, I know you love each other, I know you're committed to each other, but are you really in sync financially? Take the quiz below and find out.

| | Me | | My partner | |
|---|---|---|---|---|
| | YES | NO | YES | NO |
| 1. I haven't started to contribute to my 401(k) even though I am eligible for a company match. | | | | |
| 2. Gifts for family and close friends are so important, it's okay to spend more than I can afford on them. | | | | |
| 3. I want to buy a fancy car even if I cannot really afford it. | | | | |
| 4. I want my kids to go to private schools even if it means not saving for our retirement. | | | | |
| 5. I would never tell my friends that a restaurant they picked is too expensive for my budget. | | | | |
| 6. A weekend of gambling with friends in Vegas or a day at the racetrack is my idea of fun. I also love getting into a high-stakes poker game a few times a month. | | | | |
| 7. When I am out with friends and family, I like to pick up the bill, even if it will mean running up my credit card balance. | | | | |
| 8. I love buying a new cell phone each year so I can have the latest gizmo. | | | | |
| 9. I never sit down and pay my bills on time each month or balance my checkbook. | | | | |
| 10. I never read my credit card statement carefully to check for bogus charges. | | | | |
| 11. My closets and drawers are full of expensive items that I bought on an impulse and don't use but feel too guilty to get rid of. | | | | |
| 12. It's okay to charge a $2,000 vacation on my credit card. I deserve it, even if it means I will only be able to pay it off slowly. | | | | |

The more questions you and your partner answered yes to, the more work you have to do. Either you are too wrapped up in impressing people with money you don't have or you lack enough respect for the money you do have to make sure it is put to the right use. As a YF&Ber, you simply can't afford either. Every penny you spend on indulgences for yourself and extravagant gifts for others is a penny you don't have for paying off some credit card debt or a student loan. I am not suggesting that you live a monastic life, but I want you to be aware of how your choices today are affecting your future. If you want that future to be less stressful and more secure, you and your partner will need to find a way to change your behaviors today so you can put your money to better use.

On my website, you will find more compatibility questions that you and your partner can use to spark important money conversations.

## MERGERS AND ACQUISITIONS

In a perfect world, all couples would have their financial foibles worked out before they move in together. But I know we're not operating in a perfect world. We're dealing with your reality. So while I encourage you to continue to talk to each other about your money personalities and how they are going to impact so many aspects of your life together, we'll also need a plan for dealing with today. That means merging some, but not all, of your finances.

When you live together, your shared living expenses should be paid out of a joint checking account that you both contribute a fair share to. (More on how to figure out your shares in a minute.) But you should also keep your own separate checking accounts, too. Keeping a separate account can be a relationship saver if you've yet to achieve a mind meld on the value of balancing a checkbook. If one of you is a pathological check bouncer and the other takes pride in never having paid a bank penalty or fee, then you don't want to be merging all your accounts. I insist that you share an account that covers your living expenses, but for everything else, you can keep separate accounts.

I also want each of you to always keep your own individual credit card that is in your name only. You are not to allow anyone, including your partner, to be even an authorized user on your card. If you do this and something bad happens—say you split, are divorced, or are widowed—you will still have your own individual credit identity, which will make it possible to get credit and loans on your own.

Enough with the separate piece of this puzzle. Now we need to get into the merger strategy. You and your partner must absolutely commit to having a joint checking account that will be used to pay all your combined living costs. You must take your different incomes into account when deciding how much each person will contribute to the monthly bills. There should be no ad hoc system where one of you covers the rent and the other covers all utilities and groceries. Nor is there to be the lazy solution that you will do a 50/50 bill split. What if you are not making as much money as she is? That wouldn't be fair.

Let's say that one couple's joint living expenses are $3,000 per month. She brings home $1,500 a month and he hauls in $2,500 a month. If you went for the 50/50 solution, she would need to pony up 100 percent of her take-home pay, but he would be on the hook for just 60 percent of his take-home pay. That's a formula for instant discord, if you ask me.

We need a better plan that is based on equal shares, not equal dollar amounts. Figuring this out requires a little bit of math and an open mind.

1. Figure out your combined monthly living costs. Everything from rent/mortgage to utilities, groceries, a few dinners out, insurance, etc. Add 10 percent to that amount; trust me, everyone always underestimates their real costs.

2. Add up your combined monthly take-home pay. (Make sure you are both contributing to a 401(k) plan if there is a company match. If one or both of you isn't, you need to get that taken care of. Then factor in how that will reduce your combined take-home pay.)

3. Divide your expenses by your take-home pay to figure out the percentage of those expenses that each of you are to pay.

Let's see how this works with some real numbers to grab on to:

1. Your combined monthly living costs are $3,000.

2. You bring home $1,500 a month and your partner brings in $2,500. So your total combined income is $4,000.

3. Divide your total income by your total monthly living costs. In this example, divide $3,000 by $4,000. That comes to 75 percent.

4. Multiply your individual take-home pay by 75 percent to determine the amount you are to contribute to the kitty for your shared monthly living costs.

75 percent of $1,500 is $1,125.

75 percent of $2,500 is $1,875.

You should make sure that you each have contributed your "share" into the account at least three business days before you and your honey sit down to pay the bills. Yep, that's the next step toward financial bliss. You must pay those bills together. No excuses. Come on, sign up for online bill pay, and paying bills will cut into less than half an hour of your quality time each month. I want you to do this together so you are both completely up to speed on how the income and outflow are going. If your partner gets grumpy or balks at this arrangement, you should seriously question if this is the right person for you.

As your relationship moves forward, you will inevitably start talking about your shared future goals. It's the next big step; you move from paying bills together to saving together. Once again, you'll need an equitable plan for your contributions that takes into account how much take-home pay you have available to contribute. Remember, it's equal *shares,* not equal *dollars.*

# FINANCIAL TO-DOS BEFORE YOU SAY "I DO"

Before you get caught up in the wedding plans, I hope you'll take the time to think through all the financial decisions that come with formalizing your relationship.

Actually, let me stop for a moment and throw in my two cents on the wedding. If you are YF&B, why are you blowing so much money on a wedding? Whether it is your money or your parents', I am all for a celebration, but I am absolutely amazed when YF&Bers tell me they have no money for a down payment on a home, and then two minutes later tell me about their to-die-for $50,000 or $100,000 wedding. I will never forget a TV show I did with a couple of lovebirds who were about to finance a $30,000 wedding on their credit cards. Their jaws dropped to the floor when I explained that if they just made the minimum payment on that balance, it would take them more than forty years to pay it off.

So how about you and your honey consider keeping the wedding a bit more low-key. If you're paying for it yourselves, you will avoid pushing your credit card balance into the stratosphere. That's my idea of a great wedding present to give each other. Or if Mom and Dad are footing the bill, talk to them about whether they would consider going for a more modest shindig and then using some of their "saved" money to help you with a down payment on a home. Seems to me that's a nice combo of romantic, celebratory, and practical.

Okay, back to the pre-wedding financial planning.

When you marry, you do not take on any of the debt that your spouse amassed before you wed. But everything you accrue during the marriage is a joint responsibility. And not just the stuff on your joint accounts—I mean *everything*. If, after you marry, your spouse opens a credit card account that you know nothing about, and then runs up a $10,000 credit card balance, it's still your problem, even if the account isn't in your name. The credit card company can come after you for payment, even if the card is in only your spouse's name. Romantic, isn't it? I want you to make a simple vow to each other: Twice a year, you will log on to the computer and check both your FICO scores. It's a good practice to make sure all your information is correct and up to date, and this will also assure both of you that there are no new accounts that one of you is in the dark about. Just another reason to make sure you have complete financial trust and respect for each other before you are married.

## PROTECTING YOUR FAMILY

Once someone becomes financially dependent on you, you need life insurance. That dependent could be your partner, who has stopped working and gone back to school, or your kids, or an aging parent who needs some help with the bills. You haven't yet accumulated enough of your own assets (investments, equity in your home, etc.) to take care of your dependents if something happens, so life insurance is your Plan B if you die. Yeah, I know, confronting your own mortality is a real upper. But you cannot afford to tune this out just because you feel healthy and invincible. Anything can happen to any of us at any time. I don't think you need me to get more specific than that, right? So if your death would leave your dependents financially in the lurch, you need to get life insurance. Just think through how your loved ones would handle all their expenses if they didn't have your income to help out.

Before I continue and explain how to buy insurance, I also want to make it very clear who *doesn't* need life insurance. It kills me when I see people wasting money on coverage they don't need. If you are single with no dependents—young or old—do not buy life insurance, even if you're offered a deal at work. You don't need it. And please do not buy life insurance on your kids. This is such a rip-off. If anything were to happen to your kids, the emotional impact on your life would be absolutely devastating, but there would be no financial impact. Life insurance is financial protection, period.

Okay, back to the buying tips. I am going to make it incredibly easy for you. All you need to know is that you are to buy term life insurance. There are a slew of other types of life insurance, such as whole life, universal life, and variable life, which are typically known as cash-value policies. Ignore them. Don't listen to anyone, especially an insurance agent, who tells you that cash-value is better than term. They are flat-out wrong.

Term insurance provides coverage for five, fifteen, twenty, or thirty years. You choose the "term," based on how long you expect that your dependents will rely on you. You want to get a guaranteed level premium, which means your annual cost will not change for the entire policy term. If you die during the term, your beneficiaries get the payout of the death benefit. The beneficiaries usually are your family members or friends who are financially dependent on you. If you die after the term is up, they get nothing. There's a new type of term called "return of premium." I do not want you bothering with this at all. You are to just shop for plain old level term insurance.

The term you choose should take into account how long you need to provide protection. If you are buying the policy to protect your kids, you will usually want a policy that provides coverage until your youngest child is twenty-three years of age, or at least until you feel you will have enough time to accumulate money on your own so that they would have enough to live on if you were to die prematurely. For example, let's say you have two kids, ages five and three. If you want to make sure they are covered until they are through college, a twenty-year level term policy would do the trick. But if your youngest is thirteen years old, you might only need a ten-year level term policy.

Before I get into why I like term life insurance so much, I can't resist laying out just a few reasons why I don't like whole life and other cash-value policies. Unlike a term policy, the insurance in a cash-value policy is in place for the rest of your life. If you keep up with the premium payments while you are alive, your beneficiaries are guaranteed a payout, no matter when you die. And the insurance companies are banking on you living a long time. They study the life expectancy charts and know a YF&Ber today who makes it to age sixty-five has a pretty good chance of sticking around until age eighty-five. That gives the insurance company plenty of time to collect premiums from you; their goal is to eventually earn about three times more from your premiums (the annual payments you make) than they will have to pay out in the death benefit. Oh, sure, some of you may die early, before the insurance company has a chance to collect all its juicy premiums and earn enough from investing that money. But trust me, these folks are good at what they do. They are working on the law of averages, and they have a long history of making nice, fat profits by playing those odds correctly and getting you to pay big premiums for a very long time.

But here is what you really need to know about life insurance. Life insurance was never meant to be a permanent need. It is only meant to be there temporarily until you can build up enough of your own assets to take care of the people dependent on you if you were to die. A term policy gives you coverage for the time when you need it, period.

But if you simply listen to an agent, they are going to push hard for the cash-value policy. That's because the premium can be five times or more the cost of a term policy. Since agents can collect 90 percent of the first-year premium of a cash-value policy as a commission, the more expensive your premium, the more they will pocket.

How about we put this in dollar terms? Let's say you are a healthy thirty-year-old guy. A $500,000 universal life policy (I'll show you how to figure out the right amount for you in a sec) has an annual premium of $1,850. A $500,000 term policy that lasts for twenty years will run that same healthy guy about $360 a year. That $360 a year will give you every bit of coverage you need and none of the coverage that you don't need. And it's about $1,500 less a year. Given that you're YF&B, I figure you'll be glad to "save" $1,500. Even if you did have $1,500 burning a hole in your pocket, I could come up with about a million ideas for that money before I would entertain the purchase of a cash-value policy. For example, invest $1,500 a year in a Roth IRA for twenty years and you will have more than $66,000, assuming you earn an 8 percent average annual return. Or you could use the money to pay off a car loan or credit card debt, or to save for a down payment on a home.

'Nuff said. Term it is, right?

# STRATEGY SESSIONS

**PROBLEM:**

I am dating someone who I really like personally but hate financially. I can't deal with the debt, bounced checks, and crazy spending.

**SOLUTION:**

The way someone handles money is a personal character trait. A lack of respect for money is a powerful signal that can't be ignored.

It's amazing how we try to rationalize and compartmentalize when we are dating. We are so eager to focus on the positive that we gloss over the problems. Yet the problems are just as much a part of someone's personality as all the good stuff that attracted you to him or her in the first place. So if you are dating someone who has absolutely no respect for money, I have to tell you that that's someone who isn't going to respect you, either. Oh sure, he or she may have a great personality and be a lot of fun to hang out with—hey, with that carefree attitude about credit card debt, he or she is no doubt the life of the party—but he or she is also terribly irresponsible.

But I know it's so hard to listen to your head when your heart is pounding. So how about you sit down for a talk? This problem is not going to vanish on its own; the only chance you have is if you open the lines of communication and start talking.

Leading with "I hate how you handle your finances" is not a good conversation starter. It is an attack. That's not what you're going for. The right spin would be "You don't seem to worry about running up huge credit card bills with your spending. Do you ever get worried about how much money you owe, and what you're spending on interest?" Your delivery is to be stripped of any bite or edge.

The goal is to invite conversation, not incite confrontation.

Maybe you'll get an answer that confirms your fears, but maybe you'll learn something interesting. Perhaps your new lover is merely repeating behaviors taught by his or her parents; what's troubling to you is "normal" to your partner. Or maybe you'll get this answer: "Yeah, I just feel so out of control. I want to do better, but I don't know where to start." In both those responses, there is room for you to talk to your partner about changing. With compassion and understanding, you can lay out your feelings about money and why it is so important to you that your partner start a financial reform program. Welcome to the world of financial intimacy!

Now, of course, one conversation is not going to do the trick. You are embarking on an ongoing conversation. And don't make it the central issue of your relationship, either. Just fit it in as one of the areas you are exploring together. You are there to help but without being overbearing. Look for ways you can encourage new behavior. If your partner always insists on going out to eat every night, why not suggest that you start eating in together three nights a week? One night you cook, one night your partner cooks, and one night you cook together. If you're not kitchen-inclined, head to the bookstore together and find a fun, simple cookbook for folks just like you. You get the point. Create opportunities to help curb the spending. Quite often, what you come up with can be even more fun and intimate while costing you less.

If you are seeing progress, be patient but firm. Be very specific about what constitutes deal-breakers for the relationship. If your partner truly loves you, it will not be hard to make the changes to keep you. If not, then you know it's time to leave. Someone who is not able to treat their money with respect will ultimately be unable to give you the respect you deserve.

**PROBLEM:**
I want to ask my brother for a loan, but I don't want money stuff to mess with our great relationship.

**SOLUTION:**
Make your brother comfortable by offering loan terms that show you respect him and the value of his money.

Asking for a loan from friends or family members is one of the trickiest balancing acts you will ever encounter in your financial life. The repercussions of a deal gone bad are not merely financial; they can ruin the most treasured relationships you have. Let's face it, you turn to your family and friends when you've got no other option, right? They are your safety net.

That's okay, but what kills me is when I see so many people ask a dear friend or family member for a loan and then treat them like crap. You get your brother to loan you money and then you don't sweat it if you never pay him back. You figure blood is thicker than money. I am here to tell you that's not the case. How you handle that loan says everything about how much love and respect you have for your brother. If you don't pay him back on time, whenever you see your brother you will feel so small and embarrassed, and your brother will feel so let-down.

So if you really feel the need to ask a bud or family member for a loan, it is all on your back not to screw up the relationship. Here's how to negotiate a loan and keep the relationship intact.

You are to only ask for money that is for a truly important financial need. Asking for $5,000 for the down payment on a hot new car? I don't think so. Asking for $5,000 so you can get your credit card balance paid off and start saving for a down payment on a house? Now you're talking.

The fact that your brother or best friend would do anything for you is not a good enough reason to ask him or her for money. It is your responsibility to ask only if you know the person can truly afford it. If loaning money to you will be a stretch, don't even ask. That's just selfish.

If you have family members or friends who can loan you the money, you are to treat them as if they were loan officers at a bank. Show them what a great client you will be.

There is to be nothing casual about a loan agreement. Put it in writing, and be as specific as possible. I want you to lay out the exact terms of the loan: when you will start paying it back, how often you will make payments (weekly, monthly, quarterly), on what day of the month you will make the payments, and what interest rate you will pay. Yep, you are to pay interest. First, it shows your respect for their money. And it's actually required by Uncle Sam. If you don't charge interest, the money could be considered a gift rather than a loan. And the IRS will slap a gift tax on anyone who gives someone more than $11,000 in a single year. You can pay a low interest rate, but you must pay something.

If possible, you should also offer to "protect" the person who is lending you the money, in the event that you die before the loan is paid back. If you own a home, one possibility is to suggest that the person loaning you the money put a lien on your house for the amount of the loan. This would ensure that if you die, they would be entitled to repayment from any assets in your estate. Or if you have a life insurance policy, offer to put the person loaning you the money on the policy as as a beneficiary for the amount of the loan. It's just another way to offer protection.

The bottom line is that you are putting the most precious of gifts—the love of a family member or friend—on the line. Yeah, the $5,000 you need might not be more than a rounding error on the checking account of your super-rich brother, but it's not so much about the money. It's about how respectful and responsible you are. If you blow it, you are going to do irreparable damage to the relationship.

**PROBLEM:**
My partner and I both work, but now that our first baby is on the way, I want to stay at home, even though I'm worried about not contributing to our income anymore.

**SOLUTION:**
Hello? You'll be contributing a ton to the relationship. Make sure you and your partner realize that before you stop working.

This is one topic that I wish couples would talk through early in a relationship. Once the baby is on the way, it is too late to start the conversation. You need to dig deep and really make sure that you both agree that it is a good thing for one of you to stay home, and that you both respect that you both will still be providing equally for the relationship. The partner who keeps working will provide the financial means for the family to thrive. The partner who is staying home will provide the environment for the family to thrive emotionally. Both are work, and both are of equal value in your relationship. If you and your partner aren't in sync on that, you're going to create a lot of stress.

Even if you agree that it's a great idea for one of you to stay home, that doesn't mean it will be feasible. You and your partner must sit down months before you plan to make this decision and walk through the logistics. On one income, will you still be able to pay all your bills and keep up with your investing? Sure, having one of you stay at home will cause some costs to shrink—you've cut out commuting and professional wardrobe costs for one of you. But that's going to be more than offset by the extra cost of raising your kid(s). Be very careful in figuring out how the change will affect your family's finances. Maybe you decide that the partner who will continue to work needs to get a new, higher-paying job for your plan to make sense. Or perhaps you agree that you need to move to a less expensive home and area, so you can truly afford this huge lifestyle change.

If you both decide that this is the right move for your family, I want you to have a serious talk about how the stay-at-home partner is going to continue to have income. In a more perfect world, stay-at-home partners would be getting big, fat salaries to match their huge jobs. Instead, they end up with a feeling of less value because they don't have a paycheck to deposit every two weeks. And that's compounded by having to ask their "working" partner for money. You are not to fall into that trap. You are to agree ahead of time how much of your joint disposable income (what you have after paying your bills) is to be deposited in the stay-at-home's checking account each month. It is to be an automatic deposit, so there will be no need for one partner to have to remind the other partner every month. The point is that the stay-at-home partner is to have a fair share (see, there we go again) of any disposable income. All the other family costs can continue to come out of the joint account.

## PROBLEM:

My parents will not talk about money. I am worried that they are spending more money than they have and that I will be responsible for all the debt they leave behind.

## SOLUTION:

You aren't personally responsible for their debt, but their estate will need to pay off any debt before doling out any assets that you inherit.

Unless you cosigned for any of your parents' loans or credit cards, you are not at all responsible for their debts. But their "estate" is. Let's say they die with $20,000 in credit card debt and $30,000 in a home equity line of credit. The credit card company and the HELOC lender have every right to get repaid. Any assets your parents left behind—their estate—will first be used to pay off the $50,000 in debt. If they leave behind enough cash to cover those debts, great. But if not, you will have to sell every asset they have, including the house and its contents, to come up with the money to pay off the debt. If, after you sell off everything, there are still unpaid debts, don't worry. You're not on the hook.

But to be honest, you need to be more concerned about the impact their debt is going to have on you while they are alive. If your parents are in a huge financial mess, that is going to become your mess pretty soon. They sound so out of control that it wouldn't surprise me (or you) if they screw up and fall behind on their mortgage or a home equity line of credit. If they lose the house, they will be a knockin' on your door. Are you ready to have your parents move in, broke and penniless, just when you are beginning to move out of your own broke-and-penniless years? You've also got to be concerned that if they are such big spenders, they are also probably lousy savers. So when they retire, they aren't going to have nest eggs to live off of. If they are old and broke, you are going to stay young and broke longer, because you will need to take care of them.

Look, I know you still see yourself as just a kid when it comes to family dynamics. But you are the adult here. The fact that you are reading this book is evidence that you know how important it is to be financially responsible. Now it's time for a bit of role reversal; you are to teach your parents well. With care and respect, you need to let them know that you won't be up for taking care of them financially if they don't first make a serious attempt to take care of themselves. In a way, your parents are the other "relationship" in your life where you need to create financial intimacy. That means opening up the conversation lines and expressing with love your concern for their future. Explain why they need to get their credit card debt under control, and why they should pay off the mortgage if they are in a home in which they intend to retire. Hell, give them this book. The advice on credit card management, mortgages, and investing is just as useful for them as it is for you.

**PROBLEM:**
My partner says we need to start saving for our kids' college educations right now, but we can barely pay our own bills.

**SOLUTION:**
You need to save for your retirement before you save for your kids' college costs.

There are plenty of loans and scholarships for college. But there is absolutely no loan available to help you finance your retirement. That means you must save for your retirement before you tackle saving for your kids' college costs. And, my goodness, you never are to run up a credit card balance or not pay all your bills so you have money to put in a college fund. That's insane.

I know you want the best for your children, and you are convinced that good parenting means footing the bill for your kids' college costs. But if the only way you can do that is to ignore saving for your own future, or to take out a massive home equity line of credit, you get a big fat F in parenting. Let's fast forward thirty years. Your kids are done with college, and you are oh, so proud you paid for it all. But now you're fifty-five, and you have zero in your retirement kitty and a $50,000 HELOC that you used for the last two years of college costs. You aren't worried, though, because you are at the point where your career is going gangbusters, and you figure you will be able to rake in enough income in the next ten years to get everything taken care of before you retire....

Except that you get laid off. The only job you can find is for much lower pay. But that's not going to work, because you still have that HELOC to pay off. So you go back to your kids and say you need help. If they are in their YF&B years, how much help do you think they will be?

Do not let your incredible love for your children fog your decision-making. One of the greatest lessons you can hand down to your kids is how to be financially responsible. I think staying focused on your long-term needs is the best lesson, and gift, you can give your kids.

You can also use this as a great opportunity to teach them about their own financial power. When they are ten or twelve years old, start talking to them about your situation: that you expect to be able to contribute a portion of their college costs, but not all of them. You will not be letting them down. You will be letting them in on what it's going to take. Teach them that the better they do in school, the more scholarships they will be in line for, and that a part-time job when they turn fourteen or fifteen is a great way for them to save up a little for school. Any shortfall you can deal with together, by taking out loans that are made available to both students and their parents.

## PROBLEM:
My ex claimed bankruptcy after we got divorced, and the debt collectors are coming after me to pay his bills.

### SOLUTION:
You are responsible only for debt he rang up during the marriage.

When you say "I do," one of the vows should be that you understand that you are taking on the financial behavior of your spouse. Every penny your spouse runs up during the marriage (but not before or after) is your responsibility—even debt you didn't know about. A secret credit card account to wine and dine an extramarital affair is still "joint" debt if the money was spent while you were married.

If the debt collectors are coming after you for money that your ex spent after the divorce, you just need to wave that divorce decree in front of their faces. Typically, the date of separation stated in the decree serves as the end date for your financial responsibility for your spouse. If debt collectors continue to bug you, file a formal

When you say "I do," one of the vows should be that you understand that you are taking on the financial behavior of your spouse.

complaint with the Federal Trade Commission. You can reach the FTC at www.FTC.gov or 877-382-4357.

But you can also do a lot to minimize the chances that your ex will cause you these huge financial headaches. Hopefully, you already have at least one credit card in your name only; if not, get one ASAP. If there are no outstanding balances on your joint accounts, I want you to close the accounts. Yes, this is going to hurt your FICO score, because you are wiping out some of your credit history, but in this case, taking that small hit is worth it (your credit history accounts for 15 percent of your FICO score). You should also send a letter to any professionals that you use on a regular basis, such as lawyers and doctors, to make sure they know you are separated and will no longer be responsible for any charges incurred by your soon-to-be ex. And please, if you retain the house as part of the divorce, make sure you refinance the mortgage so it is in your name only and get the title on the house changed the minute the divorce is finalized. That is one huge asset that you don't want your ex's name to remain on.

**PROBLEM:**
My mom wants to leave her house to me; we don't know if a will is all we need or if it makes sense to pay for her to leave the house to me in a trust.

**SOLUTION:**
A will may seem less expensive to create, but it will cost you more once your mom passes. A trust is the better move.

There's a dangerous misconception that all anyone needs to do is spend a few hundred dollars to have a simple will that spells out who inherits what. That's just flat-out bad advice.

Let's say Mom's house is worth $200,000, and she has $190,000 left on the mortgage. She leaves the house to you in a will. But when she dies, you discover that the title to the house is still in her name. Mom isn't around to "sign" the title of the house over to you, so that means you will need a judge to bless your inheritance by approving the will and signing the title over to you. This process is known as probate.

Not only can it take months (or even a few years) for a will to work its way through probate court, it can also cost you some serious money. You will need to hire a lawyer to represent you in probate court. Whenever you see the word "court," there are filing fees and legal fees to deal with. There are also probate fees you will have to pay to the lawyer and the executor of the will, based on the value of the assets that are going through the probate process. That fee will be based on the value of the house ($200,000), not the equity you have (just $10,000). In California, that could come to a fee of about $10,000. If you are the executor of the will, you would still have to pay half of the amount to the lawyer, so that reduces your hit from $10,000 to a still-hefty $5,000. You can see why lawyers love wills; they can lead to nice probate fees.

Given that you may be YF&B when you inherit an asset via a will, you could be in big trouble. You're not going to have the cash to cover those costs. So guess what? You might have to sell the house and use the proceeds to settle up with the lawyer.

Instead, I want you to save yourself the time and cost of probate by having your mom put the house in a living revocable trust.

Let's break this down into nice, manageable bites. The word "trust" refers to the document itself. "Living" refers to the fact that it kicks into affect while you are living. That's the first big difference between a trust and a will; the will comes into play only once you pass. "Revocable" means you can make changes to the trust any old time. Nothing is written in indelible ink here. The person who creates the trust is the trustor. In this example, that's Mom. And we're going to have Mom stay in control of the trust while she is alive. So that makes her the "trustee." And Mom is the beneficiary of the trust while she is alive. She should name a "successor trustee" who can take over when she dies or if she becomes too ill to take care of things herself (more on this soon). And she needs to name a beneficiary for when she dies; in this case, it would be you.

Once the trust is set up, Mom's lawyer, or Mom herself, "funds" the trust by transferring the title of all her assets to the name of the trust, so it becomes the Mom Trust, with Mom as trustee. In reality, nothing changes. She still owns every asset in the trust, because she is in charge of the trust. But when she dies, rather than needing to transfer the title of her assets to you, it's already taken care of. The assets are in the "name" of the trust, and you take possession of the assets because you are named as the beneficiary who succeeds your mother. There is no need to hire a lawyer and go through the often-costly probate process.

Now, I know some of you are saying you don't need this; you don't have kids to leave your assets to, so a simple will is all you need. Not so fast. As I mentioned earlier, the will only kicks in when you die. What if you fall into a coma or become too ill at some juncture to take care of your financial assets? A will ain't going to help out. But a trust that includes an incapacity clause will provide perfect protection for you. You will be the trustee of your trust, but if you become incapacitated, the person you have designated as your successor trustee can take over and handle the assets in the trust. You can make absolutely anyone your successor trustee: your partner, your parent, your sibling, even a friend. Just make sure it is someone you trust to make the best decisions for your family.

While we're on the subject of incapacity, I also want you to have a durable power of attorney (DPOA) for health care. In this document, you spell out what your wishes are in regard to life support and other medical issues if you cannot make those decisions for yourself. You do this by appointing an "agent" to represent your wishes if you are unable to express them yourself. With a DPOA for health care, both the doctors and the entire family have your wishes in writing, and it clearly designates who you want to represent you in those tough conversations. Now, while I know you think nothing can happen to you, the minute you have a family, your job is to anticipate any potential situation that could cause hardship for your loved ones. And no one is invincible. Let's say you are in a tragic accident that leaves you on

YF&B

On my website, you can get a DPOA form for free.

life support. If your wish is that in such a tragic situation you be taken off life support, the only way it can happen is if you have spelled out your position in a DPOA for health care. And the "agent" you appoint for the DPOA for health care will represent your position with the staff at the hospital. Although you only appoint one agent, I recommend discussing your DPOA for health care with all your family members so everyone clearly knows what you want to happen.

**PROBLEM:**
We are hearing all sorts of conflicting advice on how big a life insurance policy we need; it's all so confusing, we don't know if we will have too much or too little.

**SOLUTION:**
I have a simple formula that is super-conservative. If you don't yet have any other big assets you can rely on, your death benefit should be twenty times what your loved ones need to live on each year.

There are all sorts of formulas that can be used to figure out how big a death benefit you should have for your term life policy. But I have a fairly straightforward way to estimate what you need: take the amount of money that you want to replace and multiply by twenty. So if your family currently needs $35,000 a year to live on, then I would suggest buying a policy with a $700,000 death benefit ($35,000 x 20). This formula works whether your loved ones need $35,000 or $135,000 a year. Now, I know a $700,000 death benefit sounds like it would be way too expensive, but for a healthy thirty-year-old male, it could run about $450 a year. That's less than $40 a month. Not so bad, eh?

Let me explain why I want you to aim for a death benefit that is twenty times the amount of money you feel your loved ones will need in a year. That's a lot higher than most folks would tell you. But I want your family to be truly secure. The whole idea with insurance is to assume the worst (your premature death) and make sure your loved ones will be okay financially. The best way to do that is to give them a death benefit that assures that they will never have to work. Maybe they are too devastated by the loss, or perhaps it was a horrible car accident that killed you and severely injured them. Sorry for being so bleak, but that's what's required when you are figuring out life insurance.

So you want the death benefit to be big enough that your beneficiaries can invest it conservatively and generate enough annual income that they will never need to touch the principal (the death benefit amount). I think a 5 percent return is a reasonable return to aim for. If we multiply $700,000 by 5 percent (0.05), we get $35,000. Your beneficiaries have replaced your income without having to touch the principal.

Websites such as www.selectquote.com, www.accuquote.com, and www.term4sale.com are good resources where you can shop for term policies. I would be careful about relying only on life insurance that is offered through your employer. If your employer foots the bill for the policy, that's a nice perk that you shouldn't pass up, but I also doubt it will be a sufficient amount to cover all your needs. So you may need to buy additional term insurance to make sure your loved ones are truly protected. If you have to pay for the insurance offered through your company, do some shopping around. Quite often, you can get a better deal on your own than you would if you opt for the group policy offered through work. If you are in the U.S. military, check the deals offered through your armed services division; as you age, the military policies can beat what is available in the general insurance market.

**PROBLEM:**
I have been married for almost ten years, and as a stay-at-home parent, I don't know what I need to do to protect myself financially if I choose to divorce my spouse.

**SOLUTION:**
Hang in there until you have a full ten years of marriage; it could make a big difference in your retirement.

I know I said earlier in the book that you shouldn't count on Social Security for your retirement years (see page 176), but you still want to make sure you are in line to receive as much as possible, no matter how much they scale it back in the coming years.

The length of time you are married has a large impact on the benefits you will receive. If your soon-to-be ex earns more than you do, you want to be able to get Social Security benefits that are based on your ex's salary. And to get those benefits, you have to have been married at least ten years. So if you are anywhere near that big anniversary, I would try to tough it out a bit longer.

It's also important to understand that in most states, the date that you separate is considered the final date of your marriage. But when it comes to figuring out your eligibility for Social Security benefits, the actual divorce date is used as the end date of the marriage. So be careful. If you divorce before the ten-year mark, you could put your Social Security at risk. Your separation date can also affect your share of any year-end bonuses. Let's say you separate in November, your partner gets a big bonus in December, and your divorce becomes final the following June. Because you separated before the bonus was paid, you may have no claim to a portion of the bonus, even though the divorce didn't become final until seven months after the bonus was paid.

At the point that you separate, you will want to close all joint checking accounts and divide the assets. Same with any joint credit cards, or any card you have on which your partner is listed as an authorized user. This can get thorny if there is a balance on your cards. You need to have your respective lawyers hash out how the debt will be shared. But at the very least, put a freeze on the account to prevent either of you from making any additional charges on the account. And during the divorce proceedings, make sure the minimum balance due gets paid on time. I also want you to make copies of all important financial documents, such as investment statements and credit card statements. It can be especially helpful to have the most recent credit card statement at the point that you separate. That helps your lawyer—and the courts—determine your share of any outstanding balances when the marriage ends.

You need to keep track of your spending during the separation—those costs will be part of the final agreement. Your lawyer will also work with you, and with your partner's lawyer, to determine the value of your combined assets and to negotiate a settlement. If you live in a community-property state, the assets (and debts) are split 50/50. And you should have your lawyer carefully walk you through the difference between receiving alimony and receiving a onetime settlement. It's often tempting to go for the closure that comes from a lump-sum settlement, but you may be shortchanging yourself over the long term.

**PROBLEM:**
I am about to remarry and want to make sure the house I own now ultimately goes to my kids, even if I die before my new husband does.

**SOLUTION:**
Pre-nups are a must for all second marriages.

I have to come clean on something. A few pages ago, when I talked about financial issues to consider before you marry, I thought long and hard about making my pitch for everyone to get a pre-nuptial agreement. As important as I think they are, and I think everyone should have one, I realized that the $2,000 or so it would take each of you to hire your own lawyers when you are YF&B wasn't going to fly. So that's why I didn't push the pre-nups for the truly YF&B.

But if we're talking about your second marriage, I get to assume that you may have assets and children that you want to financially protect, so a pre-nup becomes a nonnegotiable necessity.

For a pre-nup to stand up in court, you will both want to hire your own lawyers, and everyone, the lawyers included, is to sign the final document. In some states, the document also needs to be notarized. If you ever move to another state during the marriage, have a lawyer in your new state review the document and make any necessary adjustments.

Do not create a pre-nup on the way to the wedding. It needs to be done well in advance of the marriage, in a calm environment. What you want to avoid is either one of you saying down the line that you were rushed into signing the document during a stressful time, and therefore it should not be enforced.

You can include every financial issue in your pre-nup: debts and assets. For example, you are both responsible for credit card debt accrued on a joint credit card account during the marriage, but in a pre-nup, you can make it clear that neither of you will have any responsibility for debt run up on a credit card that is solely in the other spouse's name, even if the debt was accrued during the marriage. That said, getting this to hold up in court can be tricky; you need a good lawyer to help you draw up the agreement and get it recorded, and you may need to file written statements with the creditors to make it abundantly clear which debts you are responsible for.

On the asset side, anything goes. You can spell out how you want to divide basic investments, such as mutual-fund accounts, stocks and bonds, and the future value of any stock options you may be granted. The puppy is fair game to be included in a pre-nup, as is artwork, jewelry, and any valuable collectibles you snag on eBay.

When it comes to your house, you'll need a lawyer to lay out the pre-nup according to the rules in your state. In some states, you must leave a portion of all your assets to your spouse. But you can still make sure that your kids are included, too. Spell out in the pre-nup that you want your kids to inherit whatever portion of your home you are not required by law to pass to your spouse. You can stipulate that if your new husband survives you, he can remain in the house for as long as he wants. The kids are to inherit the house only after he moves or dies. Be super-careful that you keep the title to the house solely in your name. If you switch it to **joint tenancy with right of survivorship**—a common way that couples own assets together—that agreement supercedes any wishes you lay out in the pre-nup or trust. And with a JTWROS agreement, the surviving spouse (in this example, your new hubby) will become the sole owner of the home when you die. Then, when he dies, the inheritance of the house would be determined by what he says in his trust or will. If he doesn't specifically name your kids as the heirs, then your kids are effectively disinherited. Keep the title to the house in your name only, don't use the JTWROS route, and spell it all out in the pre-nup.

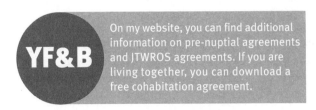

On my website, you can find additional information on pre-nuptial agreements and JTWROS agreements. If you are living together, you can download a free cohabitation agreement.

YF&B

Do not create a pre-nup
on the way to the wedding.
It needs to be done well in
advance of the marriage.

A solid relationship requires financial intimacy. That means no secrets, and merging your money as well as your lives.

You want to merge but not completely lose your personal financial identity. Always keep a checking account and at least one credit card in your name only. It is a healthy amount of independence, and it will also protect you if your relationship ends.

All living expenses are to be paid out of a joint checking account.

To split your expenses fairly, calculate your monthly combined living expenses and divide this by your combined take-home pay. Take that percentage and multiply it by your individual take-home pay. That is how much you are to contribute to pay your joint living expenses.

Once you have anyone dependent on you—a partner, a kid, or even an elderly parent—you need term insurance. To play it safe, consider buying coverage that is twenty times your current salary. Do not listen to anyone who tries to sell you a cash-value policy.

A living revocable trust that includes a durable power of attorney with an incapacity clause is the best way to protect your heirs. A will may be cheaper to draw up, but it can end up costing your heirs a ton of money and time to get it approved.

Before you agree to loan money to a family member or friend, make sure you understand the emotional and financial risk you are taking. If you can't afford (emotionally or financially) for the loan not to be repaid, just say no.

don't

do it

I can't end this book without a small dose of what I call "Suzefication," so you're going to have to indulge me for just a moment. I have a saying that your parents have probably heard me say time and again, but it's important for you to hear it now, too, after we've spent more than three hundred pages figuring out how to move you past broke. It goes: *People first. Then money. Then things.* So what's it mean? The nature of money is that it will come and go in your life. And the last time I checked, there's no way you can take a penny of it with you when you finally exit this world. I can also promise you that when you are on your deathbed, you are not going to be thinking about how great your life would have been if only you had bought that latest and greatest car, plasma TV, or fabulous outfit you always wanted.

There's a lot more to life. And the first person you need to focus on—to truly value—is yourself. If you were motivated enough to read this book, I know you have what it takes to master your career and your finances. You just need to give yourself some time to put your plan into action.

I hope you feel that I have delivered on my promise to equip you with the info it takes to handle your finances, as well as new solutions that deal with the realities of being YF&B. Yet for all the action plans I have laid out here, I am also quite aware that one of the best bits of advice I can leave you with is to tell you what *not* to do. Simply avoiding bad financial moves will have a huge impact on your bottom line and the quality of your life, so I'm going to offer up a "Do Not" list. If you follow this list, I can promise you that your route to financial security is going to be faster, smoother, and more permanent.

# do not...

**SCREW UP YOUR FICO SCORE.** It's your winning ticket to every financial move you will ever make when you need to borrow money for car loans, mortgages, or credit cards.

**FOCUS ON YOUR PAYCHECK.** Instead, focus on making your mark.

**MISS A CREDIT CARD PAYMENT.** Always pay at least the minimum on time.

**THINK YOU CAN BACK OUT OF REPAYING YOUR STUDENT LOANS.** Your lender will track you down, and you will need to repay sooner or later; not even bankruptcy will protect you.

**START A SAVINGS ACCOUNT IF YOU STILL HAVE HIGH-RATE CREDIT CARD DEBT.** Get the debt paid off first.

**INVEST MONEY THAT YOU'LL NEED IN LESS THAN FIVE YEARS IN STOCKS.** Use CDs and money markets for savings that you intend to tap for a shorter-term goal.

**PASS UP YOUR EMPLOYER'S 401(k) OR 403(b) COMPANY MATCH.** It's free money.

**TAKE A LOAN FROM YOUR 401(k) PLAN TO PAY OFF YOUR CREDIT CARD DEBT.** You will end up paying tax twice on the loan amount.

**INVEST IN A MUTUAL FUND WITH THE LETTER A OR B AT THE END OF ITS NAME.** That's a sign that there will be a sales commission attached—it can be 5 percent. That's a silly waste of your money.

**PURCHASE A VARIABLE ANNUITY.** This investment makes a lot of money for your financial adviser, but not for you. Just say no thanks to anyone who offers you one.

**LEASE A CAR.** Finance it instead.

**TAKE OUT AN INTEREST-ONLY OR NO-DOWN-PAYMENT MORTGAGE.** If you have to use either of these options, it's a sign that you really can't afford to own a home just yet.

**USE AN ADJUSTABLE-RATE MORTGAGE** if you intend to stay in the house for more than a year or two. A hybrid or fixed-rate mortgage is safer.

**PAY OFF YOUR CREDIT CARD DEBT WITH A HOME EQUITY LOAN (HEL) OR HOME EQUITY LINE OF CREDIT (HELOC).** Transferring an unsecured debt to a secured one makes no sense at all.

**ASK A FRIEND OR FAMILY MEMBER FOR A LOAN** unless you are confident that you can pay it off. No amount of money can buy back a busted relationship if you flake on repaying.

**THINK OF BANKRUPTCY AS THE LIFE RAFT THAT WILL SAVE YOU.** The financial and emotional impact of bankruptcy is devastating. Work with a credit counseling agency to devise a plan to pay your way out of your financial hole.

**BUY WHOLE LIFE OR ANY OTHER TYPE OF CASH-VALUE LIFE INSURANCE.** Stick with term insurance, and only buy insurance if someone is financially dependent on you.

**RELY ON A WILL.** A living revocable trust, along with a durable power of attorney with an incapacity clause, will give you and your family the best protection.

Okay, that's a big enough list for you to concentrate on at this point in your life. But whenever you're stuck wondering if a financial move is a do or a don't, or if you need some guidance, don't forget about the YF&B section of my website, **www.suzeorman.com**, where you can get more personalized information and exchange tips and questions with other YF&Bers.

So, my job is done, and now yours begins. Don't worry—you have more than what it takes to create anything and everything that you want. Never forget that.

Now get out there and create some magic in that young and fabulous life of yours.

**GLOSSARY**

**A-share fund:** Shares of a mutual fund that stick you with a sales commission when you invest. The commission is used to pay the broker or adviser who sells you the fund. A typical A-share commission—also known as a "sales load"—is 4.5 to 5 percent. YF&B ADVICE: Never pay a sales load. Invest in no-load mutual funds.

**Actively managed fund:** A mutual fund where a manager, or multiple managers, makes daily decisions about which stocks to buy, sell, and hold in the fund portfolio. YF&B ADVICE: Index funds are unmanaged. Because of their lower costs, index funds can often be a better investment than an actively managed fund.

**Actual cash value coverage:** A provision in a home insurance policy that pays you just the market value of your home and depreciated value of your insured possessions. YF&B ADVICE: Forget ACV when insuring your home. You want a replacement-cost-value policy so you will be paid what it costs to rebuild your home and replace damaged possessions.

**Adjustable-rate mortgage (ARM):** A type of home loan where the interest rate can be adjusted by the lender, based on what is happening with interest rates in the general economy. YF&B ADVICE: Even though ARMs offer enticing low rates, be very careful. You could get hit with as much as a 2 percent bump in a single year, and a max 6 percent boost over the life of the loan. Fixed-rate mortgages and hybrid mortgages are less risky.

**After-tax:** What remains after Uncle Sam takes his bite out of your earnings. YF&B ADVICE: Investing isn't simply about what your investments earn—what you keep on an after-tax basis is what matters. While your 401(k) contribution is made with pretax dollars, when you go to withdraw your money, it will be taxed at your ordinary income tax rate, thereby reducing your after-tax gain. Conversely, Roth IRA contributions are made with after-tax money—so there is no up-front tax break, but your qualified withdrawals are absolutely tax-free; that can make a Roth a better investment over the very long term than a 401(k).

**Amortization schedule:** The scary-looking spreadsheet you get when you take out a mortgage; it shows you how much of each monthly payment goes toward paying off your principal and how much goes to paying interest. YF&B ADVICE: Check out the total interest charges over the life of your loan; once you are in a home you intend to stay in, speeding up your principal payments can save you thousands of dollars in interest charges, because you will get the loan paid off faster.

**Annual percentage rate (APR):** A confusing interest rate on mortgages, car loans, and even your credit cards; it includes additional fees you pay. All mortgage lenders must show you the APR next to your standard interest rate. YF&B ADVICE: Forget the APR when comparing mortgages; it is based on the assumption that you will remain in the house for the entire length of the mortgage. Just stick with the straight interest rate.

**Average annual return:** A way of expressing the long-term performance of an asset (such as a stock, mutual fund, or piece of real estate) that converts the total performance over many years into an annual average. YF&B ADVICE: A 10 percent annualized return over five years does not mean you earned exactly 10 percent in each of those five separate calendar years. You may have been up 20 percent in one year and down 7 percent in another year.

**Average daily balance method:** The arcane math that credit card companies use to calculate the balance on your credit card when you run past the grace period and owe interest. YF&B ADVICE: If you carry an unpaid balance from time to time, make sure your card uses this billing method; it is less expensive than the two-cycle average daily balance method.

**B-share fund:** Shares of a mutual fund that stick you with a high annual expense ratio and a commission if you try to sell the shares within a defined period of time (typically, five years). Also known as "contingent deferred sales charge funds" and "back-end load funds." The surrender fee can be 5 percent or so if you leave after one year, 4 percent after two years, etc. YF&B ADVICE: Just like A-share funds, B-share funds are too expensive. Stick with no-load funds with low expense ratios.

**Back-end load fund:** A mutual fund that charges you a commission when you sell your shares (see **B-share fund**). YF&B ADVICE: Loads are a load of you-know-what. Stick with no-load funds.

**Balance transfer:** Moving your credit card balance from one card to another card. YF&B ADVICE: Doing a balance transfer from a card you pay high interest on to a new card with a zero-percent interest charge—or low rate—is one of the keys to smart debt management.

**Bankruptcy:** The legal process of petitioning the courts to make your creditors "forgive" your debts. YF&B ADVICE: Bankruptcy is only a last-ditch resort. It will ruin your FICO score for years. Work with a consumer credit counseling agency and try to dig out of your debt rather than fall into bankruptcy.

**Biweekly mortgage:** A commitment to make half your mortgage payment every two weeks rather than the entire payment once a month. The net effect is that you make the equivalent of thirteen monthly payments. That can reduce a thirty-year mortgage to 24.7 years, saving you interest costs over the life of the mortgage because you are paying it off faster. YF&B ADVICE: Fugghedaboudit. Lenders can charge $500 to set up this plan, plus an administrative fee for each payment. You can do it yourself—for free—by sending in the equivalent of one extra monthly payment per year. But do this only if you plan to stay in your home forever; there's no need to speed up payments on a home that you intend to sell in a few years.

**Blend fund:** A stock mutual fund that combines the growth and value investment styles. YF&B ADVICE: For one-stop shopping, a total market stock index fund is a blend fund that further diversifies for you because it includes small-cap, mid-cap, and large-cap stocks.

**Bond:** A way for corporations and governments to borrow money. You buy a bond, and the issuer agrees to pay interest on the principal (what you invested to buy the bond) until the bond reaches maturity and the principal is returned to the investor. YF&B ADVICE: Bonds issued by the U.S. Treasury are the safest type of bonds, because there is no risk that the U.S. government will punk out on its payments, which can happen to a corporation that runs into financial trouble.

**Capital gains tax:** A federal tax levied when you sell an asset, such as a stock, bond, or piece of real estate. Assets that you owned for at least one year before you sell are eligible for the long-term capital gains tax rate, which is 5 percent for individuals in the 15 percent income tax bracket or lower, and currently 15 percent for everyone in a higher income tax bracket. If you have assets that you have held for less than twelve months, you must pay the short-term capital gains tax, which is simply your income tax rate. When you sell a home, the first $250,000 in gain (or $500,000, if you are a married couple filing a joint return) is exempt from this tax. YF&B ADVICE: Know that the current tax law reverts this capital gains tax to 20 percent in 2009.

**Capital loss:** In a rare bit of empathy, Uncle Sam helps out when you sell an investment at a loss. Any asset you sell for less than your original purchase price is a capital loss that can be used to offset any capital gains that you have made in the same tax year. If you have no gains to report, then you can subtract your loss from your ordinary income, which will lower your taxable income. YF&B ADVICE: Only $3,000 per year in capital losses can be applied to offset ordinary income. If your loss is bigger than the $3K, you get to use the leftovers in subsequent years—again, at a max of $3,000 per year.

**Cash advance:** Money you can draw off of your credit card; the amount of your advance is subtracted from your available credit limit. YF&B ADVICE: Do everything humanly possible to avoid taking out a cash advance. There is no **grace period** on your withdrawal; you begin paying interest the second the money shoots out of the ATM, and the rate is typically 20 percent or more.

**Cash-value life insurance:** A brand of life insurance that combines the classic role of insurance—providing economic protection for your loved ones if you die prematurely—with an investment component. Because of that investment component, cash-value policies can be more than five times as expensive as basic term life insurance policies. YF&B ADVICE: Just stick with term insurance. It gives your loved ones all the coverage they need, without breaking your bank account.

**Certificate of deposit (CD):** A super-safe bank investment for your savings. The interest rate you earn on a CD depends on how long you will keep the money invested. Generally, the longer the period, the higher the rate you will get. If you withdraw the money before your CD matures, you will be hit with an interest penalty. YF&B ADVICE: If you want the flexibility to take your money out anytime, try a money-market deposit account or money-market mutual fund.

**Closing costs:** All the fees and charges associated with taking out a mortgage. Your total closing costs can equal 2 to 3 percent of your mortgage amount. On a $150,000 mortgage, that's another $3,000 to $4,500. YF&B ADVICE: When saving up for a home, make sure that in addition to the down payment, you will have cash handy to cover the closing costs; another option is to roll the costs into the mortgage.

**Commission:** 1. The fee charged by some financial advisers and brokers to buy or sell an investment. 2. The fee that all real estate agents are paid when a home is sold. The real estate agents for the buyer and seller typically split the commission, which is paid solely by the home seller. YF&B ADVICE: Don't ever work with a stockbroker who lives off of your commission; that's a crazy conflict of interest. If you want professional investing advice, work with a fee-only adviser.

**Company match:** The annual contribution your employer makes into your 401(k) account (also known as the employer contribution). The match can be a flat fee—say, $1,000—or a percentage of your contribution, such as 50 percent of your contributions up to a set annual limit. YF&B ADVICE: A company match is akin to a bonus; if you aren't participating in your plan, you are turning down free money. The only exception is if you anticipate you will job-hop in the next year or so. Since the company match typically **vests** over a three- or four-year period, you would be better off skipping the 401(k) and concentrating on maxing out on a **Roth IRA**.

**Consolidation:** A student loan repayment move where you pile together all your school debt into one mega-loan. YF&B ADVICE: The interest rates on student loans are readjusted each year according to the general direction of rates in the economy. When you consolidate, you lock in a fixed interest rate for the duration of your repayment period. When rates are low, consolidation is a smart way to avoid the annual financial anxiety of having your loan rate change.

**Contingent deferred sales charge:** See **Back-end load fund**.

**Credit bureau:** The Big Brother of the consumer finance world. The three credit bureaus—Equifax, Experian, and TransUnion—keep a credit report on you that tracks your credit card and loan payments, what you owe, whether you pay on time, and which debts you have punked out on. YF&B ADVICE: You must check your credit reports at least once a year to make sure there are no mistakes; the information in your credit report is used to calculate your FICO score. Mistakes can kill your score.

**Credit history:** How long you have had a particular credit card, and your past habits with that card. When computing your FICO score, a long credit history will help boost your score. YF&B ADVICE: Don't cancel any credit card with a long history, because you will "lose" all that history. If you need to avoid temptation, give the card the scissors treatment.

**Credit limit:** How much you can charge on your credit card. YF&B ADVICE: If you are very careful in how you use your card, ask your card company to boost your credit limit. It's a nice "emergency" fund, and it will also help lower your debt-to-credit-limit ratio, which will help your FICO score.

**Credit report:** Your financial report card, which includes a record of whether you have been diligent or delinquent in making your loan and credit card payments. The information in your credit report determines your credit score. The three credit bureaus share your credit report with lenders and landlords who want to size up whether you are a good credit risk. YF&B ADVICE: Check your credit report at least once a year to make sure all the info is correct; any errors can send your FICO score reeling.

**Credit score:** The Rosetta stone of your financial life. Your credit score is used by mortgage lenders, car loan lenders, credit card companies, landlords, cell-phone companies, and even prospective employers to size up whether you are a good or bad credit risk. Also known as your "FICO score." YF&B ADVICE: A good credit score can save you big bucks, because you will qualify for the best rates from lenders.

**Credit union:** It looks and smells like a bank, but it is actually a cooperative run for the benefit of its members. Credit unions are organized around a shared profession or religious affiliation. For example, there can be a credit union for local firefighters, another one for school teachers, and another for members of your church. You may be able to join a credit union if you know someone who is already a member. YF&B ADVICE: Quite often, you can get the best loan deals and highest interest rates on savings investments from credit unions.

**Death benefit:** No, it's not an oxymoron. It's the payout on a life insurance policy. A $500,000 term life insurance policy will pay your beneficiaries a $500,000 death benefit if you die during the policy's term. YF&B ADVICE: When you have yet to build up other assets in your life (investments, home equity, etc.) and someone is financially dependent on you, consider buying a term policy with a death benefit that is twenty times your beneficiary's annual income needs.

**Debit card:** A bank card that takes money directly (and immediately) out of your bank account to pay for any purchase you have made with the card. YF&B ADVICE: Be careful in using a debit card; many charge small fees for usage, and if you aren't on top of your bank account balance, you can inadvertently run up expensive bank fees if you use your card and don't have money in the bank to cover the charge.

**Debt:** Money that you owe and that you pay interest on. An unpaid credit card balance is debt. The outstanding balance on your student loan is debt. A mortgage is debt. YF&B ADVICE: Debt isn't necessarily bad. Debt where you are paying a high interest rate is definitely bad. A high FICO score and timely payments on your debt will qualify you for lower interest rates on many of your debts.

**Debt-to-credit-limit ratio:** An important factor in computing your FICO score. Your debt-to-credit-limit ratio measures the combined unpaid balances on all your credit cards compared to how much total credit you have. The lower this ratio, the better your FICO score will be. YF&B ADVICE: In the month or two before you intend to apply for a mortgage or auto loan, keep your purchases as low as possible so your debt-to-credit-limit ratio will be more favorable. That could help your FICO score.

**Deductible:** What you pay out of your pocket before your insurance kicks in. Your health insurance deductible is your total annual out-of-pocket expenditure for any expenses incurred during the year, assuming you owe no copayments. Home insurance and car insurance deductibles are charged on each claim. YF&B ADVICE: On any insurance policy where you—and not your employer—pay for the policy, opt for the higher deductible. You never want to make a ton of claims on your insurance policies for relatively small expenses; it will end up backfiring on you, because the insurer will boost your premium or possibly refuse to renew your policy.

**Default:** The failure to live up to your end of a loan agreement. When you don't pay your student loans for at least nine months, you go into default. YF&B ADVICE: If you are having trouble keeping up with any student loan or credit card payments, call the lender before you give up. Explain your situation and ask if there is a way to lower your payments for a period so you don't fall into default. If they are smart, they will want to get some money from you rather than have you default.

**Deferment:** A temporary reprieve from paying back student loans. If your loan is subsidized, no interest will accrue during your deferment. YF&B ADVICE: If you are financially stressed, ask your student loan lender about a deferment; it is a far smarter move than simply punking out on your payments and falling into default.

**Direct rollover:** The absolute best way to move your money out of an old employer's 401(k) plan and into an IRA at a discount brokerage or mutual fund company. You never touch the money; it goes straight from the company handling your old 401(k) to your new account, which saves you a ton of hassle and protects you from a huge tax headache. YF&B ADVICE: Brokerages and mutual fund companies will fall over themselves to make it super-easy to roll over your 401(k); just fill out the form, and they can handle it from there.

**Discount brokerage:** A financial-services firm that charges lower commissions and fees than a traditional full-service brokerage. YF&B ADVICE: Discount brokerages—and no-load mutual fund companies—are the best choices for your Roth IRA or regular investment account; the less you pay in commissions and fees, the more money you will keep.

**Dollar cost averaging:** An investment process where you commit to making periodic payments—monthly or quarterly—into an investment account. YF&B ADVICE: Over the long term, DCA puts you ahead of the game. You will end up buying more shares at a lower average price; the more shares you own, the more you will make when the markets rise.

**Dow Jones Industrial Average:** What everyone is referring to when they say "the market." This granddaddy of stock-market gauges follows the performance of thirty large-cap stocks. YF&B ADVICE: In addition to "the Dow," other popular indexes include the Standard & Poor's 500, which tracks 500 large-cap stocks, and the NASDAQ Composite, a benchmark for smaller companies and tech stocks.

Down payment: The cash you need to bring to the table to get a loan for the purchase of a home or car. YF&B ADVICE: Do not be tempted by the zero-down mortgage offers; if you can't afford even a small down payment—say, 3 to 5 percent—it is a sign that you are not yet ready for the responsibility of home ownership.

Durable power of attorney (DPOA): A document that designates someone you appoint to act on your behalf. A financial DPOA allows your agent to carry out bill paying and other financial-management issues that you clearly lay out. A DPOA for health care gives your agent the responsibility to represent your wishes regarding treatment and life support in the event that you are not able to communicate for yourself. YF&B ADVICE: DPOAs should be included in every living revocable trust; you also want to make sure the DPOA includes an incapacity clause, which will ensure that your agent can continue acting on your behalf if you become unable to act on your own behalf.

Early-withdrawal penalty: Investments in most retirement accounts, such as 401(k)s, require you not to touch your loot until you are at least 59½. If you want to get your hands on your money before then, you most likely will be hit with a 10 percent penalty on the amount of money that you withdraw, as well as ordinary income tax. YF&B ADVICE: There are no early-withdrawal penalties on the money you contribute to a Roth IRA; you can raid that money anytime without paying any penalty or tax.

Emergency cash fund: Your rainy-day fund to cover all the unknown but inevitable expenses that always hit at the wrong times. It can be used for things such as covering your rent or mortgage if you get laid off, or to pay the deductible on your auto insurance if you are in a fender bender. YF&B ADVICE: Ideally, you would have at least six months of living expenses stashed in an emergency cash fund. Give yourself time to build it up by committing to socking away a small sum each month in a savings account.

**Equity:** 1. In the investing world, this is the fancy-pants term for a stock. 2. In the housing world, this is the percentage of your home's appraised value that exceeds the value of your mortgage. YF&B ADVICE: You shouldn't measure your gain by what your home can be sold for. Your bottom line is your equity position—what you will pocket after you sell the home and pay off your mortgage and the agent's commission.

**Escrow:** A special account, also known as an "impound account," required by some mortgage lenders. You deposit your annual home insurance premium and property tax levies in the account, and the lender then takes care of the payments. YF&B ADVICE: Shop around for a mortgage where you don't have to set up an escrow account. It's better to handle the payments yourself and be able to earn interest on the money during the year.

**Exchange-traded fund (ETF):** A fund that tracks a market index but trades like a stock, meaning you can buy and sell during the trading day based on the current market price. (A mutual fund can only be traded at its closing price at the end of the trading day.) YF&B ADVICE: While ETFs offer more immediate liquidity, you must pay a commission every time you buy and sell ETF shares. So if you are **dollar cost averaging,** stick with no-load mutual funds.

**Expense ratio:** An annual fee charged by all mutual funds, which is deducted from each fund's gross return. Stock funds have an average expense ratio of 1.5 percent. YF&B ADVICE: The higher the expense ratio, the lower your net return. A stock fund that gains 10 percent but has a 1.5 percent expense ratio delivers you a net return of just 8.5 percent. An index fund with an 0.20 expense ratio will return 9.8 percent. When picking a fund, go for the lowest expense ratio.

**FICO score:** The gold standard of credit scores, developed by Fair Isaac Corporation. YF&B ADVICE: Lenders use your FICO score to determine if you are a worthy credit risk, and what sort of deal they are going to offer you. A higher FICO score puts you in line for a lower interest rate on a loan or credit card.

**Fixed income:** In the investing world, this refers to bonds. YF&B ADVICE: Your 401(k) and Roth IRA should be invested in equities (stock), not fixed income. You need the higher return potential of stock over the long term. As you reach your forties and fifties, you will want to add fixed income to your investment mix to provide a bit more stability as you get nearer to retirement.

**Fixed-rate mortgage:** A loan for a home purchase in which the interest rate you pay will not change for the life of the loan. A thirty-year fixed-rate mortgage is the most popular home loan. YF&B ADVICE: Fixed-rate mortgages are far less risky than adjustable-rate mortgages, but if you think you may stay in your home for less than ten years, you don't need a thirty-year fixed rate. You can get a lower interest rate with a hybrid mortgage, where your interest rate is fixed for three, five, seven, or ten years.

**Forbearance:** A temporary reprieve from paying back your student loans. During forbearance, interest will continue to accrue on all your loans. YF&B ADVICE: It's easier to qualify for forbearance than deferment. Check with your lender for its rules on seeking forbearance.

**Foreclosure:** The process by which a mortgage lender will force the sale of your home if you fail to keep up with your mortgage payments. YF&B ADVICE: Failure to keep up with payments on a home equity loan or home equity line of credit can also lead to foreclosure; be very careful before taking on this added risk.

**Foreign fund:** A stock mutual fund that invests in companies outside of the United States. YF&B ADVICE: Before you invest in a foreign fund, check to see if your stock fund has a portion of assets in foreign stocks; you may not need to buy a foreign fund to get the recommended 20 percent exposure to foreign markets.

**401(k):** A retirement savings account offered by employers. You invest in your 401(k) through automatic pretax withdrawals from your paycheck. You get a nice tax break on your contributions, and your money grows for years tax-deferred. YF&B ADVICE: Always contribute to a 401(k) so you can get the maximum company match; but if you have limited income, you might then switch to paying off your credit card debt, saving for a down payment on a home, or funding a Roth IRA for the rest of the year. A Roth offers a better tax deal than a 401(k) when you get around to making withdrawals.

**403(b):** A kissing cousin of a 401(k) that is used by nonprofits. YF&B ADVICE: Always invest enough each year to get the maximum matching contribution from your boss.

**Fraud alert:** The first step in dealing with identity theft. Contact any of the three major credit bureaus, and they will forward your request to the other two bureaus. YF&B ADVICE: An initial alert is typically good for 90 to 180 days; once you have an alert, ask for the seven-year extension.

**Full-service brokerage:** The old-line Wall Street firms where your adviser offers advice on what you should buy or sell, and is compensated by the commissions you pay when you make a trade. YF&B ADVICE: "Full-service" is a euphemism for full price on commissions and fees. Stick with a discount brokerage.

**Fund category:** All mutual funds are assigned to a specific category, such as large-cap, value, foreign, or small-cap blend. YF&B ADVICE: When evaluating a fund's performance, you want to compare it to its category average.

**Grace period:** 1. In credit card land, the period between the end of your billing cycle and the day your payment is due; you will incur no interest charges during this period. If you carry over a balance from the previous month, there is no grace period. 2. In student loan land, the six-month period between the time you leave school and the time you must start paying back your loan. YF&B ADVICE: Credit card companies love to shorten the grace period; always check your payment due date when you receive your statement to make sure you know when you need to get the payment in to avoid interest charges.

**Growth:** A stock investment approach that looks for companies whose earnings and revenues are growing at a rapid pace. YF&B ADVICE: A balanced investment portfolio includes mutual funds that own both growth and value stocks.

**Home equity line of credit (HELOC):** a secondary loan on your home, based on the equity you have built up. You can open a HELOC at any time, but you will owe interest only once you actually "tap" the line, meaning you take some money out of the line. YF&B ADVICE: The interest rate on HELOCs is variable; it moves up and down based on changes in a benchmark index that it is tied to. So be careful you don't get caught in a squeeze with a big HELOC balance when rates rise.

That said, if you do not have an emergency cash fund and you own a home, open a HELOC. It can help out in a true financial emergency.

**Home equity loan (HEL):** A secondary loan on your home, based on the equity you have built up. Unlike a home equity line of credit, a HEL comes with a fixed interest rate, but you receive the entire amount of the loan up front, and therefore, interest charges start immediately. Typically, you can borrow up to 80 percent of the equity in your house. YF&B ADVICE: HELs protect you from interest-rate shock, but again, don't use these for indulgent expenses, such as buying a sports car or putting a hot tub in the backyard; if you fall behind on the payments, you could lose your home.

**Hybrid mortgage:** A home loan where the interest rate is fixed for a few years before it morphs into an adjustable-rate mortgage. A 5/1 hybrid has a fixed interest rate for five years before it converts to an adjustable. YF&B ADVICE: Hybrids are a great option if you intend to stay in your home for less than ten years. The interest rate on a 3/1, 5/1, 7/1, or 10/1 hybrid is lower than the rate on a thirty-year fixed-rate mortgage, yet you have peace of mind that your rate will not waver for the initial period. The trick is to move or refinance before it converts to an adjustable mortgage.

**Identity theft:** When a criminal steals your personal information—a credit card number or Social Security number—and then poses as you when making charges on your existing accounts, or opens fraudulent accounts using your name and info. YF&B ADVICE: ID theft is a national epidemic. Check your credit reports at least once a year to see if there are any bogus accounts or charges in your name. To protect yourself, be very careful in sharing your financial information, and shred all statements before tossing them in the trash.

**Incapacity clause:** An addition to a durable power of attorney that ensures your self-appointed agent will be able to continue to act on your behalf if you become incapacitated. YF&B ADVICE: Without an incapacity clause, your DPOA becomes useless the minute you become too ill to handle your affairs. Give yourself and your family peace of mind by making sure your DPOA includes an incapacity clause.

**Income tax:** The portion of your earnings that are forked over to Uncle Sam. In addition, some states and local governments levy an additional income tax rate.

The rate you pay depends on your taxable income (what's left after you subtract a bunch of tax breaks and make some arcane adjustments). Currently, the lowest income tax rate—also called your tax bracket—is 10 percent for individuals with taxable yearly income below $7,150 and couples filing joint tax returns with yearly income below $14,300. The highest tax bracket is 35 percent, for individuals and couples with yearly income higher than $319,000. YF&B ADVICE: Always pay your income tax on time. If you skip out on your payments, the IRS can raid your bank accounts and stick you with wage garnishment, in addition to penalties and extra tax.

Index fund: A mutual fund that tracks the performance of a specific index. An index fund is considered to be unmanaged, because there is no manager making buy, sell, and hold decisions. YF&B ADVICE: Good stock index funds charge less than 0.20 percent per year for their expense ratio. That gives them a huge leg up on actively managed funds, where the average expense ratio is 1.5 percent. Low-cost index funds are a smart and simple way to invest.

Individual retirement account (IRA): An investment account that offers tax breaks to induce you to save for your retirement. See **Traditional IRA** and **Roth IRA**. YF&B ADVICE: If you qualify for a Roth IRA, it is simply the smartest investment move you can ever make to invest in it.

Insurance premium: The annual fee you pay for insurance coverage. YF&B ADVICE: You can reduce your premiums by choosing a higher deductible. And that's a smart move because if you make too many claims on a low-deductible policy, your insurer will eventually boost your premium or refuse to give you future coverage.

Interest: The money lenders collect from borrowers who they loan money to. You pay interest on your credit card balance, auto loan, student loan, or mortgage. You earn interest on investments such as certificates of deposit, money-market accounts, and bonds. Interest rates fluctuate based on what is happening in the general economy. When the economy is very strong, rates tend to be higher; when the economy is slowing down or struggling, rates tend to be lower. Different types of loans base their rates on a variety of leading interest rates. For example, the prime interest rate is what banks charge their best commercial customers.

Consumer credit card rates and HELOC rates are typically tied to the prime rate. Your credit card rate could be prime plus ten, meaning your rate will be ten percentage points higher than the prime rate. Changes in the federal funds rate, which is set by the Federal Reserve Board, affect short-term interest rates, such as CD and money-market rates. YF&B ADVICE: The higher your FICO score, the better (lower) the interest rate you will qualify for on your loans and credit cards. Over the course of your life, that is going to save you tens of thousands of dollars.

**Interest-only mortgage:** Traditional mortgages include two elements: your principal—the loan amount—and the interest you pay on the principal to compensate your lender for being nice enough to front you the money. With interest-only loans, you make no principal payments for a set period of the loan, which helps reduce your monthly costs. YF&B ADVICE: If the only way you think you can afford a home is to go for an interest-only mortgage, the hard truth is that you can't afford the home. These loans are just too risky. You will eventually need to start paying back the principal, and that will mean a steep climb in your payment. And there's no way you can guarantee that you will have enough appreciation before that happens to allow you to refinance to a standard loan.

**Introductory rate:** The big tease—the low interest rate that credit card companies offer to get you to do a balance transfer to their credit card. YF&B ADVICE: If you don't intend to pay off the balance before the intro period expires, make sure the "regular" rate is going to make sense for you. Or consider doing another balance transfer again. Also, always pay your bills on time; if you are late, your intro rate will skyrocket to 20 percent or more.

**Invoice price:** The price that the car dealer paid to buy the car from the auto manufacturer. YF&B ADVICE: Auto salespeople will always want to negotiate on the higher **manufacturer's suggested retail price (MSRP);** your job is to steer the negotiation so it is based on the invoice price. Quite often, dealers get additional money from the auto manufacturer (known as the "holdback") if they sell you the car, so their net cost can be below the invoice price. So don't think the invoice price is necessarily the lowest price a dealer will accept.

**IRA rollover:** See **Direct rollover.**

**Joint tenancy with right of survivorship (JTWROS):** The way you and your partner can choose to take title to your home. With JTWROS you agree that you are equal partners in the home, and that when one of you dies, the other partner automatically inherits the deceased's half of the property. YF&B ADVICE: A JTWROS agreement trumps anything in a will, and makes transferring ownership much faster, without the cost of **probate**. In addition to your home, you can also hold other assets, such as investment and bank accounts, in JTWROS.

**Keogh:** A tax-deferred retirement plan for self-employed individuals. YF&B ADVICE: If you are eligible for a Roth IRA, make that investment first. After that, you can choose between a Keogh or a SEP-IRA; the SEP can be simpler and less expensive to maintain.

**Large-cap:** A stock of a big, established company. "Blue-chip" stocks are large-caps. YF&B ADVICE: Large-caps are the solid core of a smart investment strategy that you can round out with mid-caps and small-caps.

**Lease:** An agreement to "borrow" a car from an auto dealer for a set period of time in return for making monthly payments. The typical lease period is three years. YF&B ADVICE: Buy, don't lease! When you lease, you will most probably get trapped into a never-ending cycle of constantly returning your car at the end of the lease period and leasing another car. That means you will always be making monthly car payments. Buy a car, and after your loan period—say, three, four, or five years—you can then keep driving the car while you owe no money on it. Moreover, you will make some money when you finally do sell or trade in the car.

**Living revocable trust:** A legal document that outlines the ownership of your assets while you are alive, and designates how those assets are to be handled once you die. The trust can be changed throughout your life; that's what "revocable" means. YF&B ADVICE: With a living revocable trust, your estate can pass to your heirs without having to go through the time-consuming and costly probate process.

**Load mutual fund:** A mutual fund sold by a broker or financial adviser, for which you, the investor, pay a commission. **A-share funds** charge a load, typically 5 percent, when you initially invest your money. **B-share funds** charge a very high annual expense ratio that covers a commission paid to the the broker. In addition, the B-share fund will hit you with a back-end load if you leave the fund before a set period—typically, five years. YF&B ADVICE: You want 100 percent of your money to be working for you, not paying someone else. Stick with no-load mutual funds.

**Loan consolidation:** For student loans, the process of rolling all your loans into one mega-loan for which you can then lock in a fixed interest rate for your entire repayment period. YF&B ADVICE: When you consolidate, you can choose among various payment periods; check with your lender to see which consolidation and payment plans are available.

**Manufacturer incentives:** What car makers offer both car dealers and car buyers to get their cars sold. YF&B ADVICE: Check websites such as www.edmunds.com to see if there are holdbacks—incentives to the auto dealer that are not advertised to you. If you know the dealer will get a $1,000 holdback once he sells you the car, let him know that you know. There's no reason you shouldn't "share" in that by having the price knocked down another $500.

**Manufacturer's suggested retail price (MSRP):** The price that an auto dealer wants to sell you the car for. YF&B ADVICE: Unless you are looking at a super-popular car with a waiting list, you shouldn't pay MSRP; negotiate to get the price below MSRP.

**Market index:** A group of stocks that serves as a benchmark for investors. The S&P 500 is an index of 500 large-cap stocks. The Morgan Stanley EAFE is an index of foreign stocks. There are literally dozens of market indexes. YF&B ADVICE: An index is another good way to measure your fund's performance. Most online financial websites that offer mutual fund performance information include data on the performance of a benchmark index for those funds.

**Maturity date:** No, it's not some sort of financial rite of passage, just the date that a bond ends and your principal investment is returned. YF&B ADVICE: Right now, your primary investing focus should be on stocks, not bonds. But in ten or fifteen years, when you start adding bonds to your mix, it is important to understand that the longer the maturity of a bond, the higher the interest rate it will pay you. But you also have the risk that if interest rates rise during that period, you will be stuck with your lower-rate bond.

**Mid-cap:** The stock of a medium-sized company. YF&B ADVICE: The midpoint in the stock world; mid-caps are bigger than small-caps, and thus a bit more stable, yet they aren't yet big, lumbering large-cap stocks that offer more moderate growth prospects.

**Minimum balance due:** The smallest monthly payment you can make on your credit card. Typically, your minimum balance due is computed as 2.5 percent of your credit card balance. YF&B ADVICE: When you are ready to tackle your credit card debt, commit to paying more than the minimum due each month. Adding as little as $20 or so a month will greatly reduce the time (and interest payments) needed to get your balance down to zero.

**Modified adjusted gross income (MAGI):** For your federal tax return, what's left after your gross income is "adjusted" for various types of deductions. YF&B ADVICE: You are eligible to make the full contribution to a Roth IRA ($4,000 in 2005) if you are single and your MAGI is less than $95,000, or if you are married and file a joint tax return and your MAGI is below $150,000.

**Money-market deposit account (MMDA):** A safe savings vehicle offered at banks and credit unions. Unlike a certificate of deposit (CD), your money will not be tied up for a specified period, and you can write checks against your account (though there is typically a minimum dollar amount allowed). The rates on MMDAs are typically higher than what you can earn in a savings or checking account. YF&B ADVICE: You may be able to get a better interest rate on your MMDA if you stick with the bank where you have your checking account and any loans or credit cards.

**Money-market mutual fund:** Similar to a money-market deposit account, except it is offered through a brokerage or mutual-fund company. Because it is not offered through a bank, there is no "insurance" on your investment. (A federal program insures all bank accounts up to a $100,000 max.) YF&B ADVICE: Despite the lack of insurance, there is little risk with money-market funds, especially if you stick with a conservative brokerage or fund company. And you can move your money from your money-market fund into other funds with a click of your mouse or a phone call.

**Mortgage:** A loan to purchase a home. You must make a down payment to the lender to cover a small portion of the purchase price; the mortgage covers the remaining cost of the home. You pay interest on the mortgage amount. YF&B ADVICE: Hybrid mortgages can be the smartest option if you intend to move in ten years or less; you will get a lower rate than with a standard thirty-year fixed-rate loan, yet you won't have the rate risk of a regular adjustable-rate mortgage.

**Mortgage broker:** A middleman who shops around to find you the best mortgage deal. Mortgage brokers can collect a fee from the consumer (it can be a straight fee or points on your loan; 1 percent of the mortgage amount, or 1 point, is typical), as well as from the lender. YF&B ADVICE: A good mortgage broker can literally save you tens of thousands of dollars over the life of your loan by getting you the best rate on the mortgage that fits your needs. Old-fashioned personal referrals are the best way to find a talented mortgage broker.

**Mortgage interest deduction (MID):** A nice tax break from Uncle Sam. The interest payments on a mortgage for your primary residence (not a vacation home) are deductible on your federal tax return. In the early years of your mortgage, the vast majority of your payments are for interest rather than principal. YF&B ADVICE: While a tax break is nice, don't be snookered into thinking you are "saving" money. If you are in the 30 percent federal income tax bracket, for every dollar you pay in interest, you will get 30 cents back on your taxes. But you still are out the 70 cents. The MID merely reduces your net out-of-pocket expense, but that mortgage will still cost you big-time.

**Mortgage refinancing:** Trading in your existing mortgage for a new mortgage. Refinancing is most popular when rates are falling; you can reduce your monthly payments by getting a lower-rate mortgage. Another refinancing scenario is to get out of an adjustable-rate mortgage for the certainty of a fixed-rate or hybrid mortgage. YF&B ADVICE: Pay attention to all the fees when you refinance, including any prepayment penalty for getting rid of your original mortgage. Ask the lender to do the math for you and show how long it will take you to recoup your refinancing fees if you move to the lower-cost loan.

**Mutual fund:** An investment vehicle that holds dozens, if not hundreds, of individual stocks (or bonds). An actively managed mutual fund employs a manager (or managers) to decide which investments the fund will buy, sell, and hold. **YF&B ADVICE:** A mutual fund is the smartest investment when you have limited money. With one investment, you get the great diversification of owning a share of many different firms; that protects you if any one company craters.

**NASDAQ:** The big electronic stock market where many smaller and more tech-oriented stocks trade. For you trivia buffs, it stands for National Association of Securities Dealers Automated Quotations. **YF&B ADVICE:** NASDAQ stocks often offer higher return potential, but with that comes higher risk. From the bubble high in early 2000 through late 2002, an index of NASDAQ stocks fell 77 percent. No matter how big a tech-head risk-taker you are, never have all your money riding on a NASDAQ investment, such as the QQQ ETF, which tracks the performance of the NASDAQ 100 index.

**No-load mutual fund:** A mutual fund that does not charge you a sales commission when you buy or sell your shares. **YF&B ADVICE:** No-loads are the way to go. But you also want to make sure your no-load charges a low annual expense ratio.

**Piggyback loan:** A second mortgage you take out in tandem with your primary mortgage when your down payment is less than 20 percent. With a piggyback loan, you can get around having to pay private mortgage insurance. The piggyback covers the difference between your down payment and the magic 20 percent figure that lenders require you to pay to avoid PMI. For example, in an 80-10-10 arrangement, your primary mortgage covers 80 percent of the cost of the home, you make a 10 percent down payment, and your piggyback covers the other 10 percent of the down payment. **YF&B ADVICE:** Ask your mortgage broker to compare the costs of a piggyback loan to the costs of rolling your PMI into your primary mortgage; the cost of rolling the PMI into the primary mortgage can be the financially better move.

**Points:** A fee that is charged when you get a mortgage. Not all mortgages have points. One point = one percent of your loan amount. **YF&B ADVICE:** Points are part of the closing costs that you need to pay in cash when you sign for your mortgage. Sometimes you may be offered a deal where you pay more points to get a lower interest rate. But don't take the deal if your down payment is going to be less than 20 percent. If you have extra cash, it makes more sense to use it to make a bigger down payment so you can avoid paying for private mortgage insurance (PMI).

**Prepayment penalty:** A fee that is sometimes charged when you choose to pay off your mortgage ahead of schedule. When you refinance, you can get hit with a prepayment penalty on your "old" loan, since you will essentially be paying it off and taking out a new mortgage. YF&B ADVICE: If you are refinancing, ask the lender to compute how long it will take to recoup the cost of the prepayment penalty in the lower payments on the new loan. If you think you may move before you would reach the break-even point, it doesn't make sense to refinance.

**Pretax:** Money you invest before you pay taxes on it. When you invest in a 401(k), your contributions are made pretax, meaning the money is deducted from your paycheck without first having a portion deducted for your federal tax. YF&B ADVICE: If you are in the 15 percent federal income tax bracket, each dollar of pay would normally have 15 cents subtracted to pay your federal tax, but all 100 cents of every dollar that you contribute to your 401(k) go into your account. That's like getting a 15 percent bonus on your investment. Moreover, your contribution reduces your taxable income. For example, if you make $40,000 a year and contribute $4,000 to your 401(k), your taxable income for the year will fall to $36,000, which will give you another nice tax break.

**Principal:** 1. In the world of mortgages, the size of a loan. You pay interest on the principal. 2. In the bond world, the value of the bond that you earn interest on. YF&B ADVICE: With a mortgage, the majority of your monthly payments in the early years of the loan go toward paying interest, not reducing your principal. If you decide to send in extra payments during the course of the year to get your loan paid off faster, instruct the lender that your extra payments are to go only toward reducing your principal.

**Private mortgage insurance (PMI):** Insurance that mortgage lenders require if your down payment is less than 20 percent. The monthly payment runs about $45 or so per $100,000 of mortgage, and the payments are not tax-deductible. YF&B ADVICE: See if you can roll your PMI costs into your mortgage; it will typically cost you just 1 percent of your loan amount. So on a $200,000 mortgage, paying PMI up front could cost just $2,000. Your net PMI costs will be lower and tax-deductible. A piggyback loan will enable you to avoid PMI altogether.

**Probate:** A court process that is required to validate your will. Putting a loved one's estate through probate can be costly and time-consuming; it also makes public the deceased's financial holdings. **YF&B ADVICE:** You can completely avoid probate if you outline your wishes for your estate in a living revocable trust rather than a will.

**Refinancing:** Swapping an existing loan for a new loan. This is most commonly done when the current interest rate on your mortgage is higher than the rates that are being offered, or when you want to "take out" some of the equity in your home. **YF&B ADVICE:** When you refinance, there usually are closing costs. You have to make sure that you will be staying in the house long enough that even with the reduced monthly payments, you will recover your closing costs.

**Replacement cost value coverage:** Insurance that covers the cost of rebuilding your damaged property and pays you the replacement cost—not the depreciated value—of any lost or damaged possessions. This is the only coverage you are to accept on your homeowner's insurance policy. It's a lot better than actual cash value, which will merely repay you the current market value of the damaged or lost property. **YF&B ADVICE:** Insurers are squeezing homeowners by limiting the extent of the replacement coverage. Your best move is to ask your agent to review your policy annually to make sure you have enough coverage to truly replace your home and possessions. Ask for a special rider (feature) to your policy that will automatically adjust your coverage (and your premium) each year so you can keep up with the rising cost of replacement.

**Rollover IRA:** What your 401(k) becomes when you move it from an old employer's plan into your own account at a brokerage or mutual-fund company. A rollover is a great idea if the funds offered in your old employer's 401(k) plan are lousy; when you do a rollover, you can invest the money in any combination of stocks or mutual funds. **YF&B ADVICE:** A direct rollover is your smartest move. By having your brokerage or mutual fund handle the transfer, you will not run afoul of some tough IRS rules that can create a tax headache for you.

**Roth IRA:** A retirement account that you fund with after-tax contributions and on which you will owe no tax when you take any or all of the money out, assuming you are at least 59 ½ and have had the account for five years. The great thing about a Roth is that you can take out your original contributions (though not earnings) anytime you want without taxes or penalties, regardless of how old you are when you do so or how long the money has been in the account. YF&B ADVICE: If you are single and your adjusted gross income is less than $95,000, or if you are a married couple that files a joint tax return and your adjusted gross income is below $150,000, you can—and should—invest the max in a Roth each year. The one exception: If you have high-interest credit card debt, pay that off first.

**Savings account:** A low-risk investment in a certificate of deposit (CD), money-market deposit account (MMDA), or money-market mutual fund. Savings accounts offer modest returns—just 2 percent at most in late 2004—but they are the "safe" investments for money that you will need within the next five years. YF&B ADVICE: If you are saving for a down payment, you can't afford the risk of putting your money in the stock market and then seeing it fall in value just when you need it. Your money belongs in a savings account, not a stock investment account.

**Secured credit card:** A credit card that requires you to make a hefty deposit to the card issuer; your credit limit is typically the amount of your deposit. YF&B ADVICE: For those rare birds who don't have a FICO score—because they don't have a credit card and haven't taken out any loans—a secured card can be a first step toward qualifying for a regular credit card. Do not run a balance on a secured card; the interest rates can be high. And shop around for the card with the lowest fee. Your goal is to use the card responsibly a few times a month and then pay the bill ASAP. Make sure your secured card reports to at least two of the major credit bureaus. You want to be building a good credit report so that within a year or so, you will be able to ditch the secured card for a regular card that has no fees and a lower interest rate.

**Secured debt:** A loan in which your asset—be it a car or a home—is used as collateral. If you fail to keep up with your loan payments, the lender can take possession of the asset to settle your loan. YF&B ADVICE: When you buy a home, your equity in the home is the collateral. If you fail to keep up with your mortgage payments, the lender can force you to sell the home to pay off the debt. The same is true if you fall behind on payments for a home equity loan or home equity line of credit.

**Simplified Employee Pension (SEP):** Also known as a SEP-IRA, this is a tax-deferred retirement account for the self-employed (and their employees), in which you can contribute up to 25 percent of your annual income to a current max of $41,000. **YF&B ADVICE:** If you are self-employed and eligible for a Roth IRA, fund that first, since your investment will grow tax-free. Then you can invest any additional money in a SEP; you will get a tax break on your contributions, but when you withdraw the money, you will owe tax at your ordinary income tax rate.

**Small-cap:** Stocks of smaller companies, many of which trade on the NASDAQ. **YF&B ADVICE:** The allure of a small-cap is that it will grow into a large-cap of tomorrow. If you are along for the ride, you will pocket some big gains. But small-caps can also be quite volatile and risky. Large-cap stocks should be the core of your investment portfolio, with less allocated to small-caps (and mid-caps).

**Standard & Poor's 500 stock index (S&P 500):** An index of 500 large-cap stocks that is considered one of the best market barometers. **YF&B ADVICE:** A mutual fund that tracks the S&P 500 is a solid choice for your 401(k) or Roth IRA.

**Stock:** A small share of a company, also known as **equity**. On average, stocks have returned about 10 percent a year over the long term, while bonds average about half that return. **YF&B ADVICE:** Until you reach forty-five or fifty, your money should be invested in stocks, not bonds, so you have a chance to earn higher returns.

**Subsidized loan:** A student loan for which the interest is paid by the government while the student is in school, in the grace period, or when the loan is in deferment. Subsidized loans are awarded based on financial need. **YF&B ADVICE:** Even if you have a subsidized loan, your interest payments will accrue when you are in forbearance.

**Tax-deferred:** A temporary reprieve from paying tax on an investment gain, but at some point, the tax collector will come knocking on your door. Money you invest in a 401(k) grows tax-deferred for the entire period that you have it invested. But when you make withdrawals, you will be hit with a tax bill. Moreover, the tax will be at your ordinary income tax rate rather than the more advantageous capital gains tax rate. YF&B ADVICE: Tax-deferred is nice. Tax-free is nicer. Withdrawals from Roth IRAs are tax-free if you meet certain basic criteria.

**Tax-free:** When you don't have to share with Uncle Sam or any state or local tax man. YF&B ADVICE: Gains from a Roth IRA can be withdrawn 100 percent tax-free if you have had the account for at least five years and are 59½ when you start tapping your account.

**Term life insurance:** The only type of life insurance you should ever buy. It provides all the coverage you need and is far less expensive than cash-value policies such as universal life, whole life, and variable life. YF&B ADVICE: Purchase a policy for which the premium is a guaranteed level term for the entire length of the policy. That means your premium will never increase during the period your policy is in effect.

**Traditional IRA:** The only individual retirement account that was available, until the Roth arrived on the scene in 1997. With a traditional IRA, you may qualify for a tax deduction on your contribution, and your money grows tax-deferred. But when you withdraw money from a traditional IRA, it is treated just like a 401(k): You owe ordinary income tax (not capital gains tax) on your withdrawals. YF&B ADVICE: Roth IRAs are a smarter choice than traditional IRAs. With a Roth, you have no tax due on your withdrawals, and during the time you are invested, you have greater flexibility in that you can always withdraw your contributions— though not your gains—without any tax or penalty.

**Two-cycle average daily balance:** A billing method that credit card companies use to compute the interest you owe. YF&B ADVICE: If you typically pay off your card in full each month but carry a balance once in a while, make sure your card uses the average daily balance method rather than the two-cycle average daily balance method. The two-cycle system will end up costing you more in interest.

**Universal life insurance:** A type of cash-value life insurance that you are to steer clear of. YF&B ADVICE: Term insurance is the only type of life insurance you need.

**Unsecured debt:** Debt for which you do not have to put up any asset as collateral. If you default on your payments, the creditor cannot seize any asset to settle your debt. **YF&B ADVICE:** Credit card debt is unsecured. Therefore, it makes no sense to use a home equity loan or home equity line of credit—both of which are secured—to pay off your credit card debt. You could lose your home if you fall behind on your home loan payments.

**Value:** An investment strategy that focuses on bargain hunting. Value stocks are often beat-up or out-of-favor stocks that look "cheap" to investors, based on estimates of their fundamental worth. **YF&B ADVICE:** Growth stocks are sexy; value stocks are boring. But value stocks tend to outperform growth stocks over long periods. You should have both in your portfolio.

**Variable annuity:** A combo of a mutual fund and some life insurance benefits. Your money grows tax-deferred. Because of the insurance component, variable annuities can be much more expensive than regular mutual funds. And withdrawals on variable annuities are taxed at your ordinary income tax rate, rather than the lower capital gains rate. **YF&B ADVICE:** Don't bother with variable annuities. A low-cost index fund or ETF is a tax-smart investment, and your gains will be taxed at the lower capital gains rate.

**Variable life insurance:** A type of cash-value life insurance. **YF&B ADVICE:** Do not buy variable life insurance. Term life insurance is the only type of life insurance you need; it provides the right coverage and is much less expensive than a cash-value policy such as variable life.

**Vesting:** The time it takes for a financial benefit you receive from your employer—such as stock options or company matching contributions to your 401(k)—to become 100 percent yours. Typically, a portion of the benefit vests each year; a typical vesting schedule is for 25 percent to convert to ownership each year, so at the end of the fourth year, all of the money (or stock) is yours to keep. If you leave the company before you are fully vested, you will forfeit any unvested assets. **YF&B ADVICE:** If you don't intend to stay at your job for more than a year or so, it can make sense to skip the 401(k), since none of your company match will have vested by the time you leave. Invest in a **Roth IRA** instead.

**Wage garnishment:** When a portion of your paycheck is automatically docked to cover a loan or tax that you have punked out on. YF&B ADVICE: If you fail to pay debts such as your student loans or your income tax, you run the risk of having part of your paycheck automatically siphoned off to cover that loan or tax. It is far smarter to contact your lender or the IRS and ask about special plans to help you keep up with your obligations, even when you are financially strapped.

**Whole life insurance:** Along with universal life and variable life, this is a type of cash-value life insurance. YF&B ADVICE: Steer clear of whole life. Term life insurance is the best (and cheaper) option.

**Wilshire 5000 Index:** A broad market index that includes the 5,000 largest stocks traded in the United States. An index fund tied to the Wilshire 5000 is often called a total market index fund, because within those 5,000 stocks, you have large-caps, mid-caps, and small-caps. YF&B ADVICE: A total market index fund is a great one-stop-shopping choice that provides you instant diversification among different types of stocks.

**Zero-down mortgage:** A mortgage that does not require any down payment. YF&B ADVICE: If lenders offer this, don't bite. If you don't have the discipline to save even a small down payment of 3 to 5 percent, you clearly aren't ready for the responsibility of a mortgage.

**INDEX**

# ABOUT THE AUTHOR

Suze Orman is the author of four consecutive *New York Times* bestsellers: *The 9 Steps to Financial Freedom*; *The Courage to Be Rich*; *The Road to Wealth*; and *The Laws of Money, The Lessons of Life*; as well as the national bestsellers *You've Earned It, Don't Lose It* and *Suze Orman's Financial Guidebook*. Suze hosts her own national award-winning CNBC-TV show, which airs every Saturday night. She is a contributing editor to *O, The Oprah Magazine* and is the featured writer on Yahoo! Personal Finance with her biweekly Money Matters series. She has written, coproduced, and hosted four PBS specials based on her bestselling books, which are among the network's most successful fund-raisers ever. The most recent special, inspired by *The Laws of Money, The Lessons of Life,* premiered nationwide in March 2003 and earned her an Emmy Award.

A Certified Financial Planner Professional®, Orman directed the Suze Orman Financial Group from 1987 to 1997, served as Vice President–Investments for Prudential-Bache Securities from 1983 to 1987, and from 1980 to 1983 was an account executive at Merrill Lynch. She was selected as one of the five distinguished recipients of the 2002 TJFR Group Business Luminaries Award, which honors lifetime achievement in business journalism. In 2003, she was inducted into the Books for a Better Life Awards' Hall of Fame in recognition of her ongoing contributions to self-improvement. A highly sought-after public speaker worldwide, she was profiled in *Worth* magazine's hundredth issue as among those "who have revolutionized the way America thinks about money." She lives in south Florida.